W9-DFM-993

THE STRUCTURE AND REGULATION OF FINANCIAL MARKETS

The Structure
and Regulation
of Financial Markets

PETER D. SPENCER

OXFORD
UNIVERSITY PRESS

*This book has been printed digitally and produced in a standard specification
in order to ensure its continuing availability*

OXFORD
UNIVERSITY PRESS

Great Clarendon Street, Oxford OX2 6DP

Oxford University Press is a department of the University of Oxford.
It furthers the University's objective of excellence in research, scholarship,
and education by publishing worldwide in

Oxford New York

Auckland Cape Town Dar es Salaam Hong Kong Karachi
Kuala Lumpur Madrid Melbourne Mexico City Nairobi
New Delhi Shanghai Taipei Toronto
With offices in
Argentina Austria Brazil Chile Czech Republic France Greece
Guatemala Hungary Italy Japan South Korea Poland Portugal
Singapore Switzerland Thailand Turkey Ukraine Vietnam

Oxford is a registered trade mark of Oxford University Press
in the UK and in certain other countries

Published in the United States
by Oxford University Press Inc., New York

© Peter D. Spencer, 2000

The moral rights of the author have been asserted

Database right Oxford University Press (maker)

Reprinted 2008

ISBN 978-0-19-877610-9

To my mother

Preface

The study of financial markets and institutions has changed beyond recognition over the last thirty years. Over this period, the theory of asymmetric information has transformed what was a rather dull and descriptive subject into an attractive and analytical one. At the same time, the increasingly important role played by financial markets and institutions in the economy has made the subject highly topical.

Teaching this subject in recent years has certainly been an interesting experience. There has been no shortage of newspaper cuttings to enliven classroom discussion. However, the pace of theoretical development, financial innovation, and the regulatory response has made it difficult to keep abreast of the subject. The absence of a textbook covering both capital markets and financial institutions from the new theoretical perspective has also been a problem.

Now that the dust is beginning to settle, I think it is possible to provide the student with a more comprehensive analysis of these developments. This book offers my attempt at this, based upon lecture notes provided for the final year B.Sc.(Econ.) Financial Regulation course at Birkbeck College, London, which I have been teaching since 1995. I keep the mathematics to a relatively basic level by focusing upon a binomial value model. I also find that it is easier to analyse capital market microstructure using a simple zero-profit condition rather than Bayes's Law, which is the standard textbook approach.

I have found it more difficult to devise a simple model for lectures on insurance markets. Consequently, Chapter 3, which deals with this topic, is more difficult than the rest. I normally avoid this material when teaching undergraduate students but use it on a financial structure module which is offered as part of our new Postgraduate Certificate in Finance course at Birkbeck. Lecture notes for these—and the B.Sc.(Econ.)—lectures can be found on the College website.

This work benefits from countless conversations with colleagues, friends, and others in recent years. Chapter 3 strongly reflects discussions with Andrew Scott and Richard Blundell about the papers by Barbara Mace and John Cochrane. Sudipto Bhattacharya has been a major influence upon my thinking about financial intermediaries. Norvald Instefjord and Giles Keating have also influenced my views about the UK and the US financial systems and their differences. I am grateful to Stephen

Davies for pointing out the significance of the work of Charles Calomiris and for comments on an early draft of this book. My thanks are also due to Isaac Alfon, Malcolm Hyatt, and Joe F. Pearlman for pointing out many problems with this draft. Remaining errors are of course my own.

Peter D. Spencer

London, March 2000

Contents

1. Introduction: Asymmetric Information in Financial Markets

Financial economics is regarded as a special branch of economics because financial products are different from other goods and services. This book analyses these products from the perspective of information theory and shows why financial markets and institutions are prone to failure. This analysis is used to see how regulation can reduce the risk of failure and how legal and regulatory constraints help shape a country's corporate and financial structures.

Seen from this perspective, financial products are contracts that allow investors to delegate the management of their assets to others. Fund management represents a straightforward example of such delegation, in which investors retain full legal title to their assets. In the case of an open-ended fund like a US mutual or a UK unit trust, investors can get a *pro rata* share of the fund back upon demand. In the case of equity, bond, and bank-mediated instruments, investors surrender their assets in return for control rights that constrain directors and motivate them to pay dividend and interest payments. This form of delegation is less well defined and precipitates difficult principal–agent problems. The financial markets have to find ways of solving these effectively given the legal, accounting, and regulatory systems in place.

This chapter provides an introductory review of these problems and establishes the basic framework for the analysis of later chapters. We begin by discussing a standard model of an economy without asymmetric information, imperfect competition, or other imperfections. This ideal economy forms a benchmark for the definition and analysis of financial market failure. We then discuss the complications that can arise under asymmetric information: adverse selection, moral hazard, and the problem of *ex post* verification. The final section gives an outline of the remaining chapters and the assumptions upon which they are based.

1.1. Ideal market structures

Markets allow economic agents to separate the consumption and production of goods and services through trade. Ideally, markets produce a

Pareto-optimal allocation of resources: a situation in which no individual can be made better off without making someone else worse off. An elegant description of the conditions which precipitate this ideal solution is for example provided by Arrow and Debreu (1954). They show that when preferences and production sets satisfy basic convexity and continuity conditions and:

1. there is full information,
2. agents are atomistic (too small to influence prices),
3. there are no externalities (unpriced side effects like pollution),

there are prices which clear markets and make individual plans consistent. Furthermore, the first welfare theorem states that under these conditions a competitive equilibrium is Pareto-optimal. Similarly, the second welfare theorem says that any Pareto-optimal allocation of resources can be replicated under competitive equilibrium by manipulating initial endowments.

The basic Arrow–Debreu (1954) general equilibrium model describes commodities in very abstract terms, without worrying about time or uncertainty. The market opens once, equilibrium prices are found, exchanges are made and that is the end of the story. However, the high level of abstraction means that the model can be used to handle a situation in which individuals arrange consumption and production across future time periods and states of nature by exchanging claims on future output.

Consider for example the case in which there are T time periods and G goods produced and consumed in each period, but there is no uncertainty about the future. A competitive market trading simple futures contracts (called Arrow–Debreu securities) that offer one unit of a particular good $g \subset G$ at a particular time $t \subset T$ is then sufficient to allow agents to separate consumption and production decisions and achieve a Pareto-efficient allocation of resources. Uncertainty can be handled by allowing agents to trade insurance, options, and other contracts which have payments that depend upon the state of nature. By providing income in 'bad' states, these contingent claims allow agents to insure against adverse outcomes. For instance, if someone is worried about bad weather spoiling an outdoor event that they are organizing they can take out weather insurance.

The Arrow–Debreu (1954) model can be used to describe a market structure which is *complete* in the sense that it allows individuals to hedge against *all* such contingencies. In this version of the model, S states of nature are possible in each period. The financial markets now trade

Arrow–Debreu securities that pay out one unit of a particular good $g \subset G$ in a particular state $s \subset G$ at a particular date $t \subset T$ (and nothing in other date-states). These securities are traded for every good-date-state combination and the market is complete. Trade in contingent claims allows an agent to completely separate consumption and production decisions and plan them consistently, subject to a single first-period budget constraint. These plans can be implemented by buying and holding a set of contingent claims in one period and then settling them as they fall due.

Interpreted in this way, the Arrow–Debreu general equilibrium specification provides a theoretical model of a complete financial market. It follows immediately from the first welfare theorem that competitive equilibrium with a complete market is Pareto-optimal. This means that there is no need for financial regulation, only a need for a legal structure that enforces contracts *ex post* and ensures a competitive market structure. Regulation can only be justified if one of the underlying assumptions is invalid, destroying the property of Pareto-optimality. A simple two-dimensional version of the Arrow-Debreu model is analysed in Section 3.2.

Nevertheless, we should be careful when using the Arrow–Debreu paradigm to model financial markets. It describes a static equilibrium in which markets open only once and then close permanently. An implausibly large number of markets would be necessary to achieve a Pareto-optimal outcome under this sort of once and for all contracting.[1] In practice, financial markets open every working day, and in some cases trade continuously. Breeden (1984) shows that if preferences can be described by von Neumann–Morgenstern utility functions (see Section 3.2) then the Arrow–Debreu allocation can be replicated by continuous trading of G unconditional commodity futures contracts. A similar 'dynamic spanning' theorem is obtained by Duffie and Huang (1985). These theorems make the complete markets assumption much less implausible.

---

[1] A complete market in Arrow–Debreu securities requires $T \times G \times S$ contracts. Arrow (1964) shows the Arrow–Debreu allocation can be replicated using $T \times S$ conditional futures markets which exchange 'Arrow securities' that deliver one unit of money in each date-state (nothing in other date-states) and $T \times G$ quasi-spot markets that exchange forward contracts for delivery of goods contingent upon a particular date-space outcome. Agents can then transfer money between periods and states using the Arrow securities and then allocate this money across goods in each date-state using the forward commodity markets (Eichberger and Harper 1997: section 4.4). Even so, the numbers of securities necesary to span the dimensions of a modern economy would be astronomic.

1.2. Asymmetric information

General equilibrium theorists normally assume that there is full information: specifically, all agents attach the same subjective probability to each
state of nature. Otherwise, the situation becomes much more complicated
and the standard welfare theorems cannot be applied. However, one of the
characteristic features of a financial market is that prices reveal private
information, helping to reduce information asymmetry. Indeed, it can be
shown (Allen 1986; Radner 1969, 1986) that if the market is complete,
agents condition their expectations upon market prices and have von
Neumann–Morgenstern utility functions, then they will share the same
(posterior) beliefs in equilibrium even if their initial expectations (priors)
are different. This type of solution is known as a Rational Expectations
Equilibrium (REE). As in the basic Arrow–Debreu model, it is assumed that
agents are too small to make strategic behaviour worthwhile. In this case
there are large numbers of agents with the same information who do not
gain anything by behaving in a way which hides information.

This complete market REE is exactly the same as the one that would
emerge if instead everyone held the common posterior beliefs a priori.
Conditional upon the disclosure of this information, the first two welfare
theorems still apply. However, the disclosure of information can itself
destroy *ex ante* risk-sharing opportunities as Hirshleifer (1971) shows (see
Section 6.6). A simple illustration of this effect can be provided when
there is 'no aggregate uncertainty' in the sense that the total allocation of
a good at time *t* is known but its distribution is uncertain. A claim which
is contingent upon this state or allocation allows everyone to hedge their
exposure and eliminates uncertainty at the individual level too (Section 3.3).
However, if some agents know for sure that a particular allocation or state
s will occur then all contracts for delivery in other states will be priced at
zero in a complete market REE. This reveals the state to be *s* and makes
it impossible for agents to insure against this eventuality. Exercise 6.6
provides an illustration.

Chapter 3 analyses some of the other characteristics of the complete
market model. The Fisher Separation Theorem states that shareholders can
unanimously agree to instruct company managers to maximize profit in
this situation.[2] The welfare-reducing effects of idiosyncratic (personal)

---

[2] If there are missing markets, it can be optimal for a shareholder to instruct the manager to
produce instead some idiosyncratic consumption bundle that cannot be purchased in the market
(Eichberger and Harper 1997: chapter 5). Delegation is potentially complicated in this situation
by friction between shareholders with different objectives.

shocks are eliminated costlessly through diversification. Individuals are perfectly insulated from the financial implications of unemployment, hospitalization and other personal risks. The effect of systematic (non-diversifiable) risk is minimized by spreading it optimally across the community. Although exposure to common shocks like recession or natural catastrophe depends upon tolerance to risk, all consumption flows are perfectly correlated. Any financial system which does not approximate this theoretical benchmark is Pareto-inefficient, leaving risk-sharing opportunities unexploited.

1.3. Why do financial markets fail?

Judged against this theoretical benchmark, even the most sophisticated contemporary systems are hopelessly inefficient. International business cycles are divergent and portfolios are not sufficiently diversified to share this risk internationally (Obstfeld 1994; Melitz 1999). Even within local state communities, consumption patterns are only weakly correlated (Bayoumi and McDonald 1994, 1995). Although Mace (1991) suggests that there is a high degree of risk sharing at the national level in the USA, this finding is controversial and has not been replicated on other data sets.

Shiller (1993) has argued that welfare could be improved by introducing a much wider set of financial and insurance instruments, helping to complete the financial market. He proposes futures in GDP and other macroeconomic variables. However, it is not clear that this would greatly expand the range of hedging and other instruments which are already available in the financial markets. Stock and bond prices are strongly influenced by macroeconomic variables like GDP and surely provide good proxies. Moreover, his proposal begs the question of why the market is incomplete. If these markets would be welfare improving, then in the absence of some impediment, financial exchanges would already have found it profitable to introduce them.

Many explanations have been put forward to explain the deficiencies in the range of hedging instruments available in practice. Transaction costs are undoubtedly an important factor, which can make it difficult to establish markets in exotic instruments or remote risks. However, the theory of asymmetric information provides a much more plausible explanation of missing markets. Akerlof (1970) shows how this phenomenon can prevent a market from being established. This idea has found many applications in the financial markets over the last 30 years.

The basic problem is that when individuals have access to private information that is known only to themselves or their close associates, they become information monopolists. In an insurance market for example (Section 3.5), clients will typically know much more about their own risk characteristics than the insurer does. Individuals then have an incentive to behave in a way which hides this information from the rest of the market. Markets only become fully revealing when there are large numbers of agents with the same piece of information, removing the incentive to hide information. Akerlof (1970) shows that when individuals have private information, adverse selection can prevent a market becoming established, or lead to a low-quality market. Moral hazard and other problems can also precipitate a suboptimal outcome. If the market fails for these or any other reasons, there is a case for regulation.

Economists say that a market fails whenever it does not deliver a Pareto-efficient allocation of resources. The first theorem of welfare economics tells us that perfect competition will achieve such an outcome, provided that there are no unpriced side effects (called externalities) like contagion or pollution. Perfect competition in turn assumes large numbers of buyers and sellers as well as full information. Financial markets can fail to deliver this outcome if any of these conditions fail to hold. They are dogged by contagion, free riders and other externalities. Financial institutions (especially banks) tend to be very large and may not be competitive. However, in the case of financial markets, economists are mainly concerned about the adverse effects of asymmetric information. This occurs if buyers and sellers have different views about the future, violating the first welfare theorem.

The first part of this book focuses upon the way in which asymmetric information affects financial markets, assuming away imperfect competition, transactions costs, and other frictions. Competition issues are introduced only in Chapter 7. Transactions costs are introduced in Chapter 8, which shows how the modern explanation of financial intermediation combines the new theory of asymmetric information with the old theory of lump sum costs and economies of scale in portfolio management.

1.4. Classifying markets using information theory

The consequences of asymmetric information depend upon the structure of the market. Information theory identifies three broad types of product:

1. 'Search goods': their quality is known *ex ante* i.e. in advance of purchase (e.g. basic commodities like flour, baked beans, petrol).
2. 'Experience' or 'taste' goods: their quality becomes obvious *ex post* i.e. after purchase (e.g. food, wine, and second-hand cars).
3. 'Credence items': their quality may never be established, even *ex post* after outcome is observed (e.g. surgical operations, legal advice).

Case 1 is the simplest. Products are homogeneous and everyone is familiar with their attributes. We know what we are buying and in principle we simply search out the lowest price: hence the name 'search goods'. The basic textbooks naturally focus upon this case in order to develop relatively simple theories of competition and market equilibrium.

In case 2 products are heterogeneous. The price that we are prepared to pay depends upon the quality as well as the quantity purchased. However, even upon close inspection, it is hard to discern quality, impossible to know exactly what we are getting for our money. In the case of an experience good, quality becomes apparent upon consumption. The label on the bottle may say Mouton Cadet 1983 and the wine guides may give this a high rating. However, can you be sure, until you open it, that the bottle has been properly stored over the years? Even if it has, is it going to be to your taste? This is an asymmetric information situation, in which the seller typically knows much more about quality than the buyer. It is found in durable as well as non-durable goods markets. Indeed the best-known example is perhaps that of a second-hand car, used by Akerlof in his seminal (1970) paper on asymmetric information. The quality and reliability of a car may be hard to judge even on the basis of a professional examination and a road test, but soon becomes apparent when we pay up and drive off. The housing market gives another example of a durable good or asset market with heterogeneity and asymmetric information.

In the case of credence products, it is hard to know what the standard of quality and performance was even after the outcome is known. The classic examples of this kind are drawn from professional services like medicine and the law. Car repair and airline services also provide good examples. These are situations in which there is a serious imbalance of information and we have to have faith in the judgement and competence of the professionals who provide the service: hence the name 'credence' goods. We are practically blind to the process involved. In the case of a surgical operation for example, we may eventually know whether this was successful or unsuccessful. We can be given comfort and reassurance and may be pleased with the service. But we can never be absolutely sure that the recommendation to proceed with the operation was good or bad advice or that the surgical procedure was performed well. Even if we can determine the surgeon's success rate, there is always going to be an element of luck involved, unless the sample of cases is very large.

Markets in credence goods are made on the basis of trust, which is usually maintained by professional bodies and trade associations. Industrial and individual reputations for quality and probity are built up over long periods of time but, like any reputation, are quickly forfeited by bad behaviour. The recent experience of the British beef industry gives a notorious example. In this case a reputation for a high-quality and wholesome product was ruined by bad practice by a minority of farmers which culminated in the BSE crisis. Personal pension misselling gives an example from the financial arena, which is analysed in Box 2.1. in the next chapter.

1.5. Financial products as credence goods

We have to be careful in classifying financial assets and services using this taxonomy, because they are fundamentally different from non-financial goods and services and even physical assets like cars and houses. That is because a financial security represents more than a title to an asset or portfolio: there is invariably an element of professional management involved. First, as I argue in this section, this means that all financial securities should be classified as credence goods. Second, as I argue in Section 1.11, it involves the delegation of management to another party or agent.

Take government stocks or large company shares for example. These are homogeneous because they offer the same returns and (within each class) identical voting rights. Financial futures and exchange-traded options contracts are deliberately standardized in order to achieve homogeneity. Buyers and sellers typically search for the best price and it might seem reasonable to classify these instruments as search goods. However, with an equity we are buying the right to a share in a company's dividend stream and not just the assets of the company. This claim has to be enforced under the law and depends critically upon voting rights, corporate governance and the quality of management. Management quality may only become apparent, if at all, long after purchase. We only buy equities if we believe that the company is sound and trust the management. Similarly, the value of government bonds and financial futures depends upon the quality of monetary management and ultimately (in the case of a price-indexed bond) the probity of government. For this reason, stocks, shares, and futures should really be classed as credence items, even though they are dominated by well-informed professional investors who search for the best price. Market models with these features are analysed in Chapters 4 to 7.

Some financial markets exhibit a high degree of heterogeneity. For example, the Eurobond market saw a proliferation of securities with 'bells and whistles' in the 1980s, tailored to specific clienteles, which made them very idiosyncratic. This now makes them difficult to sell. They are typically traded through 'boutiques' or brokers who find buyers in the same way that estate agents sell houses. Over-the-counter (OTC) options are also designed for specific clients. But unlike cars and houses we should also classify these securities, like the underlying stocks, shares, and futures, under the credence heading.

Fund management and advisory services clearly come into the credence category. In this case there is a wide gap between the knowledge of the general public and that of the fund managers and financial advisers selling the service. Fund management performance is difficult to assess, even *ex post*, because unless the sample is very large, it is impossible to distinguish good luck from good management. A study of British fund management data by Brealey and Hodges (1972) suggests that even with managerial continuity, it would take 80 quarterly observations of return to discriminate between good and bad managers at the usual level of statistical significance. Carhart (1997) finds that there is little persistence in US mutual fund performance, suggesting that the past performance is little guide to the future. Skill is involved even in the provision of funds that are indexed to specific stock market indices. The market for fund managers is considered in the next chapter.

The only obvious exception to this rule is a technical service like market making which is relatively straightforward and executed quickly. Nevertheless, we have to be careful to distinguish here between the *service* which is arguably a search good where minimum commissions are identified by clients and the *security* which is arguably a credence good. Even in the case of an execution-only transactions service, things may not be as they seem. Execution and counterparty risks leave a residual possibility of management error. The case of Griffin Securities in London in December 1998 gives an example. Clients trading through this firm on LIFFE thought that their balances were safeguarded against counterparty risk by LIFFE's margin requirements, but Griffin allowed one large client to trade beyond the limits. His losses bankrupted the firm and other clients lost considerable sums of money as a result.

1.6. Information as an endowment

The type of informational defects seen in financial markets depend critically upon whether or not it is easy to improve the available information through research: screening, monitoring, and auditing activity (see Table 1.1). If it is, we say that information is *endogenous* and if it is not, that information is *exogenous*. In the case of exogenous information, there is (as we shall see) a tension between market efficiency and the informativeness of prices. In the endogenous case, there are free rider problems which mean that these various research activities are likely to be underprovided by the market.

In the case of exogenous information we think of information as a fixed endowment. Everyone has access to public information. Some may be better informed, because they are company insiders for example, or because they are market professionals. But the idea is that they are stuck with the information at their disposal, and cannot increase this in any cost-effective way. Of course, it is usually possible to find out more about a product or company than we read in the newspapers. Even if it is not cost-effective for individual investors to undertake research, there are usually information providers that can do this for us. In the case of the wholesale markets there are bond rating agencies like Moody's and for equities organizations like Extel which provide information summaries. For the retail market there are 'Consumer Reports' in the USA and 'Money Matters' and 'Which' magazine in the UK. But in the case of retail finan-

Table 1.1: Problems of asymmetric information and their solution

	Transaction		Outcome
Time frame:	*ex ante*	Contract period	*ex post*
Problem	Adverse selection	Moral hazard	State verification
Solution			
(a) contract:	Two-tier	Equity participation	Debt contract
(b) research:	Screening/selection	Monitoring	Accounting and audit
	(Once and for all)	(Continuous)	Equity: all states
(c) other:	Customer relationship	Customer relationship	Debt: bankruptcy
	(Continuous)	(Continuous)	
	Self-regulation	Self-regulation	
	Intermediation	Intermediation	

cial services like insurance the imbalance of information or expertise between sellers and buyers is normally very large, even when these recommendations are taken into account. In this case it is reasonable to characterize the situation as one of exogenous information, because further information gathering is not worthwhile for an individual.

Primary security mechanisms, which bring companies to the market for the first time, also have to bridge a wide knowledge gap (Section 4.1 discusses this problem). On one side of the market, venture capital investors and managers in these companies know a great deal about them, while on the other side, the wider financial community may only have a few years of accounts and general knowledge of the sector to go on. Secondary markets in small company shares often remain very asymmetric.

1.7. Pooling equilibrium

In this kind of situation, it is reasonable to assume that information endowments are fixed. This simplifies the analysis considerably. Even so, a variety of complications are likely, depending upon how flexible agents are in their behaviour.

The basic problem is that if buyers cannot discriminate between good and bad products, but are *only aware of average quality*, the best they can do is to offer to buy at a price that reflects average quality. In other words, they pay a 'pool' price, which reflects the *average* quality of the market 'pool'. They take their luck with the quality in exactly the same way as they do if they borrow a car at random from their company car pool.

The pool price effectively subsidizes low-quality and penalizes high-quality suppliers. *Ex post*, those who happen to buy high-quality items are better off than expected, while those who buy low-quality items are worse off. This may be unfair, but as long as demand and supply are fixed the effect on resource allocation is trivial.

An illustration may help. Consider a market in second-hand company cars. Suppose that output quality variation means that there are two vehicle qualities. One fifth are 'lemons' in Akerlof's (1970) American terminology, meaning that they run poorly and are unreliable. The rest are 'peaches', running smoothly and reliably. If the second-hand buyer could distinguish the two types, the value of a two-year-old peach would be say £10,000, while a lemon would fetch say only £5,000, reflecting the maintenance and inconvenience costs. However, these are experience goods and there is no way buyers can tell until they get to know the car.

How much would you be prepared to pay for a two-year-old company car in this situation? Theory tells us that in the absence of risk aversion and other complications, you should be prepared pay a price that reflects the average quality of car: the pool price. If all companies buy new and always sell after two years, the pool price reflects the population-weighted average quality: £(0.2 × 5000 + 0.8 × 10,000) or £9,000. *Ex post*, most buyers are lucky and get a £10,000 vehicle for £9,000, while a fifth are unlucky, paying £9,000 for one worth just £5,000. The market works and all cars are sold at a price which is statistically fair.

If behaviour is flexible, the consequences of asymmetric information are much more serious. For instance, in our example, the sellers of reliable units know they are getting a bad deal, and may revise their policy. Table 1.1 shows the complications which can arise over different time spans: before a contract is made, after it has run to an end, and the interim. The lower section of the table indicates the way in which their effects can be mitigated by the market, essentially by using different types of contract structure or (if possible) research activity.

1.8. Adverse selection and the problem of hidden information

Since the pool price reflects average quality, the high-quality suppliers know that they are treated unfairly and may decide *ex ante* to withdraw from the market. Indeed, if they are high-cost producers, they may be forced to leave the market. This is the phenomenon of adverse selection. If adverse selection takes place, the average quality and hence the pool price falls, which may cause medium-quality suppliers to leave and set up a cumulative downward spiral in quality and price. An example of this is described in the next chapter, based on Akerlof's (1970) model.

Adverse selection tends to occur *before* any transaction takes place, as indicated in Table 1.1. Indeed it may prevent any deals taking place, by extinguishing the market. However, a market will be maintained as long as there are some forced sellers with high-quality products. The exogenous information model of the security market analysed in Chapters 4–5 illustrates this point, as does Question 2 at the end of this chapter. However, if behaviour is flexible, informational problems can distort the allocation of resources, as the example of the next chapter demonstrates.

I have assumed that the sellers know more about the risks involved in the transaction than do the buyers. However, in many cases the buyers are at an advantage. In the case of insurance transactions, the buyers naturally know more about themselves and the risks they are exposed to than the provider. So the insurer has to charge a premium that reflects the average or actuarial risk in a particular category of client. Adverse selection can then occur as the low-risk types decide that the premium is too high to make the insurance cost-effective for them, and leave the market. Insurance practitioners were familiar with the phenomenon in the last century, although the term adverse selection was only introduced into economics by Akerlof as recently as 1970. Similarly, in the bank credit market analysed in Chapter 9, the borrowers typically know more about the risks than the lender, leading to adverse selection. Stiglitz and Weiss (1981) originally demonstrated this effect, which they used to help explain the phenomenon of credit rationing.

The distribution of information in the capital market is more asymmetric in the sense that it is multilateral. In this case, market makers and their professional clients have a high level of expertise, compared to retail investors. Yet investors buying or selling on the basis of inside information have a further advantage. It is not realistic to assume that information is exogenous in this case.

Financial companies can try to minimize the effect of adverse selection using screening devices. For example, banks can use information systems to identify clients with poor credit records. Similarly, stockbrokers can employ company analysts to vet new companies coming to the market and make recommendations about shares trading in the secondary market.

Rothschild and Stiglitz (1976) show how it is possible to get clients to reveal private information by offering a range of different contracts at different prices. In their model, low-risk clients select insurance contracts with limited cover at a low price, while high-risk clients find it optimal to buy more cover at a commensurately higher price. This multi-tier contract solution is known as a separating equilibrium. Similarly, Easley and O'Hara (1992) show that two-tier contracts can help resolve asymmetry in a secondary capital market. In this case, liquidity trades with small demands select a small trade size at a low price spread, while insiders who want to 'trade large' go for a bigger contract size with a wider spread.

This is a second-best contract structure because it reduces welfare below the full information contract, essentially by preventing full insurance. Moreover, these devices reduce the dispersion of risk characteristics within any risk category, but they are unlikely to eliminate it entirely. This means that there is still some scope for adverse selection within any group, once these clients face a price dictated by the average for the group.

1.9. Moral hazard and the problem of hidden action

Moral hazard occurs when a contract changes the incentives and behaviour of the parties that enter into it. While adverse selection takes place *before* the transaction as a result of 'hidden information', moral hazard takes the form of 'hidden actions' which occur *during* the period of the contract (Table 1.1). The best-known examples are insurance contracts, which can reduce the incentive for the client to take care. Stiglitz and Weiss (1981) also discuss the way in which this can impinge upon the credit market, after a bank grants a loan.

A contract is a formal or informal agreement that specifies when and how payments, products, or services are transferred between two or more parties. Moral hazard occurs if actions are not immediately observable (or inferred from observable variables like the final state or outcome) and can be hidden from the other party's sight. It is inherent in situations like insurance where the outcome (say a car crash) depends upon the behaviour of the parties involved as well as chance. Like adverse selection, early references to this term can be found in the insurance practitioner's literature, but it was not until the 1960s that Arrow (1965) introduced it into financial economics. Arrow used it in the context of insurance, but it is now used much more widely, to describe the effect which hidden action can have in any product or factor market.

Although actions may not be immediately observable, it may be possible for one party to find out what the others are doing by monitoring their behaviour. However, this is likely to be intrusive or costly. Moreover, unlike the once and for all screening exercises that help remove the effect of hidden information, monitoring needs to be conducted on a permanent basis.

If information is exogenous and monitoring is not possible, payments can only be specified in terms of outcomes rather than actions. The parties to the agreement then have to adopt a second-best contract structure that builds in incentives to minimize the adverse incentives set up by a first-best solution. This is known as the principal–agent problem and is discussed in Section 7.3. The second-best structure has to balance moral hazard against the risk-sharing objectives the contract is designed to achieve. For example, giving company executives equity-based remuneration contracts helps maximize effort, but exposes them to risk. Similarly, car insurance companies routinely introduce no-claims bonus schemes in an attempt to reduce moral hazard. But this only works because it exposes clients to some of the risk the contract was designed to share.

Many different principal–agent problems arise in the financial markets. Chapter 7 looks at the case of shareholders who delegate the management of a company to a board of directors, while Chapter 8 looks at the way in which depositors effectively delegate the management of their assets to a bank and its shareholders. As we shall see, the shape of the financial system is strongly influenced by the relative effectiveness with which the legal, accounting, and regulatory system resolves these two important principal–agent problems. The bias of the Anglo-American system towards diffuse capital markets suggests that a system of common law, accounting standards, and lightly regulated markets does somehow resolve these informational problems. On the other hand, the tendency of continental systems to gravitate towards investor concentration and reliance upon bank-mediated finance appears to be the result of their different legal, accounting, and regulatory control systems (La Porta *et al.* 1998).

1.10. The problem of *ex post* state verification or hidden outcome

Frequently the final outcome of a venture is not apparent to all parties to a financial contract. In this case the uninformed may have to expend resources confirming this rather than believing what they are told by the informed parties. These are known as audit costs, as indicated in Table 1.1. For example, an equity contract or 'share' allows outside investors to share in the outcome of an investment. However, only insiders may know the true outcome. They have an incentive to *understate* this, in order to minimize the distribution to outsiders. The classic example of this is 'Hollywood accounting', which means that actors and other contributors who agree to share in a film's 'profits' rarely see any. On the other hand, the project's managers may have an equity-linked remuneration contract, in which case they have an incentive to *overstate* the outcome. Either way, all outcomes have to be verified or audited by outside parties. One of the important roles of the government in the financial sector is to ensure that there are sensible accounting standards, to facilitate this verification process. These problems are discussed further in Chapters 7 and 8.

Fixed- or floating-rate debt contracts offer a return which is independent of the outcome of a project, providing that the return (plus any collateral the owners dedicate to the venture) is sufficient to meet the loan principal and interest. If the return (and collateral) is insufficient, the lender takes over the management and ownership of the venture and keeps the residual value. The original equity participants get nothing in this case. This contract offers an efficient mechanism for dealing with the veracity problem and getting managers and equity holders to tell the truth about the outcome. That is because the only way they could try to cheat the lender is by declaring that the outcome was insufficient to repay the debt when it was not. But in that case they would lose ownership and get nothing at all. Another important background role for government is to ensure that there is an efficient legal procedure for this change in ownership.

With debt financing, only bankruptcy states have to be audited (Table 1.1). This places less reliance upon the accounting system than equity financing. However, it does not solve the moral hazard problem. If the project is simple, well-defined, and easily monitored, that may not matter. But if the manager can switch high-risk for low-risk projects, debt contracts will encourage substitution. This form of moral hazard is known as asset substitution or excessive risk-taking. Debt contracts are extensively used in banking markets, which are analysed in Chapters 8–11.

1.11. Endogenous information and security research

In the case of retail investment products, described in the next chapter, it is realistic to assume that information cannot be significantly expanded by research. This is also a reasonable assumption to make about retail banking products. However, professional investors dominate the markets for trading stocks, shares, financial futures, and their derivatives. A great deal of background information is published for these securities, which can be effectively researched by sophisticated investors. In the case of these capital markets it is more realistic to assume that information is endogenous.

Chapter 6 develops a market microstructure model that allows for research and analyses the way in which this information is revealed through open market trades and prices. It shows how this market transparency can reduce the value of research, essentially by moving prices against those who are known to transact on the basis of such analysis. This effect can lead to underinvestment in research. Ongoing company monitoring by capital investors, to mitigate the effect of moral hazard or 'shirking' by directors, is very unlikely in a decentralized market. Chapter 6 shows how these endogenous information problems can hamper the functioning of capital markets.

The consequences of endogenous information are altogether different in the case of the banking system, since banking transactions are usually conducted behind closed doors. A bank is in a much better position to justify screening and monitoring activity than equity investors are, as Chapter 8 argues. Similarly, as I have suggested, the fixed interest or floating rate contracts which are found in banking markets offer an effective way of handling the costly state verification problem. Thus intermediation provides a cost-effective way of dealing with the informational problems that beset the capital markets.

1.12. The structure of the book

Most financial textbooks begin by discussing bank deposits and fixed rate instruments, analysing equities, derivatives, and other financial products later. This is because in the absence of default risk, securities like bank deposits and bonds are easier to understand and to value than equity contracts. However, once the possibility of default is allowed for, banking markets become more difficult to analyse than capital markets. Consequently, this book begins by discussing retail products like pension plans which have uncertain values but are less prone to default risk. I then look at stocks and shares, the markets in which they trade and their regulation. This analysis reveals both the strengths and weaknesses of the capital markets and shows how financial intermediaries can sometimes be more efficient. Then I discuss the loan and deposit markets, the ways in which they can fail, and their regulation.

The next chapter begins by looking at the market for retail financial services like investment advice, investment trusts, and products such as unit-linked pension plans. The informational structure of these markets is relatively simple because clients are at a clear informational disadvantage to the provider. This means that it is reasonable to characterize these markets in terms of exogenous information. Clients also retain full legal title to the underlying investments.

In contrast, a bank deposit entitles its holder to a fixed return and the residual value of the bank's assets goes to its shareholders. This can lead to excessive risk-taking and a run on the bank. Prudential regulation is needed to minimize this risk. The discussion of retail financial services allows us to look at the effect of asymmetric information in a general setting without confronting the more complicated informational structures of capital and banking markets. It is followed by an introductory discussion of the regulation of financial services in a modern economy.

Chapter 3 looks at insurance products. These are interesting because there is usually a two-way information asymmetry. The insurer usually knows more about the product than the client, while the client normally knows more about their risk status than the insurer. I argue that analytically, mutual insurance companies are like unit and investment trust companies in terms of their ownership structure, while insurance companies are more like banks in this respect, requiring prudential regulation.

Chapters 4–6 focus upon the capital markets: which trade stocks and shares and other primary securities. This analysis is simplified by assuming that the fundamental value of these securities is exogenous and is not affected by investor behaviour. This allows relatively simple breakeven asset pricing techniques to be employed without worrying about the more complicated corporate governance and incentive feedbacks addressed in later chapters. Chapter 4 develops a simple microstructure model of the capital market assuming that information is *exogenous*. Chapter 5 looks at the way that secondary market makers and other 'uninformed' participants can learn from the trading activity of insiders and other 'informed' traders. This model is used to discuss the regulation of insider trading. Chapter 6 adapts the microstructure model to allow for security research and analyses the way in which this information is revealed through open market trades and prices. This demonstrates the way in which free rider and other *endogenous* information problems can hinder the functioning of capital markets.

The remaining chapters relax the assumption that the fundamental value of a security is given. This allows us to study the rich interplay between contract design, security values, and managerial behaviour. Realistically, as I have already argued, all security values depend upon managerial quality. Ultimately, the value of a security depends upon the control rights that are written into the contract, the legal backing for these rights, and the constraints which this imposes upon management. As Shleifer and Vishny (1997) note, assets can be worth next to nothing in countries such as Russia where these control rights are not respected.

Chapter 7 looks at the relationship between equity prices and managerial efficiency, allowing efficiency to influence prices and options and stock holdings to motivate management. This discussion provides a reason for encouraging corporate takeovers, despite the problems of market abuse and short-termism with which they are associated. That is because the threat of takeover provides a backstop mechanism for ensuring efficiency when monitoring, incentive, and other devices fail.

Chapter 8 shows how intermediation of debt contracts can overcome some of the informational and delegational weaknesses of the capital markets. To simplify the analysis and avoid the complication of moral hazard it is initially assumed that banks (and other borrowers) face large non-financial penalties in bankruptcy. This assumption is relaxed in Chapter 9, which looks at the problem of excessive risk-taking. Chapter 8 also assumes that banks issue term deposits, so that bank runs are not a problem. This assumption is relaxed in Chapter 10, which looks at the structure of the bank deposit contract, deposit insurance, and other ways of making the banking system run-proof. Chapter 11 discusses the regulation of the banking system.

Chapter 12 draws this discussion to a conclusion and looks at the implications of different corporate governance and regulatory structures for the financial architecture. Following La Porta *et al.* (1998), Shleifer and Vishny (1997), and others, we review the way in which these structures attempt to resolve the difficult incentive problems which arise in the financial markets. Finally, we discuss the potential strengths and weaknesses of the unified approach to regulation recently adopted by Japan, Britain, and other countries.

EXERCISES

Information theory

Question 1. (a) Categorize the following products from the perspective of the information theory set out in Section 1.2, outlining the reasons for your allocation: a bottle of 'Chateau Plonque 1998', a bottle of Mouton Cadet 1990, a can of Virgin Cola, a 1 kg bag of Silver Spoon sugar, the latest Oasis CD, a 'Fly by Night' charter ticket, a Qantas airline ticket, a Marks and Spencer pension plan, the Bank of England's May 1999 Inflation Report, a packet of Wal-Mart's own-label cornflakes, a packet of Kellogg's Cornflakes.

(b) Should all financial products be classed as credence goods?

Pooling equilibrium

Question 2. Assume that 10 per cent of the population of households have to sell their home every year in order to relocate for their employment. The only other reason a household may want to sell is because their residence is affected by subsidence. There is no rented market. The value to the occupier of a house without subsidence is £100,000 and of one with subsidence only £50,000. The problem is that 20 per cent of houses have subsidence and there is no way of telling whether a house is so affected before moving in. Nobody is allowed to move more than once in any year.

(a) What would you expect to pay for a house in such a market? [Suggested answers follow in a different font.]

Because purchasers cannot discriminate, all houses sell at the same price (the pool price). Good sellers subsidize bad. This pays those with subsidence to sell and buy at the same price in the hope of getting a house without subsidence. Thus the 20 per cent of the housing stock that has subsidence comes onto the market every year. So look at total supply composition and quality:

	Reason for sale	Of which:	
		Low quality	High quality
20%	Sold due to subsidence	20	0
10%	Sold due to job move	2	8
Less: 2%	(Overlap)	−2	0
100%	Total sales	20	8

Consequently, 28 per cent of the housing stock is sold annually, 20 per cent with and 8 per cent without subsidence. Taking the weighted average gives the fair price for a house under these assumptions:

$$\text{fair price} = P = \frac{20}{28} \times 50{,}000 + \frac{8}{28} \times 100{,}000 = £64{,}286.$$

(b) Suppose employers give a certificate to those moving, saying they have to move for their work. Assuming that this does not affect the composition of house types owned by these individuals, what difference should this certificate make to the price they get for their homes?

Certificates allow buyers to separate job movers from the rest. But some job movers (by assumption an average of 20 per cent) still have subsidence. So for them the fair price is

$$\text{fair price with certificate} = P = 0.2 \times 50{,}000 + 0.8 \times 100{,}000 = £90{,}000.$$

The fair price for those without a certificate is £50,000—they all have subsidence.

(c) If half of those relocating can volunteer (assume they do this only because their home has subsidence) and half are selected by their employer, how does this affect the equilibrium in (b)?

For an employee with subsidence, there is an incentive to volunteer for a job move to disguise the reason for selling. This confuses the signal given by the certificate. Consider those with certificates: half are volunteers with houses worth £50,000 (with subsidence); half are 'pressed men' with average houses worth £90,000 (from (b)).

$$\text{fair price with certificate and volunteers} = P = 0.5 \times 50{,}000 + 0.5 \times 90{,}000 = £70{,}000.$$

Again, the fair price for those without any certificate is £50,000—they all have subsidence.

(d) Discuss the general implications of your analysis for financial market equilibrium.

Adverse selection—the envelope game

(With acknowledgement to my colleague Dr Sandeep Kapur)

Question 3. Seven people each place a sealed envelope in a bag. They know how much money their envelope contains. You do not know how much money there is in any particular envelope, but you do at least know the overall distribution: one envelope contains nothing, the rest respectively £1, £2, £3, £4, £5, £6.

(a) *Pooling equilibrium.* Assuming that you are risk neutral, what is the maximum price you would offer for the right to take one envelope and its contents at random?

(b) *Adverse selection*

(i) Suppose that the money you offer goes to the contributor whose envelope gets picked. Also, that after you announce your offer each contributor is allowed to withdraw their envelope from the bag. Given your bid, which ones will withdraw their envelopes?

(ii) Would you like to change your bid now? To what value?

(iii) What if the contributors are allowed to react to your changed bid? Will there be further withdrawals from the game? Would that make you want to revise your bid?

(iv) Now collapse the game in time. If the owners are always allowed to react after you make an offer, what would you offer?

Asymmetric information

Question 4. 'Banking and financial services are not unique: medical and legal practitioners learned to live with asymmetric information centuries ago.' Do you agree?

Question 5. Describe the way in which asymmetric information in financial markets can lead to (a) adverse selection, (b) moral hazard, and (c) problems of *ex post* state verification. For each of these problems give an example of a device which these markets have developed to try to mitigate its effects. (Birkbeck College, London, Postgraduate Certificate in Finance, Final Examination, 1999).

2. Adverse Selection and the Market for Retail Financial Services

This chapter develops a simple model of adverse selection in the market for basic retail financial services like financial advice and fund management. Insurance and banking services are considered in later chapters. This model is squarely based on the one developed by Akerlof (1970). It is used to analyse minimum standard rules and other market responses to the informational problems which plague these industries. The chapter discusses the case for self-regulation in financial services and asks how government can improve upon this solution. The regulation of the industry is mainly discussed from the perspective of the British system, which now has a unified system of regulation. In the USA and many other English-speaking countries, the regulation of basic financial services is handled at the state level, making it difficult to provide a comprehensive description of the regulatory regime.

2.1. Financial services

Financial services include the whole range of services provided by financial firms and markets. However, it is reasonable to follow the approach of the British Financial Services and Markets Act (2001) and separate capital markets (which trade variable price instruments like stocks and shares) from other financial services. There are also important reasons for treating banks and insurance companies differently from other financial intermediaries like pension funds and investment and unit trusts. That is primarily because as the previous chapter indicated, clients retain full ownership and legal title to their investments in the latter case, minimizing the risk of asset substitution. Also, their liabilities are of a long-term nature, which distinguishes them from banks (discussed in Chapter 10). In the case of open-ended funds like British unit trusts, funds are invested in marketable assets which can be liquidated quickly in response to investor withdrawals. Because investor claims are related to the market value of these assets, sudden withdrawals are not normally a problem.

The basic problem with the provision of life assurance and pension products and the financial advisers who act as brokers in these retail markets is asymmetric information. Lack of expertise on the part of buyers means they find it hard to assess the quality of individual products and suppliers. This makes fraud, theft, and non-contractual wealth transfers (like churning or turnover of portfolios in order to generate commissions) a serious risk. Poor quality can be reflected in negligence, incompetence, and dishonesty, either separately or in combination. There are many notorious examples of managers who were led into dishonesty by attempts to cover up honest mistakes.

In this asymmetric information situation we are bound to see a pooling equilibrium, in which the commissions which suppliers receive reflect the reputation of the *industry* for quality and long-term value for money. Moreover, as the previous chapter argued, this is likely to lead to adverse selection, moral hazard, and verification problems. Even if research into different products is viable for individual clients, then others may attempt to free ride on this research by shadowing the purchases of these clients. This chapter focuses upon the effect of adverse selection, which is arguably the most likely cause of market failure in this area. The theoretical treatment adapts the model of Akerlof (1970). Although this was originally set out in terms of a market in second-hand cars, it lends itself nicely to the analysis of financial services.

2.2. Akerlof (1970) as a model of the fund management market

Consider the provision of retail investment products like unit and investment trusts, personal pension, and life assurance policies. These are essentially collective investment schemes that raise contributions or premia from the public and invest them in stocks and shares.[1] Although the minimum payment is sometimes guaranteed, the outcome depends upon a range of factors, notably the behaviour of the capital markets and the relative performance of the fund manager. These variables are both highly uncertain *ex ante* and hard to assess even with the benefit of hindsight. This is why I have argued that retail financial services are a credence product. The financial *service* provided by the agent who sells these

---

[1] In the case of unit-linked products, there is a direct relationship between product returns and fund performance. In the case of 'with profits' pensions and life assurance products, this relationship is much looser. The returns on these products depend upon the award of discretionary bonuses by the provider, which depend upon past fund performance, provider expectations of future performance and the assets available after meeting obligations (the free-assets ratio).

products can be viewed in the same way, but this section of the chapter focuses upon a simple model of the investment *product*.

2.3. Full information

To develop an Akerlof-style model of a retail fund management we start by defining the following supply-side parameters:

x = a fund manager's ability to 'beat the market';
c = their annual cost;
$a = x/c$ = their efficiency parameter.

Parameter (x) is the *actual* ability of the manager to secure higher (risk-adjusted) returns than the market. For ease of comparison, the parameters (x, c) and price (p) are expressed on an annual basis as a percentage of the funds under management. For example a manager with $x = 3$ and $c = 2$ would on average beat the market by 3 per cent a year and have costs equal to 2 per cent of the portfolio. Parameter x is the basic 'quality' dimension in this version of the Akerlof model and may or may not correspond to a performance measurement indicator. At one extreme, under full information, *ex post* performance measurement (by institutions like Greenwich Associates in the USA and Wood MacKenzie in the UK) could make the individual manager's ability fully observable. In this case, a suitable *ex post* statistical measure of risk-adjusted excess return like Jensen's alpha[2] would give a perfect indicator of the manager's actual ability. That is the full information assumption we make in this section. At the other extreme, analysed in the next section, these measures are uninformative at the individual level. However, the industry average is observable. A hybrid model is considered in Section 2.2.3.

To keep the model relatively simple, now assume that the efficiency parameter (a) is the same for all managers: the cost index (c) is perfectly correlated with the ability index (x). Managers know their own cost and quality indices. For the management industry to be viable we need: $x = ac > c$ or $a > 1$. We adopt Akerlof's (1970) arithmetic and assume that $a = 3/2$, so that for any fund manager with cost index c:

$$x = (3/2)c. \qquad (2.1)$$

---

[2] This is the intercept coefficient in a regression of *ex post* fund return (less the risk-free interest rate) on the market portfolio (less the risk-free interest rate). See Jensen (1968). In Section 2.5 we assume that suppliers can accurately determine each other's parameter values, even though clients cannot.

The effect of different efficiency parameter values is discussed in concluding this section.

To complete the description of the supply side of this market, we assume that the market is contestable (Baumol 1970). This means that managers can freely enter or leave the market without unrecoverable costs. Consequently, c is the supply-side reservation price, which means that if the market performance fee $p < p^s = c$ for any manager, they withdraw from the market:

$$\text{provider's reservation price: } p^s = c. \tag{2.2}$$

Turning to the demand side of the market, let us assume that retail clients are identical and have an ability and cost index of zero: $x = c = 0$.[3] They are aware of the price p of fund management (the annual percentage commission charge)[4] and will withdraw from the market if they think that this exceeds the manager's ability (since they could do better themselves, taking into account these charges). In other words, under full information the demand-side reservation price (or commission) for any (known) quality value (x) is equal to the quality index itself, which is a 50 per cent mark-up on a manager's cost:

client's reservation price
for known quality x: $p^d = x = ac = (3/2)c.$ $\qquad$ (2.3)

Since $p^d = x = ac = (3/2)c > c = p^s$ there is a potential gain from trade under full information.

In order to find a market equilibrium in this situation we must find a price p which satisfies the equilibrium condition:

market clearing price
under full information: $p^d = (3/2)c \geq p \geq c = p^s$ $\qquad$ (2.4)

where p^d and p^s are substituted from (2.2) and (2.3). Under full information two equilibria are possible in this model. In the first case, a buyers'

---

[3] This is only realistic if the client can get the same diversification and cost advantages as the fund manager and invest in the market portfolio with $x = 0$. Cost or diversification effects could however be allowed for by adjusting the x and c benchmarks.

[4] This assumes that the commissions and other charges levied by the provider are disclosed to the buyer *ex ante*. In the USA and the UK, this has always been the case for charges levied by management companies of collective funds like investment and unit trusts. Before 1995, providers of personal pensions and life assurance in the UK did not have to disclose their charges to clients, even *ex post*. However, disclosure was made mandatory by the 1995 Pensions Act (see Box 2.1 on the personal pensions misselling scandal). Disclosure rules vary from state to state in America.

market emerges because demand is not sufficient to exhaust the capacity of the industry. Seller competition then drives each provider's charges down to cost: $p = p^s = c$. In the second case, demand exceeds capacity and precipitates a sellers' market. Buyer competition drives charges up to $p = p^d = ac = (3/2)c$, and those who cannot obtain a manager at this price invest directly. In the next section we follow Akerlof and assume that this is the relevant equilibrium. When quality is heterogeneous, then this price will obviously vary in proportion to quality.

2.4 Asymmetric information

Now consider what happens at the other extreme, under (exogenous) asymmetric information. In this case we assume that there is no correlation at all between past and future performance. Retail investors simply ignore *ex post* indicators like Jensen's alpha, institutional surveys, and performance ranking tables, since research is uninformative.[5] However, the law of averages makes it easier to assess the performance of the whole industry. In this case, it is assumed that providers know their own quality but clients can only form an estimate of quality based on the historical *market average*: $\bar{x}$. Thus:

client's reservation price
under asymmetric information: $p^d = \bar{x} = a\bar{c} = (3/2)\bar{c}$. (2.5)

Obviously, if all managers have the same ability $\bar{x}$, this results in an equilibrium price of $p = p^d = \bar{x} = (3/2)\,\bar{c}$. However, if quality is heterogeneous, we cannot analyse the market as a whole. Nor can we look at the market for each skill level separately as in the previous section, because clients cannot discriminate between providers. We have to analyse a more complicated interaction of individual and market quality effects.

Statistically, the average ability $\bar{x}$ depends upon the underlying distribution of fund management skills. Suppose that at the bottom end of the scale, funds only perform in line with the market: $x = c = 0$. If management skills are uniformly distributed, the best manager will be twice as good (but twice as cost-intensive) as the average. This is a property of the

---

[5] Empirical studies of fund management returns usually find that persistence in performance is low (Brealey and Hodges 1972; Carhart 1997; Fletcher 1999). However, recent research suggests that while relatively good performance is not persistent, bad performance is.

uniform distribution. If the indices are scaled so that the average cost is unity, then the best manager will have a cost of $c = 2.$[6] In other words we assume that c is uniformly distributed on [0,2] so that $\bar{c} = 1$. The best manager's performance is then $x = 3$. If the maximum capacity of each provider is fixed we can use this as the quantity scale factor and set this to unity. The quantity of service available at each skill level x is then uniformly distributed on [0,3].

If the market price is below the best manager's reservation price (of $c = 2$) then this manager will leave the market. Market equilibrium in this asymmetric information situation depends critically upon the cost and hence the reservation price of the 'marginal' manager, defined as the best *remaining* in the market. We now use c_{max} and p^s_{max} to represent these marginal values:

$$\text{marginal provider's reservation price: } p^s_{max} = c_{max}. \tag{2.6}$$

Similarly we redefine $\bar{c}$ and $\bar{x}$ to represent the average cost and quality of the remaining managers. It follows that this average cost $\bar{c}$ is $c_{max}/2$ and the average quality (using (2.1)) is: $\bar{x} = (3/2)\bar{c} = (3/4)c_{max}$. Substituting this into (2.5) gives:

$$\text{client's reservation price: } p^d = (3/4)c_{max}. \tag{2.7}$$

In order to find a market equilibrium in this situation we must find a price p which satisfies:

$$\text{market clearing price under}$$
$$\text{asymmetric information: } p^d = (3/4)c_{max} \geq p \geq c_{max} = p^s_{max}. \tag{2.8}$$

where p^d and p^s_{max} are substituted from (2.7) and (2.6). In other words, the market price has to be at or below the demand price (or clients withdraw) and at or above the marginal provider's cost index c (or they withdraw). This is clearly impossible because $(3/4)c_{max} < c_{max}$.

This point is easy to grasp if you imagine that you are a potential client. Suppose that you observe that managers are all charging p, which could be anywhere between 0 and 3. You know that this acts as a cutoff: the best manager will have costs of p per cent per annum and will expect to outperform the market by $x = (3/2)p$. This means that average outperformance is half as great: $\bar{x} = (3/4)p$. It is not worth paying an annual

[6] The best manager's performance is then $x = 3$. Similarly, if the maximum capacity of each provider is fixed we can use this as the quantity scale factor and set this to unity. The quantity of service available at each skill level x is then uniformly distributed on [0,3].

charge of p in order to beat the market by $(3/4)p$. So no matter what the annual charges are you do not engage a manager, but invest directly yourself.

Figure 2.1 graphs these demand and supply relationships. The horizontal axis plots c_{max} and the vertical axis p. The dashed line p_0^d shows the client's reservation price under these assumptions, while the 45° line p_{max}^s shows the marginal provider's reservation price. This lies above p_0^d for all values of c_{max}: there is no value of c_{max} and no price that is consistent with equilibrium (2.8). For example, if all managers are initially in the market, the average cost $\bar{c} = 1$ and average quality $\bar{x} = 3/2$. The maximum price that clients are willing to pay is $p^d = \bar{x} = 3/2$. However, at this price, providers with $2 > c > 3/2$ (or $3 > x > 9/4$) cannot cover costs and quit the industry. The best performer has $x = 9/4$ and the average performance and demand price falls to 9/8 (since the mean of a uniform

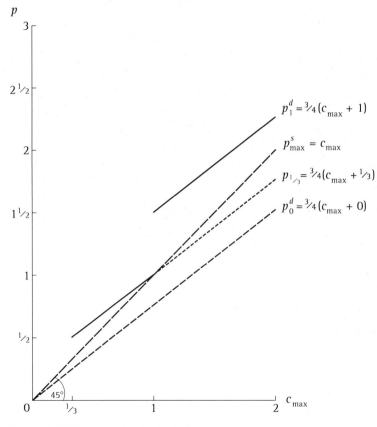

Figure 2.1 Minimum standard rules

distribution is equal to the mid-point of the range). Thus a downward spiral of quality and price ensues.

This result hangs critically on the assumption about the performance/cost ratio $a = x/c$. If $a > 2$ then the intrinsic efficiency of the fund management industry is enough to offset the averaging effect of asymmetric information. The price that customers are willing to pay is then $a\bar{c} = (a/2)p^s > p^s$, allowing a market to be established. To set against this, weakening the correlation between supplier cost and performance (which we have assumed to be perfect) makes it more difficult to establish a market. The model parameters used here are simply chosen to show how a Pareto-improving trade in financial products under full information can be extinguished by asymmetric information.

2.5 Minimum standard rules in the Akerlof (1970) model

This model also indicates the way in which industries involving professional services can combat asymmetric information effects that might otherwise drive them out of business. In this situation, suppliers have a strong incentive to think of a way of establishing a market. It is reasonable to suppose that they can accurately assess each other's quality even though the lay public cannot. Thus they have both the incentive and the ability to regulate themselves. In the legal and medical professions there are stringent entry qualifications and conduct rules that are policed by industry bodies like the American or British Medical Associations. Elements of self-regulation are also found in the financial services industry.

It is easy to see how professional self-regulation works in the Akerlof (1970) model. Take minimum standard rules for instance. Suppose that these tests effectively exclude providers with ability $x < x_{min} = 3/2c_{min}$. The market average performance and (in a sellers' market) price then increases to $\bar{x} = (x_{max} + x_{min})/2$ which means:

client's reservation price with minimum quality of x_{min}:

$$p^d = (x_{max} + x_{min})/2 = (3/4)(c_{max} + c_{min}). \tag{2.9}$$

Provided there is a market equilibrium price under full information, it is always possible to find a value of c_{min} which is consistent with equilibrium ((2.6) and (2.9)) under asymmetric information. Suppose for example that providers who are below average ($c < c_{min} = 1$; $x < x_{min} = 3/2$) are excluded from the market. The continuous line labelled p_1^d in Figure 2.1 shows the resulting client reservation price schedule.

Unlike p_0^d, this lies above p_{max}^s, indicated by the 45° line. Now all suppliers who meet the standard come to market, establishing an equilibrium at $c_{max} = 2$. Average performance and (in a sellers' market) price is $(x_{max} + x_{min})/2 = (3 + 3/2)/2 = 2\frac{1}{4} > 2$. This minimum standard allows a market to be established under asymmetric information.

This is a second-best solution because profits, the basic measure of efficiency in this sellers' market, are less than under full information. Average profit $((x_{max} + x_{min})/2 - (c_{max} + c_{min})/2)$ under full information is $(3/2 - 1) = 1/2$. With the minimum standard it is $9/4 - 3/2 = 3/4$ for those that make the grade. But there are only half as many of these, so total profits are down by 25 per cent. A Pareto-improvement could be obtained here by establishing a two-tier market, allowing those that fail to pass the standard to trade without the qualification. Indeed, a multi-level qualification would allow a multi-tier market, further increasing welfare. For example, performance measurement services might be accurate enough for wholesale investors like corporate pension fund trustees to consider broad-brush quartile measures (but note that adverse selection could occur within each quartile group of providers if they levied the same charges). Theoretically, the industry might be able to approximate the full information situation by designing and publishing an accurate index of performance. That would maximize profit, attaining the full information allocation of Section 2.3.

In a buyer's market situation however, profits under full information are zero and the gains from trade go to the consumer. In this regime the industry has a clear incentive to impose standards that restrict capacity and establish a seller's market. Consumers should be careful only to accept the minimum standard that is necessary to establish trade. In this situation, a two-tier market would be likely to develop unofficially. That is because consumers should be willing to trade at a lower price with low-quality suppliers who had failed to meet the standard. The London taxi market gives a good example: drivers of black cabs who have passed the 'knowledge' test provide a high-quality market, leaving the lower end of the market to the minicab trade.

Now suppose that we relax the minimum standard rule and restrict $c < c_{min} = 1/3$. The line labelled $p_{1/3}^d$ in Figure 2.1 shows the relevant client reservation price schedule. This crosses the suppliers' reservation price schedule p_{max}^s at $c_{max} = 1$. There is now adverse selection, because suppliers with costs in excess of $c > c_{max} = 1$ leave the market. However, a low-quality equilibrium emerges since suppliers with $1 > c > 1/3$ remain in the market at a price of $p_{1/3}^d = p = p_{max}^s = c_{max} = 1$. Average performance is also 1, below the value of 1 1/2 available under full information. Nevertheless, this minimum standard also allows a market to be established under asymmetric information.

Welfare losses implied by minimum standards and similar industrial forms of quality control are likely to be more complex than indicated here. The model assumes that buyers are homogeneous and have a fall-back option—managing their own fund (with $x = 0$). Moreover, in practice tastes are likely to differ. Some consumers place a higher value on quality, safety, and reliability than others. On the other hand, some people do not care too much about this. Minimum standards reduce the chance of the former buying a rogue product, but they prevent the rest of us from buying a lower-quality item. Also, by restricting capacity they work to the general advantage of suppliers. The campaign by the London black cab industry in 1996–7 for the regulation of the minicab trade gives a clear-cut example of a policy that would reduce welfare by reducing industrial capacity and consumer choice.

This model is designed to illustrate the effect which adverse selection can have on a credence market and show how self-regulation can mitigate its effects through devices like minimum standard rules. Leland (1979) and Tirole (1988: ch. 2) also provide interesting analysis of minimum standard rules. We now take a broader look at some of the ways in which individual providers and the financial service industry as a whole can deal with the problems caused by asymmetric information.

2.6 Market-based solutions

The problem of asymmetric information has dogged the medical profession since time immemorial. Professions like law and accounting have also been seriously affected. These services have all developed ways of dealing with the consequences. These devices are based in self-regulation at the industrial level, backed up in recent years by the force of law. They are also used in the financial service sector. In the USA the operation of the (non-bank) financial system was based upon the principle of self-regulation until the Securities Exchange Act of 1934, and despite the overarching authority of the Securities and Exchange Commission (SEC) vestiges of this system are still important. In Britain, this principle was dominant until the new Labour administration came to power in May 1997.

Sellers of experience goods have also found ways of dealing with informational problems. However, few of these methods are useful in the case of financial products which, as credence goods, trade under a high degree of information asymmetry. These individualistic solutions include:

1(a). *Reputation*: This is important if initial buyers make repeat purchases or recommendations to their associates. Black-market dealers in experience goods furnish the best examples. Since the client has no legal comeback against bad suppliers (of illegal drugs, for instance) and supplier collusion is difficult, individual suppliers have to develop effective ways of dealing with adverse selection. Long-term banking relationships, discussed in Section 8.6, offer the best example from the financial markets. However, it is hard for individual suppliers to establish a track record in the case of a credence good. Providers can use their position in the fund management league tables to signal good performance, yet studies by Carhart (1997), Fletcher (1999), and many others consistently show that the past is not a reliable guide to future performance. Moreover, in financial industries, short-term incentives to cheat or defraud are typically high compared to long-term incentives to remain in the industry. Nevertheless, companies with high-quality reputations developed in other industries are now successfully using their reputations to penetrate retail financial services, e.g. General Electric, Sears, and J. C. Penney in America and Virgin, Marks and Spencer, and Tesco in Britain.

1(b). *Signalling equilibrium*: In a signalling equilibrium, suppliers provide an associated product or service activity which signals high quality and is uneconomic for low-quality suppliers to provide. For example, markets of high-quality reliable cars can give a long-term warranty or service facility, which is cheap for them to provide, but expensive for makers of unreliable cars to provide. However, this device can only work if the outcome is fairly predictable and is revealed soon after purchase, which is not the case in retail financial services.

1(c). *Intermediation*: In this case, traders with no direct buying or selling interest use their quality recognition skills to filter out bad items. A good example is provided by second-hand car sales organizations. Also banks, which can develop expertise in screening borrowers, provide an example from the financial sector in that they effectively screen on behalf of their depositors. Independent Financial Advisers (IFAs) can do this for pension and life assurance products, but the problem is that it is hard for retail investors to distinguish good agents from bad. All in all, intermediation is not generally of much use in the case of basic financial services.

2.7. Industrial solutions

Financial services are a credence good, making it much easier for the general public to assess the long-run performance of the industry as a whole (essentially by relying upon the law of large numbers) than to assess the quality of an individual supplier. Consequently, industrial rather than individual reputations count under heading 1(a). The loss of reputation over the personal pensions misselling scandal shows how reputations are built and lost at the industrial level.

In this kind of market, the long-run performance of the industry determines the public's perception of average quality, hence (the Akerlof assumption) the price obtained by the individual supplier. So individual suppliers have a strong incentive to cooperate in maintaining this at a high level. For example, if autonomous (or 'Nash') optimization would drive the industry out of existence, suppliers would have an incentive to vote for minimum-standard rules or competence tests. Even low-quality suppliers that might be eliminated or discriminated against by such tests would have nothing to lose by supporting them.

In this situation, as the Akerlof model demonstrates, bad suppliers impose a negative externality upon the rest of the industry. Consequently, these markets naturally evolve forms of self-regulation. Historically, this has been effective in allowing markets in medical, legal, and accounting services to prosper. Until the Labour administration's reforms, the UK financial system was also based upon the principle of self-regulation. Professional associations and other self-regulating bodies, in the financial sector as elsewhere, tend to employ similar devices to control their members and regulate the industry. These devices include:

2(a). *Minimum standards and other barriers to membership*: These are universal amongst professional bodies and trade associations, with powers of expulsion acting as the ultimate sanction for misbehaviour. These controls involve the screening of new entrants, educational and professional qualifications, as well as 'fit and proper' conduct tests. Entry barriers are anti-competitive, and by raising economic rents may provide an 'equity' incentive to stay in the industry by behaving well. However, equity stakes should arguably be provided instead through equity investment. And as noted earlier, minimum standards work to the detriment of those who want to buy or sell low-quality services at a low price.

2(b). *Mutual monitoring and audit*: Industry-based monitors naturally have the expertise to monitor their peers. They allow relevant industrial expertise to be brought to bear as effectively and as flexibly as possible

Box 2.1 Britain's personal pensions misselling scandal

Background. The general reputation of the life assurance and pension industry with the British public was very high until the 1980s, based on generations of satisfied customers as well as tax advantages. Remember, industrial reputation is crucial in an industry like this selling a 'credence' good. Then in 1988 the Fowler Reform of Social Security introduced legislation with a national insurance subsidy favouring personal pensions in order to induce a switch into personal pensions from the State Earnings Related Pension Scheme (SERPS). Few of the experts thought that this would pose regulatory problems in view of the system of self-regulation which had been in place since 1986.

1988–93: Misselling. Representatives of pensions companies and independent agents encouraged 560,000 people to transfer out of occupational pension schemes into personal pensions between 1988 and 1993. They took with them total transfer payments of £7 billion. For many of the clients, existing schemes were more generous than the new personal plans. Agents were largely motivated by high commissions and exploited clients' lack of expertise. They obtained too little information about clients to advise them properly. Pension providers did not keep records adequate enough to defend themselves against subsequent misselling claims.

The consequences. 1993–94: The adverse publicity which emerged from these cases hit the industry's reputation hard. Sales of life assurance and pension products fell sharply between 1992 and 1994.

December 1993: The SIB announced that it was undertaking a review of the personal pension schemes of the people who had transferred out of the occupational pension schemes between 1988 and 1993. The review concluded that a large fraction had been badly advised.

1995: 'Hard Disclosure': a new regulator, the Personal Investment Authority (PIA), brought in a much tougher set of rules, which were legally enforceable. These were designed to ensure that clients were notified of early repayment terms, costs, commissions, and other terms on pensions and life contracts.

Firms involved have either sacked or retrained their representatives and put them on a fixed-salary/bonus system. Compensation terms for those most badly affected by misselling are currently being negotiated. The total cost to the industry has been put at £11 billion: £10 billion in compensation and £1 billion in administrative costs. (The latest indications are that this will prove to be an underestimate. See for example the article 'LloydsTSB put aside another £102 million for misselling' in *The Independent*, 23 November 1999.)

(e.g. keeping abreast of technical and financial innovation). The negative externalities mean that the monitors also have an incentive to perform effectively. A further incentive is often provided by mutual insurance schemes (2(c)). These incentives mean that it is not usually necessary to worry about who monitors the monitor. In the absence of formal mutual monitoring schemes, 'whistle-blowing' can help preserve industrial reputation, by disclosing rogue traders before they do too much damage. A recent case of whistle-blowing in a credence industry is provided by Malaysian Airlines, which was reported to the Civil Aviation Authority in May 1999 for flying into Heathrow with less than the required fuel reserve.

2(c). *Mutual industrial insurance or compensation schemes*: These are the industrial or credence good equivalent of 1(b). They go hand in hand with mutual monitoring and audit (2(b)), which helps to prevent high-quality firms subsidizing low-quality ones. It may also help to minimize moral hazard. However, mutual monitoring is not very good at detecting fraud and other dishonest practices. These leave the investor and the industry exposed to risk and form a case for government intervention.

2.8. Government intervention

It may not be realistic to rely upon self-regulation or the legal system to prevent or punish bad practice. Both of these approaches have their drawbacks. If this is the case, government regulation may provide a more cost-effective alternative.

Theft and fraud are criminal activities and should arguably be dealt with under the criminal law. Civil litigation is not appropriate. (Insider dealing is slightly different and is discussed in the next chapter.) However, the problem is that the criminal law requires a high standard of proof: 'beyond reasonable doubt' in the Anglo-Saxon countries. The jury system and the technical nature of white-collar crime make it notoriously difficult (and expensive) to secure a prosecution.

The main problem with self-regulation is that it is anti-competitive, liable to 'regulator capture'. This is a risk in any form of industrial supervision. Regulators and industrial managers normally evolve some form of *modus vivendi* and regulator capture is said to occur when this relationship becomes too close and the regulator starts to favour the industry rather than its clients. In the case of a self-regulating industry, the regulator is appointed by the producers and arguably captured *ab initio*, leading to rules devised for the benefit of producers rather than consumers. This is why the rules of self-governing bodies should at the very least be scrutinized by consumer associations and government departments. There is also a need for an external consumer representative or ombudsman to take issue with the decisions of financial firms.

2.9. The Anglo-Saxon approach to financial regulation

The elements of a self-regulating system can be recognized in most Anglo-Saxon financial systems. The USA furnishes the prime example. Until the Securities and Exchange Act of 1934, capital markets like the New York Stock Exchange (NYSE) were self-regulating, buttressed only by the civil and criminal law on fraud. Then Congress made the SEC responsible for capital market regulation. The SEC has formidable legal powers but delegates the day-to-day supervision of the industry to 'Self-Regulatory Organizations' (SROs) like the NYSE and NASDAQ which are funded by their members. Similarly, the Commodities and Futures Trading Commission (CFTC) is a federal agency that was established in 1974 to supervise the commodities and futures exchanges, which remain largely self-governing. Regulation in the USA is based on the principle of functional supervision, which means that regulatory jurisdiction is based on the type of activity rather than the type of firm (institutional supervision).

Supervision of the US monetary system, like the banking system itself, is fragmented. The Comptroller of the Currency (a department of the US Treasury) is primarily responsible for the national banks, while the Federal Reserve is responsible for bank holding companies and state banks which are members of the Federal Reserve System. Other state banks are jointly regulated by the FDIC and agencies of the various state legis-latures. The Federal Reserve is responsible for systemic stability and the operation of the lender of last resort facility (see Chapter 10).

This hybrid system provides specialized and informed regulation, tailored to different types of institution, while remaining under political control. It has been remarkably successful and has been copied by other English-speaking countries. Nevertheless, the American regime is not immune to criticism. The system of functional supervision leads to frag-mentation and has been criticized by Coffe (1995), for example.

Until recently, the British system of financial service regulation was firmly based upon the twin pillars of self-regulation and functional supervision. These principles were enshrined in the 1986 Financial Services Act.[7] Under this legislation, HM Treasury delegated powers to the Securities and Investments Board (SIB) which in turn handed them to SROs, for each sector of the industry. Significantly, the SIB unlike the SEC was a private company owned by its members, and not a statutory body. Its chairman was appointed by the Chancellor of the Exchequer and the Governor of the Bank of England. The Treasury monitored the working of the system and kept reserve powers of intervention, leaving the Bank of England to supervise banks under the 1987 Banking Act. Similarly, the Building Societies Commission supervised the building societies under the 1984 Act, while insurance companies were monitored by the DTI.

This system was designed to minimize malpractice by imposing standards and tests of competence. The sanctions included fines, suspension, and ultimately debarment from the industry, for firms as well as operatives. Internal compliance officers in each company were responsible for communicating with the various SROs and ensuring that employees adhered to their rule books. In addition, financial companies were required to invest collateral in their various subsidiaries. This collateral was known as 'dedicated capital' and designed to discourage excessive risk-taking, negligence, and theft. Supervision was arranged along functional lines. Fund managers were regulated by the Investment Managers Regulatory Authority (IMRO) and financial advisers by the Personal Investment Authority (PIA). Customer interests were upheld by an ombudsman. The Securities and Futures Authority (SFA) and the Recognized Investment Exchanges (RIEs) like the London Stock Exchange (LSE) provide the specialist supervision required by the capital markets, which are discussed in the next three chapters. There was a multiplicity of ombudsmen (which survives under the new system).

This regime of self-regulation was buttressed by the legal system. Fraud, theft, and insider dealing were exclusively dealt with under the criminal law: notably the 1984 Prevention of Fraud Act and the 1986 Companies Act. The 1993 Criminal Justice Act reinforced the law relating to inside dealers. Nevertheless, it proved very difficult to secure convictions under this system.

This system was generally thought by practitioners to be fragmented and burdensome, since it put the onus for coordination and compliance

---

[7] Prior to that, financial firms were initially vetted by the DTI under the 1958 Fraud Act, but were not supervised afterwards. One of the first acts of the SIB in 1986 was to investigate and then close the firm of Barlow Clowes, a procedure which would have been much more difficult under the 1958 legislation.

upon financial companies. The proliferation of different SROs and rule books complicated the supervisory process and made compliance more expensive. This made it hard to estimate its total cost, but various informal estimates suggest that this was of the order of £100 million during the mid-1990s. Peacock and Bannock (1995) and Simpson (1996) provide interesting analysis of these costs. Franks, Schaefer, and Staunton (1998) provide a broader perspective.

The downfall of this regulatory regime was due to a series of scandals which effectively destroyed public trust in the industry. The worst of these was pensions misselling, which affected hundreds of thousands of individuals (see Box 2.1). The 1990 Maxwell Affair had a similar impact upon public confidence. In this case, Robert Maxwell misused the access which as trustee he had to the investments of the Mirror Group Pension Fund, threatening the retirement incomes of its members. This scandal led to an inquiry chaired by Sir Roy Goode (Goode, 1993). The recommendations of his report were reflected in the 1995 Pensions Act. Meanwhile, although none of its clients actually lost money, the failure of Barings Bank in 1995 increased worries about the efficacy of the arrangements for deposit takers. Insider dealing scandals are discussed in the next two chapters.

2.10. The UK's Financial Services and Markets legislation

Britain now has a new regulatory regime. The new system is enacted by the Financial Services and Markets (FSM) Act (2001). This attempts to deal with the problems of fragmentation and self-regulation by instituting a single regulatory authority with statutory powers. This legislation amalgamates the various regulatory bodies, codifies their rule books, and gives these the force of law. Under this reform, the SIB, the SROs, the Building Societies Commission, the Registrar of Friendly Societies, and the Banking Supervision Department of the Bank of England are merged into the new Financial Services Authority (FSA) or 'super-SIB'.

In this streamlined system, the FSA is also responsible for prudential regulation of the insurance and banking systems, the argument being that financial convergence has lessened the differences between banks, insurance, and other financial institutions, making it sensible to bring their supervisors under one roof. However, the Bank of England retains responsibility for financial stability and the operation of the lender of last resort facility (see Chapters 11 and 12).

In this unitary regime there is a single industrial insurance and compensation scheme and a single tribunal to hear appeals against the FSA's rulings. Vestiges of self-regulation remain from the previous regime. For example, in deference to their expertise in the operation of their markets the Recognized Investment Exchanges (RIEs, notably the LSE, LME, and LIFFE) retain a degree of autonomy. They regulate their members on a day-to-day basis and set their own rules, while the FSA oversees their activities and ensures compliance with the recognition requirements in the FSM legislation. The FSA holds reserve powers in this case. This status is extended to Recognized Clearing Houses (RIEs, the London Clearing House and CREST). Controversially, statutory immunity from civil action extends from the FSA to these bodies for the purposes of the discharge of their regulatory functions.

The new FSM system will use the criminal law to deal with fraud, theft, and insider dealing and other forms of 'market abuse' (which encompasses market manipulation and the release of misleading information). The relevant provisions of the 1984 Fraud Act, the 1986 Companies Act, and the 1993 legislation are retained. However, the FSM legislation also gives the FSA the power to bring a case against insiders under the civil law, where the standard of proof is based on a balance of probabilities, making it easier to secure a result (see the next chapter).

This statutory framework brings the British system closer to the US regulatory regime. The autonomy granted to the British RIEs is similar to that enjoyed by the US RIEs. The separation of responsibility for prudential regulation and systemic stability is also a feature of the US system. The use of the civil law against insiders is clearly modelled on the SEC's powers of restitution, which allow it to levy fines of up to three times the profits on insiders. Controversially, no limit is set on the FSA's powers to fine, although it will have to publish a statement of the principles underlying its policies. The main difference is that the US system remains fragmented. SEC is not responsible for the regulation of insurance and retail financial services: this is conducted at the state level in the USA. Nor is it responsible for the commercial banks. This is ultimately the responsibility of the Comptroller of the Currency (set up in 1864 to regulate the national banks), and the agencies of the various state legislatures (which monitor local banks). The CFTC regulates the US futures exchanges.

The convergence and consolidation of financial firms provides a powerful argument for a single financial regulator. Besides Britain, many other countries have adopted this approach recently. However, as we shall see, insurance and banking activities are fundamentally different from other types of financial firm and arguably require special regulatory provision. An assessment of the new UK system is deferred to the concluding chapter.

2.11. The international dimension

The rationale for the single national regulator is based on the view that the activities of firms spanning different financial industries needs to be closely coordinated. Similarly, the increasing number of firms operating across national borders has forced a degree of cooperation upon regulators in different countries, even though they remain sovereign within their own jurisdictions. The best known of these international groups is the Basel Committee on Banking Supervision, which was formed in 1974 in the wake of the Herstatt and Franklin Bank failures. Less well known, the International Organization of Securities Commissions (IOSCO) was established in 1990 and the International Association of Insurance Supervisors (IAIS) in 1994. These groups provide a forum for supervisors from different countries to meet, exchange information, and agree common standards of supervision. They work by consensus but are able to exert peer pressure on recalcitrant members.

The main risk is that in the absence of international coordination, financial firms operating in different parts of the world will 'slip through the regulatory cracks', without being supervised by anyone. This problem was first diagnosed during the Herstatt failure, which involved large foreign currency exposures that had not been properly supervised. This led directly to the 1975 Concordat on supervision, which gave the bank's 'parent' country the primary responsibility for solvency, but left the 'host' country responsible for the capitalization of subsidiaries incorporated in their own jurisdictions. The Concordat was rewritten in 1983 in the wake of the Banco Ambrosiano affair.

The need for a more clear-cut approach to the supervision of international banking activities was dramatically underlined by the Bank of Credit and Commerce International (BCCI), which was closed by the Bank of England in 1991, resulting in widespread depositor losses (see Box 2.2). Prior to that, the BCCI had not really been supervised, since its charter was granted by Luxembourg, its head office was in London, and its operations were mainly in the Middle East. In order to help prevent another BCCI, the Basel Committee announced in 1992 a move to 'home country' supervision, whereby all banks are in principle regulated in the country

Box 2.2 The BCCI scandal

The Bank of Credit and Commerce International (BCCI) was founded in 1972 by Agha Hasan Abedi. It was an international bank that recruited and operated in many different countries. Initially, its main business was in raising money in oil-rich Middle Eastern countries for lending to countries in Latin America and elsewhere. However, its business activities became very varied and included money laundering operations as well as covert banking services to international terrorists and dictators. By the early 1990s its liabilities had grown to nearly $20 billion. Many of these deposits were raised from immigrant communities in Britain. UK local authorities were also attracted by the very high rates of interest the bank was offering—an indication that the level of asset risk was high. BCCI had 10,000 customers in the UK.

The main problem with BCCI was that its international character and the lack of international supervisory coordination left it unregulated. The bank's original charter had been granted by Luxembourg, which was formally responsible for supervision, although its head office was in London and it had branches in over 70 countries. However, the Luxembourg supervisors were not up to the job. In 1987 they agreed to share this work with supervisors in Britain and other countries, but even this group found it difficult to keep track of developments at BCCI. They discovered evidence of fraud early in 1990, but the Bank of England did not close the bank down until July 1991 following a damning report from the accountants Price Waterhouse.

The initial investigations suggested that depositor losses would amount to about $10 billion and the Bank of England and other regulators were roundly criticized for their failure to act more quickly. The British government was lobbied to provide more compensation to depositors than they were entitled to under the British deposit insurance scheme. (At the time of the BCCI crisis, the British scheme provided insurance of 75 per cent on deposits of up to £20,000, leaving many investors with large losses.) This spurred moves towards closer international cooperation between financial regulators and in particular the principle of 'home country' supervision, as noted in Section 2.10.

The task of liquidating BCCI has been hampered by the corrupt nature of its business. However, the liquidators have made surprisingly good progress. By 1998 they had returned 46 pence in the pound (a total of $6 billion) to creditors. This was partly financed from prosecutions of BCCI executives in the USA, the UK, and Abu Dhabi. By the end of the decade, the liquidators were planning a new payment and were saying that there was more to come. Part of this payment is to be financed by an out-of-court settlement with BCCI's auditors worth $195 million. The liquidators are also taking legal action against the Bank of England for alleged negligence. Besides the compensation provided to creditors, these recovery actions are significant because they should serve as a warning to bank executives, accountants, and supervisors that bad behaviour, whether it be corruption or negligence, will be dealt with appropriately in future. The liquidator has an important role to play in reinforcing market discipline, even when the horse has bolted.

where they are headquartered (Box 2.2). This agreement is buttressed by others that allow regulators in other countries to restrict the activities of foreign bank branches if they feel that the parent country supervision is inadequate.

Another risk is that 'footloose' organizations will migrate to the financial centres with the most lax supervisory standards, a process known as 'regulatory arbitrage' or 'drift'. This has brought international coordination and harmonization designed to minimize such distortions, the 1988 Basel Accord (Box 2.3) offering the best example. Similarly, the need to develop transparent international markets has given impetus to proposals for coordination of accounting and listing standards.[8]

The risk of regulatory arbitrage rises as technology increases capital mobility and as international barriers are dismantled. This is a great concern in Europe, which has adopted a single currency and is trying to establish a single market in financial services. These developments have increased the transparency and contestability of the market for financial services. However, cross-border competition in this area has so far been limited.

Electronic technology seems to be gaining the ascendancy in market making and is spurring international competition in this industry as we will see in the next chapter. In principle, e-commerce (direct marketing and distribution through the internet) should increase customer proximity, price transparency, and contestability of the retail market. However, the introduction of new distance selling techniques (like telephone sales) in the past has had considerable impact in the national market, but very little cross-border effect.

Market making may be unique in providing a rapidly executed service in a homogeneous product which is readily verified, as argued in Section 1.7. Insurance and banking products are generally more heterogeneous and complex. For example, anticipating the discussion of Chapter 9, aggressive new entrants into the credit market find it difficult to distinguish good and bad risks, and adverse selection means that they find themselves with a disproportionately bad selection. Credit scoring or screening techniques can reduce this effect, but in many cases local banks, relying on the long-term 'customer relationship', can do better. The experience of the American and other 'new mortgage lenders' in Britain in the 1980s provides a good illustration of the problem.

---

[8] At the moment, for example, it is not possible to trade international equities on the NYSE unless their accounts are prepared by a US firm under US accounting standards.

Box 2.3 Basel 1988: bank capital requirements

The Basel Accord was reached after a long period of consultation by the Basel Committee on Banking Supervision and marks a move towards agreed minimum standards in international banking supervision. Although this agreement is not legally binding it was endorsed by the G10 central banks, which committed themselves to enforce these standards within their own jurisdictions.

The key to this agreement was its simplicity. It produced a common definition of bank capital, subdivided into 'tier one' (share capital) and 'tier two' (subordinated debt, which ranks after other creditors but before shareholders in the event of a bankruptcy). The other element was a simple four-category system for risk-weighting bank assets. In this scheme, zone 'A' (essentially OECD) country debt has a zero risk weighting. Bank debt has a 20 per cent weight and residential mortgages a 50 per cent weight. All other assets have a 100 per cent weight. The basic idea underpinning this weighting system is that government debt is essentially default free, while the riskiness of bank debt is reduced by regulation. Mortgages are backed by collateral. Under the minimum standard, weighted bank assets should not exceed 8 per cent of tier-one plus tier-two capital. Tier-two capital should not exceed tier-one capital.

The simplicity of this system has led to its widespread adoption outside the G10 countries to which it originally applied. It has been successful in increasing the capital base of the international banking system. Recent estimates published in *The Banker* indicate that bank capital increased from $800 billion in 1990 to $1,400 billion by 1998. It is not clear how well the Accord has done in reducing regulatory arbitrage, but it has helped to level the playing-field for banks in different jurisdictions.

The shortcomings of this system also lie in its simplicity. In particular, the risk weights fail to allow properly for credit risk and this results in anomalies. For example, banks are not required to hold any capital in respect of sovereign debt issued by a Zone A country like Mexico which is rated Ba2 or 'speculative' by Moodys. Similarly, unsecured credit card debts (which typically have interest margins of over 500 basis points) are given the same weight as corporate bonds issued by top corporate names like BP-Amoco and IBM (which enjoy margins of about 50 basis points). These anomalies give banks perverse incentives to switch out of low-margin into high-margin assets in the same risk category. Securitization techniques mean that banks can take low-margin business 'off balance sheet' relatively easily to economize on capital. These criticisms have been reflected in the Basel Committee's July 1999 consultative paper on a new capital adequacy framework, discussed in Section 11.3.3.

Other financial industries are still constrained by economic geography. Investment banks for instance tend to cluster together in major international cities like New York and London. Transport and communications, language, amenities, and culture may play just as important a role in the development of these centres as the regulatory regime. Other consumer-based industries like retail insurance and investment advice are naturally found close to major population centres. It would probably need a major shift in technology or regulation to disturb the geography of these industries.

2.12. Financial regulation in the European Union

Contemporary thinking about regulation in the European Union is seriously constrained by the different approaches to regulation found in the member states. The well-publicised difficulties of harmonizing the different cultures found in the agencies merged into Britain's new FSA would be minor in comparison to those involved in a European harmonization. This problem effectively rules out the imposition of a uniform set of rules. The approach has therefore been to seek agreement on minimum standards and use these to minimize regulatory migration. This idea is found in the European Financial Services Directive which came into force in 1996. This introduced the European 'passport' which allows a financial firm recognized by any member of the European Union to undertake business in any other, subject to local business conduct rules. It is thus based firmly upon the principle of parent country regulation. Drift is reduced by the imposition of harmonized minimum standards. In addition, there are provisions which in principle require regulators in countries experiencing regulatory immigration to tighten their rules.

These rules are open to different national interpretations and have been criticized as inadequate. There have been calls for a closer harmonization of rules. However, some commentators argue that market forces will ensure that European regulatory systems converge upon an optimal form of regulation. On this view, competition between different schemes will lead to the survival of the best. Support for this can be found in the observation that the Eurodollar markets are centred in London with its system of light self-regulation by the Association of International Bond Dealers (AIBD) rather than financial centres like Grand Cayman that have little or no regulation.

Whether this will happen in the case of retail financial services would seem to depend critically upon whether customers can learn to recognize products and discriminate on the basis of a product's country of origin (as they once did with the 'made in Britain' label). On the argument of this chapter, it will be the national reputation, if anything, which allows this to happen. If this is the case, then we will indeed witness international competition between financial systems. Institutions could compete on the basis of their national reputation, in the same way that pension funds, life assurance, and other industries compete with each other for business in a national market on the basis of their group reputation. If retail customers cannot effectively discriminate, however, then regulatory drift will surely be a problem and a high degree of harmonization will then become inevitable in the new Europe.

EXERCISES

Akerlof (1970)

Question 1. Akerlof analyses the way in which adverse selection might work in the market for second-hand cars, assuming these are of variable quality. He works with reservation demand p^d and supply p^s prices (which are respectively similar to x and c in the financial services application of Sections 2.2–2.5). He assumes that marginal utilities and reservation prices are constant (utility is linear in consumption of cars and 'other goods'). The basic assumptions are:

- q (= the quality index) is distributed uniformly in the range $[0–2]$,
- buyers would be willing to pay $p^d = (3/2)q > q$ for a car of quality q,
- sellers would be willing to accept $p^s = q$ for a car of quality q.

(a) *Competitive equilibrium with full information.* Calculate the potential gain from trade in this situation. Assume that buyers have enough money to buy all vehicles so that there is a 'supplier's market'.

>We have a market equilibrium described by
>$$p^d = (3/2)q = p > q = p^s.$$
>In this situation, sellers get $(3/2)q$ for cars of quality q, a net gain of $q/2$.

(b) *Asymmetric information.* Now assume that

- individual quality q is known only to the seller,
- buyers know only average quality: $\bar{q}$,
- all cars fetch the same (pool) price.

Is a market viable under these assumptions?

>In this situation, buyers are prepared to pay only $p^d = (3/2)\bar{q}$. Given the assumption of a uniform distribution, average quality is half of the maximum quality q_{max} left in

the market: $\bar{q} = q_{max}/2$. The reservation supply price for this supplier is $p^s_{max} = q_{max}$. This is above the demand price

$$p^d = (3/2)\bar{q} = (3/2)(q_{max}/2) < q_{max} = p^s_{max}.$$

So the market is not viable for any feasible value of q_{max}.

Minimum standard rules

Question 2. (a) Suppose that in the Akerlof (1970) model of the second-hand car market (Question 1) other dealers can assess quality, even though the public cannot. Now suppose that the Ministry of Transport uses these experts to implement a scheme which effectively prevents any cars with quality $q < q_{min} = 1$ coming onto the market. Answer the following questions:

(i) What is the average quality ($\bar{q}$), assuming for a moment that there is no adverse selection?

(ii) What is the price that buyers are prepared to pay under this assumption?

(iii) Will there be adverse selection in these two cases?

(iv) Is trade possible? If so, what is the equilibrium average quality and price?

> The reservation supply price for the marginal quality supplier is $p^s_{max} = q_{max}$ as in Question 1(b). Buyers are still prepared to pay $p^d = (3/2)\bar{q}$. But average quality is now $(q_{max} + q_{min})/2$ given the assumption of a uniform distribution.
>
> (i) If there is no adverse selection, $q_{max} = 2$. Substituting $q_{min} = 1$:
>
> $$\bar{q} = (2 + 1)/2 = 3/2.$$
>
> (ii) Substituting this into the demand price, $p^d = (3/2)\bar{q} = 2\frac{1}{4}$.
>
> (iii) Adverse selection will not occur because this demand price is higher than 2, keeping the highest quality in the market.
>
> (iv) There is no adverse selection and suppliers with $q \subset [2, q_{min}]$ will all remain in the market. Quality and price are given in (i) and (ii).

(b) Now answer these questions with $q < q_{min} = 1/2$.

> (i) Substituting $q_{max} = 2$; $q_{min} = 1/2$:
>
> $$\bar{q} = (2 + 1/2)/2 = 5/4.$$
>
> (ii) In this case the demand price is
>
> $$p^d_1 = (3/2)\bar{q} = 15/8.$$
>
> (iii) Adverse selection will occur in this case because the demand price is less than 2.
>
> (iv) However, trade will occur. We can solve for the best quality left in the market by equating the demand and supply prices:
>
> $$p^d = (3/2)(q_{max} + q_{min})/2 = (3/4)(q_{max} + 1/2) = q_{max} = p^s_{max}.$$
>
> Solving this gives $q_{max} = 3/2$. This means that all suppliers with $3/2 > q > 1/2$ remain in the market. Average quality is thus $\bar{q} = (3/2 + 1/2)/2 = 1$ and price is $p = p^d_1 = (3/2)\bar{q} = 3/2$.

(c) Plot the reservation price schedules (p^s_{max}, p^d) over $q_{max} \in [0,2]$ for cases (a) and (b).

(d) Is it possible to choose q_{min} in a way that replicates the full information allocation?

> No. Minimum standards exclude low-quality suppliers.

(e) Show that minimum standards are not necessary for there to be a market when owners are forced sellers.

> In this case the reservation supply price is effectively $p^s = 0$ and all cars are sold at the pool price 3/2.

Question 3. Financial advisers are now required to inform buyers of life assurance contracts about commissions, early repayment values, and similar details. Consider the effect which the removal of such an informational asymmetry is likely to have on demand, supply, quality, and price in this market. (Birkbeck College, London, Postgraduate Certificate in Finance, Final Examination, 1998)

Question 4. If there is to be freedom for financial firms to offer services anywhere within the European Union, should the regulations applied to these firms by different member states be the same?

3. The Structure and Regulation of Insurance Markets

The previous chapter discussed the structure and regulation of basic retail financial services like fund management and investment advice. The main problem in this area is the information advantage held by suppliers, who know much more about their product quality than the buyer typically does. This is a general feature of retail financial markets. Providers of retail insurance products like holiday, house, and motor insurance as well as life assurance policies are also likely to know much more about these products than the purchaser. However, insurance markets are special in several respects. In terms of their informational structure, the purchaser is likely to know more about their own risk characteristics than the insurer. That is the main reason why insurance markets are considered separately in this chapter. Retail banking services are very special and are considered in Chapters 8–11.

3.1 Mutual insurance and other risk sharing arrangements

This chapter begins by analysing the way in which insurance can reduce the effect of risk and maximize welfare in a situation of full information: when clients understand the product and providers know a client's risk characteristics. As in the previous chapter, this full information model is Pareto-efficient and provides a benchmark against which the effect of asymmetric information can be gauged. It provides a reasonable description of small-scale mutual insurance schemes which historically allowed members of small close-knit groups like trades unions to insure each other against health, unemployment, and other personal risks. Members of such communities are arguably in a good position to know each other's risk characteristics and to monitor reckless behaviour and other forms of moral hazard.

Family or tribal groups which look after members who fall upon hard times also provide informal mutual insurance. Mutual insurance schemes allow larger groups to formalize such assistance. They allow the economic effects of personal risks like industrial accidents (which strike individuals rather than the whole community) to be reduced by diversification. The law of large numbers says that these risks can be virtually eliminated in large groups. These hazards are known as idiosyncratic risks. This leaves the community exposed to 'common' risks like contagious disease or economic recession that affect large numbers of people simultaneously. Insurance markets can reduce the welfare costs of common hazards by sharing the financial risk across the community, but cannot eliminate their effects entirely.

This distinction between idiosyncratic and common risk factors resembles that of the Capital Asset Pricing Model (CAPM, Sharpe 1964). In the CAPM, idiosyncratic (or company-specific) risks can be eliminated by diversification, leaving investors exposed to risks which are common to all companies (known as 'market' risk). Government social security schemes are another form of mutual insurance. Private insurance companies also rely upon the law of large numbers when providing personal insurance cover in line with actuarial rates.

Mutual insurance societies have a long and successful historical tradition and have developed into large commercial organizations in most developed countries. Most societies are now 'anonymous', meaning that they provide insurance to the general public and no longer confine their business to particular groups. They have lost some of the informational advantages of their original form, but have gained from the diversification and other economies that result from large scale.

As far as the general public is concerned, the mutuals are little different from insurance companies, which provide similar insurance products. There is a crucial difference, however, in that the societies are collectively owned by their members and any surplus after claims have been met and bonuses paid are added to financial reserves. In this sense they are similar to fund management companies, where ownership of the assets remains with individual clients. However, an insurance *company* is owned by its shareholders under *limited liability*. Provided that the financial reserves are adequate, it is free to distribute surplus profits as dividends to shareholders. This is why prudential controls (Section 3.10) are much more important in the case of insurance than they are for fund management services and why the legislative regime tends in practice to be a lot tighter.

The analysis becomes much more complicated when we assume that insurance providers cannot distinguish high-risk from low-risk clients. Clients then behave as information monopolists and try to hide their risk characteristics. Rothschild and Stiglitz (1976) show that in this situation insurers will provide a range of contracts to suit different types of client. In equilibrium, the high-risk clients will buy full insurance contracts at high cost, while adverse selection means that other clients buy partial insurance schemes at more favourable rates. In other words, the lower-risk individuals underinsure even if they bear the full cost of any damage themselves. Group insurance (like company membership of medical insurance schemes) avoids this adverse selection effect and can make all members better off by providing risk cover at rates reflecting the average or pooled risk characteristics of the group.

This pooling effect can make it optimal to introduce laws making full insurance compulsory. It can justify the provision of social insurance by the government. The argument for compulsion is greatly reinforced if damages to others are potentially important (as in the well-known example of car insurance). However, adverse competition and moral hazard effects are potentially much more of a problem in case of compulsory insurance schemes than in the case of mutual or partial insurance systems. The implications for the regulation of insurance markets are discussed in the final section.

As discussed in the introductory chapter, the Arrow–Debreu model of general competitive equilibrium has a complete financial market which offers insurance against all contingencies. This feature means that static optimization techniques can be used to analyse the model. This chapter begins by illustrating the properties of the complete market model using a simple two-dimensional specification which allows standard graphical devices to be used. The next section sets out the basic model and Section 3.3 uses this to analyse the efficacy of mutual insurance arrangements as a way of dealing with idiosyncratic risk. The next two sections look at the role of a competitive insurer in a complete market. Section 3.6 analyses the effect of asymmetric information in an incomplete insurance market following the seminal paper by Rothschild and Stiglitz (1976) and Section 3.7 analyses the argument for compulsion in this situation. The remaining sections draw out some of the implications for the regulation of insurance markets.

3.2 Full information and insurance

This section sets out the basic framework of the mathematical model used in this chapter. It is a simple two-dimensional example of the complete market model discussed in Section 1.1. I assume that:

1. There is just one consumption good and two future 'date-states' 1 and 2 with consumption levels denoted by C_1 and C_2. These date-states could represent (a) two future periods with no uncertainty (i.e. when there is a single future state); or (b) two states of the world in a single future period.[1]

2. There are just two types of risk averse individual. In Sections 3.2 to 3.4 they are labelled $j = 1,2$, while in the remaining sections they are $j = h,l$, indicating high- and low-risk individuals. Individuals maximize expected utility,[2] written for individual j as:

$$W = U^j(C_1^j) + B^j.U^j(C_2^j) \tag{3.1}$$

where $U^{j\prime} = \partial U^j/\partial C > 0$, $\partial^2 U^j/\partial^2 C < 0$, $B^j > 0$. Section 4.4 introduces a competitive insurance institution which is indifferent to risk.

3. Aggregate endowments (or production) are represented by Y_1 and Y_2 and individual endowments by Y_1^j and Y_2^j, $j = 1,2$. R is the relative price of output in the two date-states. The budget constraint for individual j is then:

$$C_2^j = Y_2^j + R(Y_1^j - C_1^j). \tag{3.2}$$

The intertemporal interpretation (a) of this model will be familiar to most readers. In this specification, B is a subjective discount function (so that $0 < B < 1$) and $R = (1 + r) > 1$ where r is the safe interest rate.

However, the idea of optimizing and trading between states (interpretation (b)) may not be so familiar. Suppose for example that current consumption has already been decided and that there is just one remaining future period and one good. However, there are two possible states of nature s_1 and s_2. The first is a 'bad' state in which unfavourable developments (like 'low productivity', 'bad weather', or 'high oil prices') hit spending power (through low real incomes or capital losses) and the second a 'good' state in which they do not. Then Y_1^j and Y_2^j represent the total resources available to individual j for consumption in s_1 and s_2 and C_1^j and C_2^j represent total consumption in these states.

---

[1] A hybrid state-preference version of this specification due to Diamond and Dybvig (1983) is employed in Chapter 10.

[2] The conditions under which this assumption holds are set out and discussed in Eichberger and Harper (1997) section 1.3. First, to be able to represent the preference ordering in terms of a utility function, this must satisfy the standard assumptions of completeness, transitivity and continuity. Second, to be written in the state independent form (3.1), where the argument of the function U is indexed by the state, but U is not, preferences must satisfy the von Neumann–Morgenstern independence axiom.

Once the state becomes apparent, *ex post* utility is assumed to be $U^j(C)$, where C is appropriately C_1^j or C_2^j. If d^j represents j's subjective time discount factor, p^j their subjective probability of the bad state and $(1 - p^j)$ that of the good state then their expected utility is the discounted probability weighted average $d^j p^j U^j(C_1^j) + d^j(1 - p^j)U^j(C_2^j)$. Welfare is only defined up to a monotonic transformation and so an equivalent welfare index W can be constructed by dividing across by $d^j p^j$ to get (3.1), where now $B^j = (1 - p^j)/p^j > 0$.

Technically, p^j is a posterior probability, which in principle takes into account any information that j gleans from market prices (R). Consequently, B^j should be considered an endogenous variable rather than a fixed parameter. If the market is complete, this allows individuals with different priors to effectively exchange their private information and converge upon common posterior odds in a 'Rational Expectations Equilibrium'. For this to happen they have to act as price takers, which is a reasonable assumption to make when there are large groups of individuals with access to the same information. This also means that in a complete market equilibrium it is reasonable to assume that $B^j = B$ for all individuals, even if there is asymmetric information in the sense that they start with different private information (Grossman 1981).

Now suppose that it is possible *ex ante* to substitute output and income between the states s_1 and s_2. For example, if s_1 represents a 'high oil price' and s_2 a 'low oil price' state then j can boost C_1^j at the expense of C_2^j by investing *ex ante* in energy efficient investments. Specifically, suppose that reducing energy efficiency to cut C_1^j by one unit increases C_2^j by R units. Then the budget or trade-off line is represented by (3.2).

The optimal solution C_1^{j*} and C_2^{j*} follows by substituting (3.2) into (3.1) to get $U^j(C_1^j) + B^j.U^j(Y_2^j + R(Y_1^j - C_1^j))$ and then differentiating with respect to C_1^j. This gives the first order condition $U^{j'}(C_1^j) - RB^j.U^{j'}(Y_2^j - R(Y_1^j - C_1^j)) = 0$. This can be rearranged as:

$$U^{j'}(C_1^j)/B^j.U^{j'}(C_2^j) = R. \tag{3.3}$$

We recognize this as the standard rule which states that the marginal rate of substitution in consumption must in equilibrium equal the marginal rate of transformation in the financial market or production. The geometry is set out in Figure 3.1(a), which represents the first individual's optimum in terms of a point of tangency between the indifference curve I_0 and a production frontier FF'. (For simplicity I have omitted the $j = 1$ superscripts.) Figure 3.1(a) shows the case of 'autarchy' in which there is no financial market, just a physical investment opportunity. This

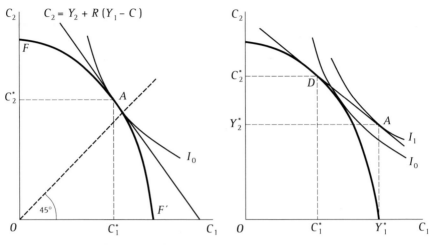

Figure 3.1a Incomplete market   **Figure 3.1b** Complete market

illustrates the case of an incomplete financial market in which consumption and production decisions have to be taken jointly. If the investment or intertemporal production function is concave, illustrated by the production frontier FF' in the figure, then R emerges as the slope of the line of separation at a point of tangency between the indifference curve I_o and the frontier FF'.

In a model of pure exchange with an initial endowment represented by the point A, the production set would be replaced by the box $OC_1^*AC_2^*$. If we adopt the two-state interpretation (b) of the model, the uncertainty disappears if this allocation point lies on the 45° line, indicating the same endowment and consumption level in each state. But if A lies away from this line, the two states differ and there is to that extent uncertainty. Figure 3.1(b) shows the effect of introducing a financial market with relative price R. This is an example of a complete market and allows the consumption and production decisions to be separated in the usual way. In the figure, the optimal production point is D and optimal consumption point is A. This 'Fisher separation' property means that in a complete market the production decision can be delegated to a manager instructed to maximize profits. The consumption decision then follows (given the resulting income) from (3.2) and (3.3).[3]

---

[3] The model (3.1) to (3.3) can also be used to describe a multidimensional Arrow–Debreu (1954) specification. Providing that investment opportunities allow an individual to shift any specific good or bundle of goods between two date-states st and $s't'$; then (replacing C_1 and C_2 by C_{st} and $C_{s't'}$) equations (3.2) and (3.3) can be used to represent a choice between the planned

3.3 Mutual insurance

The interstate problem (b) is isomorphic with the standard intertemporal problem (a) because dates and states are mathematically equivalent under the von Neumann–Morgenstern axioms. All that changes is the interpretation of B, R, C_1, and C_2. Moreover, the additive nature of the utility specifications gives the model another important feature. At any point along the 45° line in Figure 3.1, $C = C_1 = C_2$. Substituting this into the marginal rate of substitution shown in (3.3) gives:

$$U^j(C^j)/B^j.U^j(C^j) = 1/B^j, \, j = 1,2. \tag{3.4}$$

This says that the slope of the indifference curve (the ratio on the LHS) along the 45° degree line is always equal to the reciprocal of the discount/relative probability factor B. This is the case for all individuals.

This observation has important implications for the complete insurance market when there is 'no aggregate uncertainty'. Uncertainty can arise either because production outcomes or preferences are state-dependent. In this chapter we assume that preferences are not state-dependent, and that uncertainty only results from the production side of the economy. In this case there is no aggregate uncertainty when the total allocation (or profit-maximizing production) of a particular good in a particular period is the same in both states of nature.[4] All that changes between states is the output or endowments of different individuals—the distribution of resources. Chapter 10 looks at the alternative situation, in which production outcomes are known but preferences are state-dependent.

When there is no aggregate uncertainty, mutual insurance arrangements can be devised which neutralize distributional effects and remove uncertainty at the individual as well as the aggregate level. For simplicity in this section I additionally assume:[5]

---

values C_{st} and $C_{s't'}$ in terms of the current relative price, as indicated by the relevant cost ratio $R_{st,s't'}$. This relationship holds given these specific investment opportunities, even if the market set is not complete. However, the allocation is not Pareto-optimal if any potential trades are frustrated by missing markets.

[4] In a multidimensional context the total allocation of each good in each date must be independent of the state.

[5] As noted earlier, this condition emerges naturally in a Rational Expectation Equilibrium in a complete market. To allow this we need to assume that there are groups with large numbers of agents with von Neumann–Morgenstern utility and access to the same private information, which may differ between groups. These agents act as price takers, effectively pooling their private information and settling upon the same posterior probabilities. Exercises 1 and 2 give examples of fully revealing equilibria.

4. agents have the same information, interpret this in the same way, and agree the same posterior probabilities: $B^j = B$, $j = 1,2$.

This situation is illustrated by Figure 3.2(a). In this illustration I assume that there are equal numbers of type 1s and type 2s and pair up each type 1 individual with a type 2. Using the axes to represent their *total* output Y_1 and Y_2 or consumption C_1 and C_2 in the two states, a point such as T on the production frontier indicates the total output in each state. A point like A lying within the box to the left and below point T can be used as before to represent the type 1 allocation. The type 2 allocation follows by residual. In other words, Y_1^1 and Y_2^1 and C_1^1 and C_2^1 are plotted relative to the origin O, while Y_1^2 and Y_2^2 and C_1^2 and C_2^2 are plotted on the inverse axes drawn through T. As Figure 3.2(a) is drawn, the type 1 individual does relatively well in the second state.

The aggregate production point T lies on the 45° line: $Y_1 = Y_2$. This means that the Edgeworth box (showing the set of feasible consumption allocations) is square. However the allocation point A lies off the 45° line: $Y_1^1 \neq Y_2^1$. In other words there is risk at the individual but not the aggregate level. The indifference curve I_0^1 drawn through this point shows the set of consumption points which give the first individual the same level of satisfaction as the initial allocation. Similarly the curve I_0^2 plotted using the inverse axes drawn through point T shows points of indifference for the second individual. The shaded area bounded by the two indifference

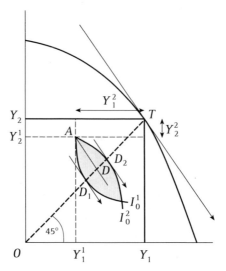

Figure 3.2a Aggregate certainty

curves shows the core, or the set of allocations which are feasible Pareto-improvements upon the initial allocation.

As in a standard two-good or two-period model, the contract curve (showing the set of efficient bargains) is generated by points of tangency between pairs of indifference curves for different individuals. In this case, the 45° line is the contract curve. That is because any pair of indifference curves drawn through a point on the 45° line have the same slope $1/B$ (via 3.4) at that point, making this an efficient outcome. (Beliefs are consistent so that $B^1 = B^2 = B$.) Note that consumption allocations along the 45° line make individual consumption levels independent of the state, providing full insurance.

The final allocation between the two individuals will lie somewhere on the line drawn between D_1 and D_2, that is on the 45° contract line within the core. In other words we observe mutual insurance because the type 1s and 2s contract to keep each other on the 45° line and this removes uncertainty. If there are large numbers of type 1 and type 2 individuals, a competitive market will ensure that the tangent to the two curves has a slope reflecting both the relative probabilities $(1/B)$ of the two states via (3.4) and the relative price r (via (3.3)).

For aggregate uncertainty to be absent from a model of pure exchange, aggregate allocations must simply be independent of the state. However, if production is flexible, then for full production and consumption equilibrium, the relative probability and price ratio $R = 1/B$ must also equal the marginal rate of transformation in production (the slope of the production frontier at the equilibrium point T).[6]

This sort of coincidence seems unlikely, certainly as a description of a multidimensional production set. However, the mutual insurance model does provide a realistic description of idiosyncratic risks like health problems, which can be very worrying at the individual level but made relatively certain in aggregate by the law of large numbers. Suppose for example that there are large numbers of individuals who are identical *ex ante*. However, with probability $p = 1/2$ an individual can fall sick. The law of large numbers means that in a large population the numbers of sick and healthy people will be effectively

---

[6] This means that any investment opportunity which allows the same output in each state must be actuarially fair. In other words, if a change in the structure of production can increase output in the first state by ΔY_1 and reduce it in the second state by ΔY_2, then: $\Delta Y_1 = B\Delta Y_2$. For example if the probability of the bad state is 3/7 and that of the good state 4/7, then starting with the same output in both, reducing output by 3 units in the good state must generate extra output of 4 units in the bad state. (Figure 3.2(a) is drawn using this ratio.)

matched, allowing us to pair any sick person *ex post* with a healthy one.[7]

This situation is shown in Figure 3.2(b). This assumes that the sick individual produces nothing and the healthy one produces one unit of output. Aggregate output for each pair is normalized at $Y_1 = Y_2 = 1$ and the aggregate output set is shown by the square box. If state 1 is defined as the one in which individual 1 is sick and individual 2 is healthy, then the allocation point A is the top left corner of the box. In this large number situation competition leads to the optimal mutual insurance contract in which whoever is sick receives a compensation of 1/2 from the other. Final consumption is thus 1/2 for all individuals in all states. This maximizes expected utility and in this *ex ante* sense is Pareto-optimal.

Generally speaking, personal risks are diversifiable and in the absence of transactions costs, moral hazard, and similar complications, could be insured in line with pure actuarial risk, without a risk premium. This leaves common shocks (aggregate or market risk), which cannot be diversified and can only be insured at a premium. If the insurance market does

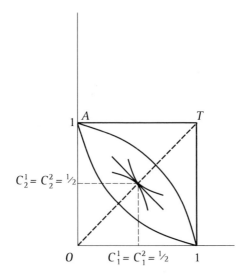

Figure 3.2b Mutual insurance

[7] When there is an even chance of an individual being sick or healthy then $p = 1/2$ and the percentage of sick people in the population has a Bernoulli (or binomial) distribution. If s is the number of sick people and n the size of the population then the expected value of the fraction s/n is 1/2. The variance of s is $p(1-p)n$ and the variance of the fraction s/n is thus $p(1-p)/n = 1/4n$ which goes to zero rapidly as n increases, allowing the numbers of sick and healthy individuals to be closely matched.

not provide effective personal insurance, mutual insurance is often implicit in family or community risk-sharing arrangements. A study by Mace (1991) using panel data for US individuals claims that idiosyncratic risk is largely diversified away by a combination of informal and formal arrangements. Remarkably, she finds that individual consumption patterns are not significantly affected by idiosyncratic effects like unemployment and hospitalization. Individual consumption is strongly influenced by aggregate consumption however, reflecting the effect of aggregate risk.

3.4 Aggregate uncertainty

We now consider the effect of aggregate uncertainty or 'common shocks'–those that cannot be eliminated by mutual insurance. If the aggregate allocation is fixed, then aggregate uncertainty obviously occurs when this differs between states. We assume that the allocations of each individual in each state are known in advance but that they do not know which state will occur. This case is illustrated by Figure 3.3(a). The aggregate allocation is again represented by the point T and (as in Figures 3.2(a) and (b)) state 1 is 'bad' and state 2 is 'good'. Individual 1's allocations are again shown relative to the origin O and 2's relative to point T.

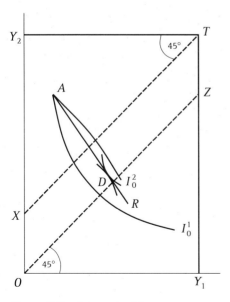

Figure 3.3a Aggregate risk

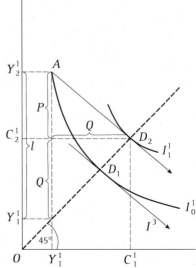

Figure 3.3b Fair insurance

The 45° line *OZ* shows situations in which 1 gets the same in both states while the parallel *XT* shows situations in which 2 gets the same in both states. *XT* lies above *OZ* if state 1 is a relatively bad state.

The initial distribution of these resources is represented by the point *A* and the core is bounded again by the pair of indifference curves drawn through this point. The trade equilibrium will lie at a point of tangency between another pair of indifference curves within this area illustrated by point *D*. If both individuals are risk averse, then it can be shown that this point will lie within the rhombus *OXTZ*, meaning that after this trade, both individuals are better off in state 2 than state 1. That is a consequence of optimal risk-sharing.

As this diagram is drawn, the curvature in I_0^1 is greater than that in I_0^2: individual 1 is more risk averse than individual 2. Reflecting this, the final consumption point is closer to *OZ* than *XT*. Figure 3.3(b) shows what happens if the type 1 individual trades with a type 3 agent who is completely indifferent to risk. This means that their *ex post* utility function is linear in *C*, allowing *ex ante* expected utility to be represented as $C_1^3 + BC_2^3$. The associated indifference curve becomes a straight line with a (negative) slope equal to the relative probability $1/B$ as shown by I^3 in Figure 3.3(b). (Remember that $B = (1 - p)/p$.) Since we know that any type 1 indifference curve I^1 has this slope along the 45° line *OZ*, this again becomes the contract curve.

This means that the equilibrium will lie at D_1 or D_2 or somewhere in between. If there are many type 1 risk-averse individuals and one monopoly insurer the equilibrium is at D_1, and all of the gains from trade go to the insurer. On the other hand, if there is a preponderance of risk-indifferent individuals, competition between them will ensure that trade precipitates an equilibrium at D_2. This point is determined by drawing a line with the slope $(-)1/B$ from the type 1 allocation point *A* to the 45° line. In other words, risk-indifferent individuals act like non-profit-making insurance institutions and provide risk-averse individuals with actuarially fair insurance. Equivalently, the rest of this chapter assumes that there is a single insurer providing fair insurance in a contestable market.

3.5 Competitive insurance under full information

To reinterpret this model as an insurance market, note that the difference $l = (Y_2 - Y_1)$ between income in the good state and the bad state can be interpreted as a loss. If the insurance market is fair then the client pays a premium of P and receives a *net* compensation for loss of Q in the bad state as shown in Figure 3.3(b). To be actuarially fair, $Q = PB = P(1 - p)/p$ (i.e. $pQ = (1 - p)P$). Since the premium is paid *ex ante*, it reduces consumption by P in both states. The *gross* compensation in the bad state is thus $P + Q = P(1 + B)$. To provide full insurance this must equal the loss of l. Thus the fair full insurance premium is simply the size of the loss times the probability of loss: $P = l/(1 + B) = lp$.

So far it has been assumed that there are just two states, which taken literally means that all clients of a particular type face losses simultaneously. However, personal risks are likely to be idiosyncratic, affecting different individuals in different states. Moreover, the probability of loss may differ between different groups. When using this apparatus to describe an insurance market it is more realistic to suppose that type 1 clients are similar in terms of their preferences and the risks they face, but can incur losses in different states. Since a fair insurer will offer them all the same rates, Figure 3.3(b) can then be replicated for any type of client. We simply need to interpret state 1 as a state in which a particular client suffers a loss, and state 2 as one in which they do not.

The indifference curve I_0^l in Figure 3.4(a) shows the pairs of consumption points which yield the same level of expected utility as the initial allocation A for a relatively *low-risk* client facing the probability of loss p^l. As in Figure 3.3(b), they are offered insurance along the fair odds line AL.[8] They move to D_1^l on the 45° line which gives them a higher expected utility. This is the point of tangency between the budget line AL and the indifference curve I_1^l which lies above I_0^l.

This low-risk apparatus is now overlaid with another showing the equivalent indifference curve I^h for a relatively *high-risk* client with the same *ex post* utility function and allocation, but a higher probability of loss: $p^h > p^l$. I_0^l is less steep than I_0^h at any point such as A and moves above I^h for points to the right of A.[9] These individuals move along the fair odds line AH to D_1^h which gives a higher level of utility than I_0^h, but a lower level of utility than D_1^l. Again, this is a point of tangency between a budget line (AL) and an indifference curve (I_1^h, which lies above I_0^h). These fair odds lines and the indifference curve I_1^h play an important part

---

[8] The fair odds line AL is constructed by drawing a line through the allocation point which is parallel with the tangent of I_0^l (or any other low-risk indifference curve) at the intersection with the 45° line. AH is constructed in a similar way, using I_0^h.

[9] Evaluating the marginal rates of substitution at any point using (3.3) shows that the slope of I^l divided by the slope I^h is $B^h/B^l < 1$.

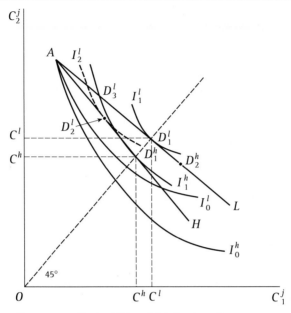

Figure 3.4a Rothschild and Stiglitz (1976)

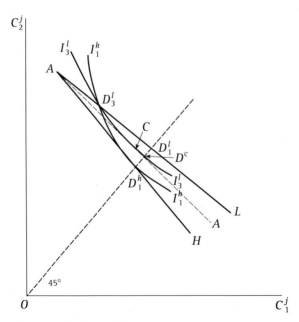

Figure 3.4b Compulsion

in the analysis and are reproduced for clarity in Figure 3.4(b), discussed in the next section.

This assumes that the insurer can distinguish different clients and offer them different but actuarially fair contracts, allowing them to insure fully. In this case the low-risk types are naturally offered a better contract with a price ratio of $R^l < R^h$. They attain full insurance by paying a premium $P^l < P^h$ and receiving a net compensation of $Q^l = B^l P^l > Q^h$. This allows them to attain the risk-free consumption point $C^l < C^h$ as shown in Figure 3.4(a). In this case, a risk-indifferent competitive insurer ensures Pareto-optimality under full information.

3.6 Rothschild and Stiglitz (1976): Adverse selection in insurance markets

The full information assumption (4) plays a fairly harmless role in the two-state model of Sections 3.2 to 3.4. That is because if the market is complete and people act as price takers they will effectively pool any private information and share the same posterior odds in equilibrium.[10] Moreover, everyone knows *ex post* which state has occurred. However, the idiosyncratic risk model developed in the previous section is very different. In this case there are effectively as many states as there are individuals and each one has private information about their own status, which they are unlikely to reveal unless it is in their interest to do so. In this situation, adverse selection and moral hazard are likely to precipitate a suboptimal outcome. Moreover, if the state has to be verified this will involve further welfare losses.

Rothschild and Stiglitz (1976) analyse the effect which adverse selection has in this situation. Following their analysis, now suppose that individuals know their own risk type but that the insurer does not. If the contract with the price ratio of B^l is offered (represented by the fair odds line AL in Figures 3.4(a) and 3.4(b)), then the insurer breaks even on the low-risk transactions, but loses on contracts with high-risk clients, who move to a point such as D_2^h in Figure 3.4(a).[11] On the other hand, if a price ratio of B^h is offered (corresponding to AH) then the insurer breaks even

---

[10] This assumes that a REE exists, which may not be true for certain parameter values. However, Allen (1986) shows that these values only occur by 'accident': they have a probability measure of zero.

[11] This would in principle be a point of tangency between the budget line AL and an indifference curve I_2^h (not shown) which lay above both I_0^h and I_1^h.

on contracts with high-risk clients but makes a profit on low-risk contracts. In this case the best that the low-risk types can do is to move to a point such as D_2^l in Figure 3.4(a). This is the point of tangency between the budget line AH and the indifference curve I_2^l (dashed) which lies between I_0^l and I_1^l.

Neither of these situations is consistent with the contestable market assumption. In the second case, another insurer can enter the market and offer a new contract just to the left of the point D_3^l shown in Figure 3.4(a). Because this line lies to the left and below I_1^h, the high-risk types will prefer the original contract and remain at D_1^h. However, because D_3^l lies above I_2^l, the new contract will be preferred to the original one by the low-risk types. This will give the newcomer all of the low-risk business, at an actuarially fair rate (since D_3^l lies along AL, which is actuarially fair for low-risk types). The incumbent will just be left with low high-risk types at the actuarially fair rate.[12] Exercise 5 provides a numerical example of this Rothschild–Stiglitz contract.

Consequently, in equilibrium, this insurance market offers the two contracts simultaneously and clients self-select. This two-tier contract structure forces the low-risk types to distinguish themselves from the high-risk types in order to gain full insurance at an actuarially fair rate. The low-risk types get partial insurance at a fair rate. In practice, this usually takes the form of a 'deductible' or 'excess' which reduces the scale of the compensation by a fixed amount. Alternatively, when losses are variable (rather than the fixed amount assumed here) 'coinsurance' (fractional compensation) can be used.

This two-tier market solution with self-selection is known as a separating equilibrium. It was originally developed by Rothschild and Stiglitz (1976) in the context of an insurance market. Other applications of the model include Easley and O'Hara (1992), who develop a separating equilibrium model of a securities market with asymmetric information. In this case, different commission rates are charged for small and large transactions, separating those trading on a small scale for liquidity reasons from those trying to trade in large size on private information. Glosten (1989)

---

[12] If the incumbent were to offer contracts with a price ratio between B^l and B^h the newcomer would still cream off the low-risk types. This would leave the incumbent making a loss dealing exclusively with low-risk types. Rothschild and Stiglitz note that if the incumbent left the market the high-risk clients would move to the new contract which would then make a loss. In this case there would be no equilibrium. However, a rational incumbent would realize that he could break even by moving the price ratio to B^l and dealing with the high risks.

develops a sliding-scale price model of a security market which achieves a partial separation between liquidity and information traders.

3.7 Compulsory full insurance

In the Rothschild and Stiglitz model, the high-risk types are fully insured, but the low-risk types are underinsured. Importantly, this is true even though they bear all of the risks themselves, without involving third parties. This solution is suboptimal compared to the full information situation discussed in Section 4.4 in which both types are fully insured at fair rates. In practice, it may be possible to distinguish broadly between different types of risk using medical or employment records, actuarial statistics and the like, but within each risk category the market only caters properly for the highest-risk types.

In this model the low-risk types prevent the high-risk types pooling with them by selecting a less expensive partial insurance contract. However, if they are sufficiently risk averse, the low-risk types could be better off *collectively* by allowing the high-risk types to pool with them. Of course, the high-risk types would always be better off if this happened.

Suppose for example that the government brings in a law which states that all individuals must take out full insurance. This contract is shown graphically by point D^c in Figure 3.4(b) which is halfway between D^h and D^l. This assumes that there are equal numbers of high- and low-risk individuals and that the contract is actuarially fair.[13] As the diagram is drawn, D^c lies on the curve I_3^l, which passes through D^h, indicating that the low-risk types are indifferent between compulsory full insurance and the Rothschild–Stiglitz contract D_3^l. The low-risk types are clearly better off than at D^h. Consequently, in this case the law brings a Pareto-improvement. Indeed, if the curvature of I_1^l is increased, the low-risk types are actually better off in the pooled insurance scheme. However, following the argument of the previous section, compulsion is necessary to prevent low-risk individuals breaking ranks and taking up a partial insurance offer (such as C) from another insurer.[14] Exercise 5 proves another numerical illustration.

---

[13] If there were more low-risk clients this would rotate the budget line in an anticlockwise direction, making a gain for the low-risk types more likely.

[14] D lies on the 45° line and so the slope of I_3^l at this point is $-p^l(1 - p^l)$. This is parallel to AL and therefore less steep than AA. Consequently, there are points such as C lying along AA to the north-west of D which would be better than D (and D_3^l) for the low-risk types.

3.8 The regulation of insurance markets

The information problems affecting insurance services differ from those affecting the basic financial services like fund management discussed in the previous chapter. Consequently, the rationale for regulation is different. In both cases, retail clients are likely to find it hard to distinguish high- and low-quality suppliers. This may make it hard for suppliers to establish a market, leading the industry to regulate itself. Minimum-standard and other arrangements have to be policed by industrial or government agencies. They can lead to a two-tier market if low-quality suppliers can trade separately.

However, insurance is special in several respects. First, it may also be hard for suppliers to distinguish high-risk from low-risk clients. As we have established, clients then behave as information monopolists and try to hide their private information by behaving strategically. The character of the market is determined by the low-quality high-risk types who in equilibrium are fully insured at fair actuarial rates. Other clients under-insure. They can be cherry-picked by insurance companies who offer partial insurance schemes at better rates. In this case, a two-tier market emerges through individual self-selection rather than industrial self-regulation. There is an argument for making full insurance compulsory in this case. Although this forces the low-risk types to pool with the high-risk types it reduces the average cost of insurance and can actually leave the low-risk types better off.

People will also tend to underinsure if their financial wealth effectively limits their liability to third party claims. This is particularly likely in the case of high-risk low-income individuals. Third party claims are an important feature of the vehicle insurance market. Cars for example can cause damages to third parties that can dwarf the financial capacity of all but the most wealthy. In this case, an uninsured owner effectively shares the risk with third parties that they cannot fully compensate in the event of a serious accident. This limited-liability effect greatly strengthens the case for compulsory full insurance against third-party damage. Consequently, most countries have laws which make third-party accident cover compulsory for vehicles.

A similar case can be made for mandatory medical and (in some circumstances) social insurance. Accidents and other health problems involve medical bills and a simultaneous reduction of earning capacity. These losses are normally borne by the victim, but they may have to forgo treatment, because they may not be able to afford to pay. In this case, contagion, empathy, and other externalities can bring distress to third parties. Reflecting this, emergency medical services do not normally establish the financial or insurance status of accident victims before providing treatment.

These considerations are more likely to be influential in the case of small tight-knit communities, which are bound together by family relationships, religious, or other affinities which make it difficult for members to walk away when one of their fellows falls upon hard times. As the introductory section argued, these communities have de facto social insurance arrangements for dealing with idiosyncratic risk. Mutual insurance societies offer a way of formalizing these risk-sharing arrangements and are often found in local communities, trades unions, and similar organizations. Members of these societies are in a good position to monitor each other's behaviour and impose informal sanctions for misbehaviour, helping to contain the problem of moral hazard.

Unfortunately, large anonymous societies are not very good at handling these problems. Moreover, groups who suffer losses (typically from say natural disasters, economic collapse, or bank failures) are in a position to lobby government for assistance even if there is no legal requirement for the government to intervene. The classic example is provided by flood insurance. People who are exposed to this risk typically reckon the government will be compelled to provide compensation in the event of a flood, so no one takes out insurance. This obliges the government to provide de facto insurance for nothing.

Bank failures provide other examples of de facto government insurance. Following the BCCI collapse in 1993, the British government was lobbied to provide more compensation to depositors than they were entitled to under the British deposit insurance scheme.[15] In the same way, individuals can come to believe that they can rely upon the rest of society to bale them out of medical and unemployment problems and support them in their old age. Once this happens it becomes very difficult to rectify the situation by refusing support and making them suffer the consequences.

---

[15] At the time of the BCCI crisis, the British scheme provided insurance of 75 per cent on deposits of up to £20,000. This has since been raised to 90 per cent and is likely to be raised to 100 per cent under new European directives.

3.9 Market structure

The alternative to de facto government insurance is to make insurance against these eventualities compulsory. This is why many countries make flood insurance compulsory. Many other countries have compulsory social insurance. However, once insurance becomes compulsory this precipitates other serious problems. It provides the insurance companies with a captive market, making it extremely important to ensure that competition forces companies to provide insurance in line with actuarial rates. The presence of non-profit-making mutual insurance societies helps in this respect. National insurance schemes, which provide universal medical and social cover through government agencies, provide another route to profit-free insurance.

Compulsory insurance schemes normally offer a standard level of cover to everyone. They thus avoid adverse selection, but can exaggerate the moral hazard problem, particularly if contributions are related to income. Moreover, the local community is unlikely to monitor behaviour in the case of a national scheme. This role falls by default to government officers who can easily get a reputation for being intrusive and heavy-handed. These institutions can precipitate a culture in which individuals do not bother about supporting themselves, but simply expect the state to provide.

3.10 Prudential regulation

Government insurance agencies typically fund their disbursements out of taxation or other levies on the working population. Because these contributions are usually linked to income they can have disincentive effects. This is likely to pose a serious problem in the developed countries as the ratio of dependents to workers increases in the next century.

In contrast, private insurance schemes support their liabilities by holding investment funds. Although they are similar in this sense to fund management companies, there is an important difference. As we have seen, pension funds and investment and unit trusts simply act as managers and their clients retain ownership of the funds under management. Their shareholders' funds are held separately. The situation is in fact similar in the case of a mutual insurance society, which legally holds assets collectively on behalf of policyholders, even though individual members may not claim anything more than their policy entitlement.

In the case of an insurance *company*, however, the shareholders enjoy ownership of the assets (net of liabilities) under limited liability. Although losses can prejudice the claims of policyholders, any profits after claims have been met accrue to shareholders and not policyholders. Moreover, shareholders' funds are usually small compared to the gross assets under management, which means that the effect of capital gains on profitability is amplified by a capital gearing effect.

This asymmetric gearing phenomenon can cause reckless behaviour on behalf of insurance company managers. This is especially likely if an insurance company gets into financial difficulties, since it then has an incentive to engage in high-risk activities. This is because if the net assets are negligible and the company is likely to fail, further capital losses will not make any difference to shareholders, while capital gains could allow the company to survive. Mathematically, shareholder profits are a convex function of fund management profits, a situation which is analysed in Chapter 9. This is the basis of the case for prudential regulation: balance sheet controls designed to prevent excessive risk-taking by managers.

A similar situation arises in the case of banks, where depositors have a fixed claim upon the loan portfolio and residual profits accrue to bank shareholders. Almost all financial systems have legal restrictions upon banks and insurance companies, which are designed to protect their clients from fraud, excessive risk-taking, and other forms of exploitation.

Prudential controls are primarily designed to ensure that insurance providers have enough financial reserves to meet potential commercial or portfolio losses. If these capital requirements are properly regulated, this means that shareholders bear the cost of losses just as they benefit from gains, removing the asymmetry which causes excessive risk. These capital requirements are buttressed by a regular inspection of insurance company balance sheets, designed to ensure that managers avoid high-risk situations. Some European countries adopt a prohibitive regime that tightly restricts the range of securities in which insurance companies can invest. However, in the English-speaking world it is typically argued that prohibition distorts the market and that capital adequacy requirements are more efficient.

EXERCISES

Fully revealing financial markets

Question 1. Using standard valuation criteria, a public utility would be worth £6 under current management. If this company is taken over by another utility this will result in economies of scale which push this value up to £9. Anticipating the discussion of Chapter 7, assume that the takeover mechanism is competitive and that a bidder will offer the full reorganization value of £10. The stock market price is currently £7. Assuming that investors are indifferent to risk, what is the probability the market attaches to a successful bid?

> If investors are indifferent to risk, the market price equals the expected or probability-weighted value. If the probability of a bid is p, the expected value is $p \times 9 + (1 - p) \times 6$. Equating this with the current price and solving for the probability of takeover $p = 1/3$.

Question 2. Consider a futures market trading two oil-based products: fuel oil (used for heating and power generation) and kerosene (jet fuel). There are two major uncertainties facing the market over the next six months. The first is the possibility of a severe winter, the second the possibility of a Middle East crisis. Both would push up product prices, but the latter would have a dispropor-tionately large effect on the price of kerosene. Market analysts say that the spot prices (measured in US dollars per 100 litres) likely in the four possible *ex post* scenarios would be:

Kerosene		Crisis?	
		no	yes
Severe winter?	prob	$(1 - l)$	l
no	$(1 - q)$	20	40
yes	q	24	44

Table Q2.1

Fuel oil		Crisis?	
		no	yes
Severe winter?	prob	$(1 - l)$	l
no	$(1 - q)$	10	14
yes	q	12	16

Table Q2.2

(a) Using l to represent the probability of a Middle East crisis and q that of a severe winter, derive two linear relationships showing the *ex ante* expected or probability-weighted value of the two futures prices. Assume that the two events are independent, so that the probability of a compound event (like a severe winter and no crisis) is the product of the simple probabilities ($q(1 - l)$ in that case). Let K represent the expected price of kerosene and F the price of fuel oil.

> Taking probability-weighted averages of the spot prices shown in Tables Q2.1 and Q2.2 gives

$$K = 20(1 - l)(1 - q) + 40l(1 - q) + 24q(1 - l) + 44lq$$
$$= 20 + 20l + 4q,$$
$$F = 10(1 - l)(1 - q) + 14l(1 - q) + 12q(1 - l) + 16lq$$
$$= 10 + 4l + 2q.$$

(b) Assuming that futures prices equal expected prices (i.e. indifference to risk), invert these relationships to show the implicit probabilities l and Q given any futures price observations K and F. Calculate the probabilities implicit in the following *ex ante* observations:

	Scenario		
	1	2	3
K	24.0	40.0	24.0
F	12.0	14.0	11.4

Table Q2.3

Inverting the two relationships derived at (a) gives

$$l = K/12 - F/6,$$
$$q = F(5/6) - K/6 - 5.$$

Substituting K and F values for *ex ante* scenarios 1–3 into these relationships gives the following results:

	Scenario		
	1	2	3
l	0.0	1.0	0.1
q	1.0	0.0	0.5

Table Q2.4

[Actually, we can infer results 1 and 2 directly from Tables Q2.1 and Q2.2.]

(c) Suppose that market prices are as shown in scenario 3. You believe that the probability of a crisis is 20 per cent and that of a severe winter 50 per cent. What trade should you make if your gross futures position is limited to $100,000? What is your expected profit?

Substituting my subjective probabilities into the equation derived in 2(a) gives average or expected spot prices of $26 for kerosene and $11.8 for fuel oil. These are higher than the prevailing futures prices shown in Table Q2.3. I choose to buy kerosene futures rather than fuel oil futures because the percentage gain is higher and there is an open position limit. I can buy 4,166 kerosene futures contracts for $99,984. This is the maximum I can buy. I expect to sell these contracts at an average future spot price of $26, yielding $108,316 with an expected profit of $8,332.

Insurance under full information

Question 3. Individuals have an income of 2 units, but can lose 1 unit in a bad state $(l = 1)$. They can take out variable insurance $0 \le x \le 1$ for an *ex ante* premium of xp which returns x in the bad state. They maximize expected (probability-weighted) utility. Their *ex post* utility is described by the natural logarithm of *ex post* consumption C:

$$U = \ln(C). \tag{3.5}$$

The probability of loss is $p^l = 1/3$ for low-risk and $p^h = 1/2$ for high-risk individuals. Suppose that insurance companies are competitive and can distinguish these types. They offer the fair premia $p = p^l = 1/3$ to low-risk and $p = p^h = 1/2$ to high-risk individuals.

(a) How much insurance do these types buy at these rates?

Depending upon their risk premium p and insurance level x, each individual experiences the following consumption levels in the bad and good states:

$C_1 = 2 - 1 + x - xp$
    $= \text{income} - \text{loss} + \text{claim} - \text{premium},$
$C_2 = 2 - xp$
    $= \text{income} - \text{premium}.$

Taking the probability-weighted average of the utility levels in these states and substituting these consumption levels, the expected utility of individual i, where $i = h, l$ is

$$EU^i = [p^i\ln(C_1) + (1 - p^i)\ln(C_2)]$$
$$= p^i\ln(2 - 1 + x - xp) + (1 - p^i)\ln(2 - xp). \tag{3.6}$$

Individuals choose x to solve the optimization problem

$$\max_{\{x\}}\{p^i\ln(2 - 1 + x - xp) + (1 - p^i)\}\ln(2 - xp)\}. \tag{3.7}$$

Under full information the premium $p^i = p$, and differentiating with respect to x gives the first-order condition

$$0 = p(1 - p)/(2 - 1 + x - xp) - (1 - p)p/(2 - xp).$$

This implies $(2 - 1 + x - xp) = (2 - xp)$ or $C_1 = C_2$. Solving for x gives $x = 1$: both types fully insure.

(b) How do their insured utility levels compare with their uninsured expectations?

To calculate the expected utility gain we substitute $x = 1$ into (3.6) and subtract the result for $x = 0$:

$\ln(2 - p) - (1 - p)\ln(2)$
fully insured − uninsured,

(using $\ln(1) = 0$). Evaluating this for $p = p^l = 1/3$ and $p = p^h = 1/2$ gives a gain of $0.5108 - 0.4620 = 0.0487$ for the low-risk types and $0.4054 - 0.3465 = 0.0590$ for the high-risk types. As we would expect the gain is higher the greater the risk.

Insurance under asymmetric information

Question 4. The situation is as described in Question 3, but now insurers cannot distinguish the two risk types. An insurer offers a contract with a premium rate of $p = p^h = 1/2$ allowing the high-risk types to fully insure.

(a) What do the low-risk types do when faced with this premium rate?

> They choose x to maximize (3.7) with $i = l$ and $p = p^h = 1/2$:
>
> $$\max_{\{x\}}\{(1/3)\ln(1 + x/2) = (2/3)\ln(2 - x/2)\}.$$
>
> The first-order condition is
>
> $$0 = (1/3)(1/2)/(1 + x/2) - (2/3)(1/2)/(2 - x/2).$$
>
> This gives $x = 0$. The low-risk types do not insure at all. They have the (uninsured) utility level of 0.4620 calculated at 3(b).

(b) Design a Rothschild–Stiglitz contract with $p = p^l = 1/3$ that restricts $x < \bar{x}$. where $\bar{x}$ is such that the high-risk types would be indifferent between the new contract $\{p = p^l = 1/3,\ x = \bar{x}\}$ and their fair insurance contract $\{p = p^h = 1/2,\ x = 1\}$.

> The high-risk types have the utility level $\ln(2 - 1/2) = \ln(1.5)$ under their fair insurance contract. Substituting $p = p^l = 1/3$ into (3.6) gives their expected utility value under the new contract:
>
> $$(1/2)\{\ln(1 + 2x/3) = \ln(2 = x/3)\} = (1/2)\{\ln[(1 + 2\bar{x}/3)(2 - \bar{x}/3)]\}.$$
>
> Equating the two utility levels gives an equation for the value x which makes the low-risk types indifferent between the two contracts:
>
> $$\ln(1.5) = (1/2)\{\ln[(1 + 2\bar{x}/3)(2 - \bar{x}/3)]\}.$$
>
> Multiplying by 2 and taking antilogarithms of each side gives
>
> $$1.5^2 = (1 + 2\bar{x}/3)(2 - \bar{x}/3).$$
>
> Finally, rearranging this as $0 = \bar{x}^2 - 4.5\bar{x} + 9/8$ gives the internal solution $\bar{x} = 0.2657$. (The second-order conditions confirm that this is a maximum.)

(c) Confirm that the low-risk types prefer this Rothschild–Stiglitz contract to the one they are offered at (a).

> We have shown that contract (a) has an expected utility value of 0.4620 for the low-risk types. Substituting $p = p^l = 1/3$, $x = \bar{x} = 0.2657$ into (3.6) reveals that contract (b) has a higher level of expected utility:
>
> $$(1/3)\ln(1 + 2 \times 0.2657/3) + (2/3)\ln(2 - 0.2657/3)\} = 0.4861.$$

(d) Suppose that the government brings in a zero-profit compulsory full insurance scheme which charges everyone the same premium rate p. Calculate the share (s) of high-risk individuals in the population which would make the low-risk individuals indifferent between this contract and the Rothschild–Stiglitz contract analysed at (b).

> For the scheme to break even averaging across high- and low-risk types with the shares s and $(1 - s)$ the premium must be $p = s/2 + (1 - s)/3 = 1/3 + s/6$. Substituting this into (3.6) with $x = 1$, $p^l = 1/3$ gives the utility of the low-risk types under

this scheme: $\ln(2 - p) = \ln((10 - s)/6)$. Equating this with the utility level of 0.4861 under the Rothschild–Stiglitz contract (b) and taking antilogarithms gives a linear equation for the breakeven share s: $(10 - s)/6 = \exp[0.4861]$. This has the solution $s = 0.2442$. We conclude that the low-risk individuals would not be hostile to the new scheme if the high-risk types made up less than a quarter of the population.

4. Capital Market Microstructure and Regulation

Financial markets allow agents to divorce their spending from their income by selling or buying securities. Capital markets are special because they organize trade in variable price securities like equities and bonds. These are primary securities that do not involve the intervention of a financial intermediary like a bank. Although their value depends upon market conditions, bond and equity contracts and the markets they trade in are actually easier to analyse than bank-intermediated instruments like deposits. Bank deposits claim to offer instant access with capital certainty, but as the intoductory chapter noted, the possibility of bankruptcy complicates matters considerably.

Capital markets perform several other important functions. They allow agents to insure themselves against unfavourable events which are correlated with security prices (by 'hedging' or arranging their portfolios appropriately). Together with the financial futures markets and the insurance industry, they help to diversify risks across the community. Capital asset prices also reflect prospective economic developments, and thus help to collect information and share it across the community. This information helps to inform investment and other key decisions taken by company directors, public officials, and other agents. For example, the portfolio switch out of conventional equities into information and communications technology stocks which took place around the turn of the century lowered the cost of capital to very small proportions in ICT companies, whilst raising it dramatically elsewhere. This signals a major switch in capital investment from the 'old' to the 'new' economy. This shift is also likely to have major differential effects upon remuneration and recruitment in industry.

The next four chapters analyse the strengths and weaknesses of capital markets using the theory of asymmetric information. This analysis tells us that the flow of information and securities through the capital markets is imperfect and that financial intermediaries can help to remedy these imperfections. This observation forms a basis for discussing the role of banks and other financial intermediaries in subsequent chapters.

This chapter begins with a brief survey of the main types of capital market found in a modern economy. I then present a simple version of the

Copeland and Galai (1983) model of dealership markets commonly used to trade bonds and equities in the Anglo-American markets. This model offers a theoretical basis for discussing the role which inside traders play in these markets, during a takeover bid for example. It offers an example of asymmetric information, since the insiders know whether a bid is going to occur, or have some other vital knowledge which is not known by the rest of the market.

This market structure differs from those analysed in previous chapters in several respects. First, this is a two-way market in which clients sell as well as buy. Second, prices are flexible rather than administered like fund management commissions. Third, the imbalance of information is more complex. Although there may be some unsophisticated retail participants, many clients are sophisticated professional investors who know as much about the market as the dealer. Indeed, insiders know more about the value of the product than everyone else and, depending upon this information, can either buy or sell. This means that security trades and prices signal this information to the rest of the market. This transparency or openness fundamentally distinguishes the capital markets from markets in banking, insurance, and other financial services.

This chapter maintains the assumption of exogenous information: insiders are endowed with exclusive information for nothing, while research by interested outsiders is unlikely to uncover this information. The dynamic analysis of the next chapter shows that a flexible security price 'pools' or 'aggregates' the information of different traders and can eventually reveal what insiders know. We then consider the implications of all of this for insider regulation. Chapter 6 shows what happens if we assume that financial research can deliver useful information about security values. This chapter also assumes, like the microstructure literature upon which it is based, that the fundamental value of the security is independent of its market price. This assumption is maintained in Chapters 5 and 6, but then relaxed. Chapter 7 looks at the relationship between managerial decisions, equity prices, and the capital markets.

4.1. Primary capital markets and their regulation

Primary markets organize new issues of securities: company flotations, privatizations, private placements, and the like. These markets introduce new companies or government agencies to a market or raise capital for existing ones. This process increases the range of securities or the quantity outstanding.

New issues are organized by investment banks who usually act as brokers to the issuer, placing the new securities directly with investors. Importantly, these banks do not usually provide finance in their own name, as a commercial bank does. Instead, they introduce issuers to investors, who then form a direct financial relationship.

A variety of different offer, underwriting, and market management techniques can be used by investment banks to achieve a successful flotation. Public fixed-price offers have been extensively used in British and other privatizations (sales of government-owned firms), while public auctions are used to sell government bonds like US Treasuries and UK gilts. Book-building techniques (where the investment bank gauges the market beforehand in order to establish an indicative flotation price range and then invite tenders) are much more common in company flotations. Bond issues are generally easier to price and in the Eurobond market for example, the issuing bank usually underwrites the issue by guaranteeing the issuer a fixed price.

In the USA, the capital markets are regulated by the Securities and Exchange Commission. However, as has been noted, the New York Stock Exchange is granted a degree of autonomy in view of the specialist nature of the stock market. The same is true in the UK, where the London Stock Exchange (LSE) has powers delegated by the FSA. The International Securities Markets Association (ISMA) oversees the Eurobond markets, while responsibility for the burgeoning swaps market lies jointly with the British Bankers Association and the International Association of Swap Dealers.

The primary markets can be characterized in terms of exogenous information. In this sense they are similar to retail financial markets. Although they are dominated by sophisticated professional investors, the imbalance of information between buyers and sellers is naturally high and it is hard for individual investors to remedy this asymmetry through research. Instead, it is more effective for the stock exchange authorities to force companies coming to the market to divulge information. This is indeed the essence of primary market regulation.

The managers and owners of small private companies typically know them inside out, while the general investor community knows practically nothing about them. This problem is particularly acute in the case of Initial Public Offers (IPOs), which introduce unquoted companies to the equity market. Privatization issues apart, these are usually young companies, with an average life of about five years in the USA, and about ten years in the UK during the 1990s. This compares with nearly fifty years in Germany. Their track record is harder for outsiders to assess, since unquoted companies only have to publish a minimum of financial information. It is hard to imagine a situation where the seller of a security has a greater informational advantage over the buyer.

Reflecting this, the LSE's 'yellow book' ('Admission of Securities to Listing'), devotes most of its massive weight to the regulation of the primary market. Treasurers of newly floated companies as well as market operators complain bitterly about the burden and responsibility which this involves. However, in effect, these regulations boil down to two simple requirements. First, the provision of financial information must be brought up to the standard required of existing quoted companies. In particular, this requires three years of audited company accounts. Second, 'due diligence' is required of everyone associated with the company. This includes its managers, regulators, and stockbrokers for example, requiring them to divulge any information germane to the value and prospects of the company. For example, this might be confidential information about a pending law suit or a forthcoming price review. This is surely the absolute minimum that could be expected in this situation.

IPOs are anomalous because these issues are usually sold at an initial price discount but then tend to underperform the rest of the market. Recent research findings (Levis 1993; Ritter 1996) indicate that there is a negative correlation between the initial price increase and the longer-term performance, suggesting that in the absence of information the market may misprice stocks initially, leading to a correction as information accumulates. This area is the subject of a great deal of research by financial economists (Jenkinson and Ljungqvist 1996). It seems clear that the way in which companies (and in the case of privatizations, governments) raise capital in the stock market and the rules which govern these issues will continue to be the subject of academic research and policy debate.

Nevertheless, our main objective in this and subsequent chapters is to analyse the informational structure of secondary markets, which is more informative than retail and primary markets. Although secondary markets in small company stocks are similar in terms of the disparity of information between management and outside shareholders, markets in large blue chip stocks are much richer in information. Large companies and their products are often in the headlines and it is not difficult for ordinary investors to form a reasonably accurate impression of their management.

Moreover, the share price itself reveals information and individual research can be worthwhile.

4.2. Secondary capital markets

Secondary capital markets organize trade in existing securities, without changing the range or amount outstanding. In effect they provide a second-hand market, allowing investors a flexibility in spending which would not be possible if they had to hold securities until they were redeemed. For example, investors who bought shares in a primary issue intending to hold on to them can nevertheless meet unforeseen cash requirements by selling securities to other investors. In this way, the issuer remains immune and the amount of securities outstanding remains unchanged, and yet the investor remains liquid.

There is, however, a price for this flexibility, which is that the price the seller receives depends upon market conditions which are uncertain. This effect may be seen by comparing an open-ended investment company (OEIC) like a British 'unit' trust which is obliged to buy its shares back from the public at a price in line with its net asset value, and a closed-end fund (a British 'investment' trust) which is not. In the latter case, the executives can get on with the job of fund management, without worrying about redemptions by investors. However, the share price is established in the market and can move to a large discount to net asset value.

On the other hand a fixed price, whether it be for a foreign exchange transaction, a deposit issued by a government body or a bank, or some other instrument, means that the issuer or some other agency must intervene in the market to meet fluctuations in demand. In the case of a unit trust, the management is required to buy and sell units at the published bid and ask prices. This necessitates liquid reserves and ultimately transactions in the underlying stock or bond markets which can be costly.

The variance of prices means that agents associated with secondary markets have to be very nimble to avoid risking their capital. If they are due to inherit some shares for example, they are exposed to the vagaries of the stock market unless they hedge them, say by purchasing put options. Similarly, if they are due to buy a holiday home abroad, they are exposed to the exchange rate unless they buy the foreign currency in advance. Secondary markets, with the associated futures and options exchanges, allow commercial traders and investors to 'hedge' or insure their portfolios and business activities by executing the appropriate transactions. They will usually be keen to cut their exposure as soon as possible, which is why Grossman and Miller (1988) call this trading motive the demand for 'immediacy'.

The role of a secondary market is to provide liquidity and immediacy in a cost-effective way. To this extent, it enhances the value of the securities it mediates, strengthening the primary market and lowering the cost of finance for companies and governments. As any market does, it performs this job by matching buyers and sellers and establishing a price at which equilibrium occurs. It offers a forum in which investors and traders interact and exchange securities according to their trade requirements and beliefs about the true value of the security. The price which clears the market therefore offers a consensus view of the underlying value of the security. However, as we will see, asymmetric information can seriously handicap a market's ability to perform these functions.

A security price is said to be informationally efficient if it reflects all of the information available to participants in the market. In this chapter, information endowments are fixed and this criterion is quite straightforward. However, it becomes much more difficult to assess efficiency if research is possible, as we assume in Chapter 6. In this case we need to ensure that research is socially as well as privately optimal and is fully reflected in prices. Anticipating that discussion, Grossman and Stiglitz (1980) prove that it is impossible to meet this criterion if information is endogenous.

4.3. Secondary market trading mechanisms

As with the primary markets, various mechanisms can be used to make a secondary market. In practice the best trading mechanism will depend upon the available technology. It will also depend upon the degree of product homogeneity and the client's need for anonymity, liquidity, and immediacy. For example, financial futures contracts are designed along simple lines in order to achieve a high degree of product homogeneity, allowing large numbers of buyers and sellers to be matched rapidly. These traders are usually exposed to price risk, which they want to hedge quickly. At the other extreme, houses are heterogeneous, making it much harder to match buyers and sellers. Prices in these markets are usually less volatile than those in the futures markets. Many clients switch from one residential property to another and are largely hedged if both legs of the transactions are conducted simultaneously. Thus the demand for immediacy is not as great as in the case of financial futures. Steil (1996) argues that the demand for immediacy is not very great in the case of the European equity markets.

Reflecting the very different characteristics of the underlying securities, we see many different trading mechanisms at work. In practice, it is very much a matter of 'horses for courses'. For example, 'open outcry' offers a relatively simple method of trade matching, which has been used for centuries in the London commodities markets (and until recently in the LIFFE financial futures market). In this case, buyers and sellers match themselves up directly by calling out bid and offer price offers in the trading 'pit'. This technique works very well for price-volatile homogeneous instruments like commodities and standardized futures. It is still extensively used in financial futures markets like the Chicago Board of Trade (CBOT).

This physical order-matching system is now being emulated electronically by new screen-based futures exchanges. Indeed, as noted in the Introduction, the trading pits are rapidly losing ground to the electronic systems, especially in Europe. Perhaps the best example of these electronic order-matching systems is the one introduced by the Deutsche-TerminBörse (DTB) in 1997. This successfully won back to Frankfurt in 1998 the trade in the Bund (German government bond) future, which had previously been dominated by LIFFE. The Stock Exchange Trading System (SETS, see Box 4.3) introduced by the London Stock Exchange (LSE) in 1997 gives another well-known example. The NASDAQ also introduced electronic trading for some securities in 1997. Earlier examples include TSA, pioneered by the Amsterdam Stock Exchange in 1994, and SWX, introduced by the Swiss Exchange in the following year. The Frankfurt Bourse has the Xetra electronic trading platform. These new electronic media are used mainly by market makers and industrial users to conduct large wholesale transactions. However, online trading systems have been extremely popular at the retail level in the USA and are now rapidly gaining ground in the UK and other European countries.

At the other extreme we find the brokerage mechanism, which is employed in thin markets for heterogeneous goods or instruments. This is quite adequate for traders with little immediacy or liquidity requirement, who trade infrequently. In this case brokers use their knowledge of the clientele to find buyers for sellers and vice versa, without taking any items onto their books. In an extreme case, where this process fails, an auction may be arranged. Realtor or estate-agency brokered housing markets illustrate this mechanism. Similarly, small company shares are usually traded on a 'matched bargains' basis by small regional stock-brokers. Another example comes from the Eurobond market, where many outstanding issues have 'bells and whistles' which were initially tailored to suit specific customer needs, but which now make them difficult to trade. Several specialist boutiques have sprung up in London to broker these instruments.

Matching methods are used by some of the smaller continental European bourses to make markets in equities. This is also how opening prices are determined in continuous auction systems like New York Stock Exchange (NYSE, Box 4.1) and in the SETS (Box 4.3). In this case, client 'limit orders', which specify the size of the trade and an acceptable price range, are collected before the market opens. These buy and sell orders are then aggregated, and the market-clearing price is found at the level at which net demand is close to zero. A market maker has the option of using this aggregate demand/supply schedule as an offer curve and can execute these limit orders against her own inventory.

This batch trading mechanism is clumsy and has been largely replaced by continuous electronic auction systems in Europe. However, aggregating orders does have the important advantage of reducing 'strategic behaviour' by individual clients. For example, it is hard for small trades to influence the equilibrium price in this sort of system. This influence would be greater if market makers published sliding scales of prices at which they were prepared to deal for individual execution. Such schedules would also make the relationship between price and quantity quite explicit. Madhavan (1992) shows that this system would be much less robust than the batch trading system in the face of strategic behaviour by insider dealers.

4.4. Dealership markets

Between these two extremes, we find dealership markets. Liquidity in these markets is maintained by dealers in return for privileges which they receive from the stock exchange. There are two main mechanisms for achieving liquidity, one being 'quote-driven', the other 'order-driven'. Although these mechanisms look very different to outsiders, we will see that they are very similar mathematically.

In quote-driven markets, dealers announce a 'bid' price (at which they stand ready to buy, up to some maximum quantity) and an 'ask' (or offer) price (at which they are prepared to sell). They then meet orders at these

Box 4.1. The New York Stock Exchange (NYSE)

The NYSE is the world's premier stock exchange. With the possible exception of the Japanese Nikkei Dow, all of the world's major stock markets follow movements in the Dow Jones index day to day. The 'open board' dealership trading mechanism is by far and away the oldest of any the world's major exchanges. It has remained in place with modifications since 1869. Gordon Gekko, the character of the 1980s film *Wall Street* would have found himself at home with the trading system in place a century earlier. The moving price strip which flashes along the walls of the major houses now is just an electronic version of the ticker tape introduced by Thomas Edison in 1867. The stock exchange itself can be traced back to the Buttonwood Agreement of 1792.

The NYSE trading mechanism is based on an order-matching process. Clients submit limit orders (price- and quantity-conditional buy and sell instructions) and market orders (unconditional as to price) to the order book. Limit orders are ranked to form the price schedule, as in any order-driven system. Market orders are immediately matched against the best limit order price in the book. The order book is organized by a specialist dealer. There is one specialist for each stock. When a new order arrives on the book, the dealer has the option of meeting it out of her inventory at a price equal to that available in the order book. Although there is only one dealer for each stock, the specialist does not have a monopoly, but competes against the book's limit orders. This system is an example of a continuous auction mechanism as analysed by Pagano and Roell (1993), Madhavan (1992), and Tonks (1996).

Opening prices are determined by matching methods on the NYSE as in other order-driven systems. Client limit orders are collected before the market opens. These buy and sell orders are then aggregated, and the market clearing price is found at the level at which net demand is close to zero. Again, a specialist can use this aggregate demand/supply schedule as an offer curve and execute these limit orders against her own inventory.

This mechanism is fairly robust, having survived for 130 years with few modifications. It works well if trade is brisk. Liquidity is effectively provided by the competition between the specialist and client limit orders. However, liquidity practically dried up during the crash of 1987, driven largely by computer-initiated 'hedge' trades spilling over from the derivatives market. The exchange responded by introducing circuit breakers, which suspend computer driven trades when the major indices have moved by more than a specified number of points. Specialists' capital requirements were also increased, as were floor space and the capacity of computer systems.

prices out of their inventory, adjusting prices accordingly. The screen-based US National Association of Securities Dealers Automated Quotation (NASDAQ) and the London Stock Exchange Automated Quotation (SEAQ) systems introduced as part of the Big Bang reforms in 1986 are prime examples of this mechanism. This trading mechanism is described in Box 4.2.

In order-driven markets, dealers (known in the jargon as intermediaries) submit limit orders on a continuous basis to the stock exchange computer. A limit order is an instruction to buy (sell) shares up to a specified maximum at a price equal or below (above) the specified level. These orders are 'crossed' or executed against existing limit orders if possible, but otherwise added to the order book, which forms the price schedule for the market. Similarly, clients can submit limit orders. They can also submit 'market orders' which are unconditional as to price and are immediately matched against the most favourable limit order price in the computer. This is the system used to organize trade in New York (see Box 4.1) and in London's Stock Exchange Trading System (SETS, see Box 4.3). SETS was introduced in 1998 and is used to deal in the top 100 London stocks, the components of the FTSE 100 index.[1] Other London stocks are still traded on the SEAQ or in the small companies markets (AIM or OFEX).

Intermediary limit orders ensure that the market remains liquid at all times, just as it does in the quote-driven system. *Ceteris paribus*, the continuous auction is theoretically equivalent to the quote-based trading mechanism (Pagano and Roell 1993; Madhavan 1992; Tonks 1996). However, in practice, as these authors acknowledge, differences in trading, transparency, and other rules could make a difference to the operation of the system. (We take up this point in Section 4.7.)

These two dealership mechanisms tend to work well if the product is homogeneous but trade is brisk. It also helps if the market is well understood by clients, and there is a lot of information about the fundamental factors influencing these securities in the public domain. However, the key requirement is for market makers to support liquidity by submitting firm price quotes or limit orders at all times, which means offering them special privileges not available to proprietary traders and others who are not obliged to support liquidity and can stop trading when this becomes hazardous. In the case of the LSE, the market maker privileges include exemption from stamp duty and the 3 per cent holdings disclosure rule (see Chapter 7). These dealership trading mechanisms have been the focus of much study by market microstructure economists. The next two sections develop a mathematical description of this market specification derived from the microstructure literature.

---

[1] It is also used to make markets in stocks which have left the FTSE 100 since SETS was instituted in 1998, as well as stocks for which there are individual equity options on LIFFE.

Box 4.2. London's SEAQ quote-based equity trading system

The Stock Exchange Automatic Quotation (SEAQ) system was introduced as part of the September 1986 Big Bang reform in London. Prior to that, security dealers known as jobbers had posted their prices on the floor of the Stock Exchange building. Clients placed market orders through fixed-commission brokers who in turn found the best price on the floor. Clients could also place price-contingent orders, which the brokers executed if the opportunity arose.

Firms were not allowed to act as both jobbers and brokers. In 1986, this restriction was abolished, opening the way to dual-capacity firms which performed both roles in a seamless way. Entry restrictions were also relaxed, allowing commercial banks and overseas investment banks into the market and providing more capacity and capital. Fixed commissions were also abolished.

London's SEAQ and SETS systems are decentralized, being based on television screens rather than a trading floor. SEAQ was modelled on the North American Security Dealers Association Quotation system (NASDAQ). These screens identify each market maker's bid and ask quotations and the 'size' in which they are prepared to deal. There is one screen for each stock. To facilitate best execution this identifies firms offering the lowest ask and highest bid prices. Institutional clients typically have these screens in their offices and telephone the market-making firms with their orders. These orders are then relayed verbally from the sales person receiving the call to the appropriate in-house dealer who executes it. In some circumstances, clients can negotiate prices which are inside the ranges shown on the screen. Alternatively, orders can be placed indirectly through agency brokers, who find the most favourable price and charge a commission.

Liquidity in these markets is provided by the dealers, who are obliged to provide firm quotes. In return, the dealers are exempt from stamp duty and disclosure requirements and have access to Inter-Dealer Broker (IDB) screens. This system was initially handicapped by settlement problems, but bedded in well after the crash of October 1987. Nevertheless, by the mid-1990s dissatisfaction with this trading system was mounting. Market makers argued that the obligation to quote to anyone placed them at too large a disadvantage. The practice of negotiating prices within the screen spreads for large institutional clients also reduced profitability. Institutional traders on the other hand argued that their trades provided liquidity, although they had none of the privileges enjoyed by market makers. They argued that they should have access to the IDB screens and were given access to this system in 1996. Regulators were concerned about the lack of transparency for large trades. The new SETS system (Box 4.3) takes account of these concerns and harnesses the liquidity available from institutional and proprietary traders.

Box 4.3. London's SETS order-driven equity trading system

The Stock Exchange Trading System (SETS) was introduced in October 1998 and used initially to trade the 100 stocks making up the FTSE index. Other stocks are still traded under the SEAQ system (Box 4.2).

In the SETS system, market makers, known as 'intermediaries', submit bids and offers which are stored electronically as price-conditional 'limit orders' in a computer. Clients can submit limit orders, adding to the liquidity of the system. They can also submit unconditional buy or sell instructions known as 'market orders'. When a client's market order comes into the system it is automatically matched against to the highest buy or lowest sale order and executed (or 'filled'). If it exceeds the capacity of the best limit order, then the remainder is filled by the next best order(s). Similarly, a new limit order is if possible executed (or 'crossed') against outstanding limit orders. Otherwise, it is stored in the computer for possible future execution. Small orders (typically of less than £5000) are not allowed onto the order book directly, but are either met out of the intermediaries' inventory or aggregated with other small orders for batch execution later.

Opening prices are struck by aggregating limit orders that are submitted before the market opens and finding the price at which net demand is close to zero. Buy orders with prices above this market-clearing level are matched with sell orders at lower prices and are all executed at this clearing price. The remaining limit orders then stay within the computer system to form the buy and sell price schedules against which new incoming orders are executed. These price schedules are displayed on screens which are available to both intermediaries and large institutional traders.

Unlike the SEAQ quotes, which identify the market maker, this electronic order book is anonymous. However, traders know who their counterparty is as soon as the trade is executed. Unlike the SEAQ system, where clients trade only with dealers, they may find that the counterparty is an institution or other trader. In this respect, the new London system differs from continental systems, where the stock exchange usually acts as an intermediary for settlement. Counterparty risks are handled by an LSE guarantee scheme.

Off-market transactions remain an issue. Market makers are still able to negotiate quotes over the telephone that lie inside the spreads displayed on the screen. There is no obligation to put these through the order book. Large block trades are protected by Worked Principal Agreements. These agreements allow intermediaries to provide a firm quote to a client for a block trade and then seek to improve upon these terms by working the order book to find better prices. These agreements remain confidential until the end of the day when the final terms are settled and published.

The new system now seems to be working well. Preliminary indications are that, as expected, there has been a significant reduction in average price spreads owing to the extra liquidity provided by client limit orders. The number of trades has also been on an upward trend, although this may have been for other reasons—the long bull run in equities for example. As with any new system, there have been teething problems. Initially, there was a lack of liquidity at the opening and close when the market was thin. This problem was frequently exacerbated by price manipulation at the close, when small opportunistic orders could sometimes be used to manipulate last trade prices and hence the prices at which options and other contracts settled. (Abuse of the order book during the last hour of trade of 1998 was sufficient to move the FTSE index itself.) This problem has been largely solved by taking an average of closing prices as representative. Another problem was the 'snake in the grass': a limit order with a very low buy or high sell price submitted on the off chance of securing a profitable trade from a market order in the absence of more realistic limit order prices. Recent changes in opening hours and the build up of volume seem to have relieved these various rogue-price problems.

Although it is hard to distinguish the effect of other influences, the move from SEAQ to SETS does appear to have improved the quality of the market in FTSE stocks. In particular, the introduction of institutional limit orders has improved the general liquidity of the system, while relieving some of the pressure on market makers. Other things being equal, simple quote- and order-driven models may be equivalent mathematically, but in practice other things are not equal. Rules regarding the submission of orders and disclosure for example can have significant implications for market structure.

4.5. Microstructure models

A major problem facing traders in financial markets is that they usually contain people like insiders or company analysts trading on better information or analysis than is available publicly. I will call these participants 'informed' or 'information' traders. As Milgrom and Stokey (1982) point out, this means that an 'uninformed trader', that is anyone speculating purely on the basis of public information, is likely to lose on average to informed traders.

This means that if they are rational, uninformed traders must be in the market for some non-speculative reason, perhaps because they have inherited shares which they want to sell or have savings which they want to invest for their retirement. They are called liquidity traders for this reason. I will regard these liquidity requirements as exogenous, fixed independently of asset prices. Moreover, in the absence of liquidity traders, no trade would ever take place: even if different investors brought different information to the market, they would be wary of revealing it, and trading with others with superior knowledge. In this case, we would have what Milgrom and Stokey call a 'no trade equilibrium'.

Dealers stand in the market and are obliged to quote realistic bid and ask prices or submit limit orders to the system. This guarantees liquidity, meaning that clients can always deal at some price. This is why dealers are also known as 'market makers'. These agents act passively and have to allow for the possibility that trades are informative. If some clients are better informed than the dealers, the dealer's buying and selling prices must allow for this.

Obviously, if they can discriminate, dealers will refuse to deal with known insiders, or pre-empt them by quoting them a very wide bid–ask spread. But they will also be wary of dealing unwittingly with clients who have superior information. They will establish a price spread which allows them at least to break even, balancing the probable losses on such trades against the probable gains on liquidity-driven trades. Because they are calculated to break even conditionally upon a client's sale or purchase, prices are regret-free in the sense that the dealer does not care which transaction occurs. This is the essential insight of the Bagehot (1971) paper.

Informational asymmetry plays a key role in this phenomenon: the market maker does not know who the insiders are or what their inside information is. Of course, this is not the only reason why market makers impose a spread. Market making is an expensive business, requiring a lot of sophisticated human and electronic resources, and these overheads are reflected in the spread. Financial capital is also needed to underpin the solvency of the firm and to finance the inventory positions which result from imbalances of order flow. Moreover, this is risk capital, which must therefore be looking for a high rate of return (Grossman and Miller 1988). Some dealers, the specialists on the NYSE for example, may be in a position to make monopoly profits. All of these influences can affect the prices which clients obtain.

The market microstructure literature furnishes a wide range of models of market mechanisms under different assumptions. A comprehensive review is provided by O'Hara (1995). The early literature such as Ho and Stoll (1981) stressed the role of risk capital and inventory movements. However, in this book we develop an information-based model that abstracts from such influences and shows how asymmetric information can affect market prices and allocation. The next section presents the basic version, based on the Copeland and Galai (1983) model. This was originally designed to show how dealers in a quote-driven market could calculate breakeven bid and ask prices. However, the simplicity of the specification means that intermediaries supplying limit orders to maintain the liquidity of an order-driven market would go through the same breakeven calculations and submit buy and sell orders at these prices. Consequently, with appropriate interpretation, we can use their model to describe either quote- or order-driven systems. Conveniently, this is also true of the Glosten and Milgrom (1985) version of the model developed in the next chapter.

4.6. Copeland and Galai (1983)

Copeland and Galai develop the basic algebra of the bid-ask price spread in a static model. The basic assumptions are:

1. There is a single trading period or 'day'.
2. The security value is realized at the end of this period.
3. The cost of carrying inventory is negligible, as are other dealer costs.
4. The market is contestable (the market maker acts competitively).
5. All agents are risk neutral.
6. Information endowments are exogenous: q per cent of clients are informed and $(1 - q)$ per cent uninformed, and they appear randomly.
7. Client liquidity needs are fixed at plus or minus one unit of stock (this unit is used as the scale variable).
8. Order size is fixed (at plus or minus one unit of stock).
9. Clients can only deal once a day.

In this situation, the market maker will quote ask P^a and bid P^b prices (valid for one unit of stock) or equivalently submit selling and buying instructions at these prices, which are just expected to break even. The contestable and costless nature of the market means that a wider spread would leave her idle, while a narrower spread would mean expected losses.

The model can be simplified by following Easley and O'Hara (1992), who suppose that the realization price can take just two values: either 'high' V^h or 'low' V^l (where $V^l < V^h$). Informed clients know with certainty whether V^l or V^h will be announced at the end of the period, and will buy or sell accordingly (assuming that $V^l < P^b \le P^a < V^h$). In this chapter we can think of them as company insiders, who know for sure whether their employer is about to mount a takeover bid at price V^h.

The market maker and her uninformed clients have access only to public information. They believe that the value can take on just two values, described by a Bernoulli or binomial distribution. Their initial belief is that there is a p per cent chance of a high (bid) price V^h emerging (and thus a $(1 - p)$ per cent chance of a low price V^l). Their prior expectation is thus:

$$\mu = pV^h + (1 - p)V^l \tag{4.1}$$

$$1 \geq p \geq 0. \tag{4.2}$$

This forms the baseline for the bid and ask prices in this model. The variance of the outcome:

$$\nu = p(1 - p)(V^h - V^l)^2 \tag{4.3}$$

is also important since this shows the uncertainty faced by the uninformed traders, a basic indicator of the information asymmetry. The Bernoulli variance[2] $p(1 - p)$ shows the variance as a single draw which yields 1 with probability p and nothing with probability $(1 - p)$. This is scaled up by the square of the value spread $(V^h - V^l)$.[3]

Suppose that the market maker first sets P^a at a level which means that sales are expected to break even. As far as she knows, there is a q per cent chance of trading with an informed agent and a p per cent chance of a high price, so there is qp per cent chance of a sale to such an agent at price P^a. This unit of stock must be replenished at the end of the trading period at a cost of V^h. The overall loss would therefore be $(V^h - P^a)$, as indicated in Table 4.1.

Table 4.1. Average profits

Market maker meets:	(a) with prob	(b) and net profit
(i) informed buyer	qp	$P^a - V^h < 0$
(ii) uninformed buyer	$(1 - q)/2$	$P^a - \mu > 0$
(iii) informed seller	$q(1 - p)$	$V^l - P^b < 0$
(iv) uninformed seller	$(1 - q)/2$	$\mu - P^b > 0$

Average profit:
of sales   a(i) × b(i) + a(ii) × b(ii) = $(P^a - V^h)qp + (P^a - \mu)(1 - q)/2$
of bids   a(iii) × b(iii) + a(iv) × b(iv) = $(V^l - P^b)q(1 - p) + (\mu - P^b)(1 - q)/2$

[2] The variance of the binomial distribution is derived by using an indicator variable that takes the value 1 in the case of a successful experiment (say a bid) and 0 otherwise. This is $p(1 - p)$.

[3] The variance ν is the squared deviation from the mean for a high outcome $(V^h - \mu)^2 = (1 - p)^2(V^h - V^l)^2$ weighted by p; plus $(V^l - \mu)^2 = p^2(V^h - V^l)^2$ for the low outcome weighted by $(1 - p)$. This simplifies to the expression shown at (4.3).

On the other hand, there is a $(1 - q)$ per cent probability of transacting with an uninformed agent. It would be reasonable for her to assume that liquidity needs net out to zero over the investor community, so that half of the uninformed clients are sellers and half buyers. There is then a $(1 - q)/2$ per cent chance of trading with an uninformed buyer. In this case the sale still takes place at price P^a, but the cost of replenishment is μ and the expected profit is $P^a - \mu$. The average profit on sales is thus: $(V^h - P^a)qp + (\mu - P^a)(1 - q)/2$ where $1 \geq q \geq 0$. Under assumptions (1) and (2) we can set this to zero and solve for the breakeven value of P^a. This is a weighted average of the high and low outcomes:

$$P^a = (V^h qp + \mu(1 - q)/2)/(qp + (1 - q)/2) \tag{4.4}$$
$$= (V^h p(1 + q)/2 + V^l(1 - p)(1 - q)/2)/(qp + (1 - q)/2)$$

using (4.1), where the weights depend upon the probabilities q and p and are non-negative. In other words, P^a is a convex combination of V^h and V^l. Inspection of the first line of this relationship shows that $V^h > P^a > \mu$.

If the market maker's purchases are to break even then repeating the analysis on the buy side using the probabilities, gains, and losses shown in Table 4.1, gives the bid price:

$$Pb = (V^l(1 - p)q + (1 - q)\mu/2)/(q(1 - p) + (1 - q)/2)$$
$$= (V^l(1 - p)(1 + q)/2 + V^h p(1 - q)/2)/(q(1 - p)$$
$$+ (1 - q)/2) < \mu. \tag{4.5}$$

where $V^l < P^b < \mu$. A little algebraic manipulation shows that the equilibrium spread is:

$$S = P^a - P^b = s(V^h - V^l),$$
$$\text{where: } s = 4p(1 - p)q/(1 - q^2(2p - 1)^2).$$

This shows how the spread depends upon the degree of informational asymmetry and uncertainty. Looking at the numerator first, we immediately see that the price spread is directly proportional to the value spread $V^h - V^l$. Obviously, the price spread disappears entirely if there is just one possible outcome $(V^h = V^l)$ and everyone knows what this is. We next recognize the term $p(1 - p)$ as the Bernouilli variance discussed earlier. This means that the information asymmetry and the spread disappears as p tends towards 0 or 1.

The spread depends critically upon the presence of insiders. Some special cases make this easy to see. First, as we would expect, if we can effectively ban insider trades then $S = q = 0$ irrespective of the residual degree of uncertainty. In this case the market is efficient because it clears with zero spread. But prices are uninformative in the sense that they reflect the uninformed expectation. At the other extreme, if there is a pre-ponderance of insiders and $q = 1$ then the dealer protects herself by mov-ing the price spread out to the value spread: $S = (V^h - V^l)$. In the limit, the market simply disappears and there is no price to observe.

Another interesting special case results if the uninformed traders attach equal weights to the high and low outcomes: $p = 1/2$. Then the price for-mulae reduce to:

$$P^a = (V^h(1 + q) + V^l(1 - q))/2 = \mu - q(V^h - V^l)/2,$$
$$P^b = (V^l(1 + q) + V^h(1 - q))/2 = \mu - q(V^h - V^l)/2 \qquad (4.6)$$

and the bid–ask spread is:

$$P^a - P^b = q(V^h - V^l).$$

This case was originally analysed by King and Roell (1988) in the con-text of a quote-driven market, and a numerical example based on their version of the model is set out in Exercise 1. In this case, the spread is the product of the value spread and the proportion of inside traders. Their result provides a very neat demonstration of the effect which insider trad-ing has on the capital markets. It suggests that insiders are unequivocally bad, just increasing the spread and making the market illiquid and inefficient. Similar arguments are to be found in Easley and O'Hara (1992), Glosten (1989), and Leland (1985).

This analysis has important policy implications. However, the results are based upon some strong assumptions and it is important not to read too much into them at this stage. In particular, information endowments are exogenous and the models are static. The next three chapters relax these assumptions and provide a rather different perspective on informed trading.

4.7. Risk aversion, inventories and other complications

All dealers in the original Copeland–Galai (1983) quote-driven specifica-tion display the same breakeven ask and bid prices P^a and P^b. In the case of the order-driven analogue, these uninformed dealers simply become uninformed 'intermediaries' and they all submit breakeven sell or buy orders at P^a and P^b respectively. Either way, when a client comes into the market with a 'market order'[4] this is executed against P^a (if it is a purchase) or P^b (if it is a sale). Anticipating the analysis of the next chapter, providing that the market is fully transparent in the sense that all trades are visible, all intermediaries revise their quotes in the same way in response to this trade. There is no difference between quote- and order-driven market mechanisms under these assumptions.

In practice, however, dealer risk-aversion, inventories, and other complications mean that dealers in quote-driven markets do not typically offer the same prices as each other. Those who have too much inventory will tend to lower their bid and ask prices so that they attract buy orders rather than sell orders. Conversely, those who are short of a particular stock will try to raise their prices in order to accumulate inventory. For this reason, the television screens used by the NASDAQ and SEAQ quote-driven systems identify the lowest ask and highest bid prices to help clients achieve the best execution. The difference between the lowest ask and highest bid prices is known as the touch or inside spread, and will usually be less than an individual dealer's price spread. This is also true of screen-based continuous auction systems like the SETS. In this system, intermediaries (and clients) submit equivalent limit orders and the stock exchange computer automatically achieves best execution.

Also, as Tonks (1996) observes, in an order-driven system, clients can submit limit (price contingent) orders as well as (unconditional) market orders. This is not usually possible in a quote-driven system. This rule does not make any material difference in our simple mathematical model. However, if market makers are risk averse and inventories are pushing prices away from their breakeven values, some of their larger clients may not submit market orders for immediate execution. They may prefer to submit limit orders in the expectation of a more favourable price. This facility would make an order-driven system more liquid than its quote-based analogue. On the other hand, the market liquidity obligations of the intermediary in the order-driven system may be less onerous than in a quote-driven system, making it less liquid. Some preliminary evidence is provided by the recent move from SEAQ to SETS in London, discussed in

---

[4] In this model it is reasonable to assume that both uninformed liquidity traders (risk-averse agents with liquidity trades to execute) and informed clients would submit market orders for immediate execution. Unlike intermediaries, who gain privileges from the exchange, uninformed clients without liquidity trades (and informed clients masquerading as such) would have no incentive to submit limit orders if they are allowed to, as in the SETS for example. In any case, such orders would make no material difference since they would be at the uninformed breakeven prices P^a and P^b.

Box 4.3. Either way, the *ceteris paribus* assumption breaks down and the theoretical equivalence of quotation and continuous auction systems demonstrated by Pagano and Roell (1993), Madhaven (1992), and Tonks (1996) may not hold.

4.8. Developing the basic model

The Copeland and Galai model provides an example of a 'pooling equilibrium'. In this case bid and ask prices reflect the average or probability weighted mix of informed and uninformed clients in the seller and buyer pools. Each pool price is available to all client types, allowing the informed to profit at the expense of the uninformed. This means that, reflecting the Milgrom–Stokey observation, uninformed agents must trade for non-speculative reasons. If there were never any liquidity trades ($q = 1$), then the market maker would move the price spread out to the value spread and trade would vanish.

Assumptions (6) to (9) ensure that the size and structure of the client pool does not depend upon the price spread. In other words, the liquidity traders are forced buyers or sellers, since they buy or sell irrespective of price quotes. Asymmetric information makes it difficult to achieve a trade equilibrium, but forced buyers or sellers make it possible to establish some level of trade. Since the number of trades is fixed, it is a trivial matter to relax assumption (3): in a contestable market running costs would simply be spread over the fixed number of transactions, increasing the price spread by a constant.

Easley and O'Hara (1992) develop a model of a separating equilibrium in a dealership market. This is similar to the model of a separating equilibrium in the insurance market developed by Rothschild and Stiglitz (1976) discussed in the previous chapter. Easley and O'Hara note that insiders can see sure profits and will, other things being equal, want to trade up to the maximum size allowed by the market maker. However, uninformed transactions will largely be driven by the needs of trade, which are typically small. In the simple model set out here the maximum trade size (of unity) is fixed in line with the standard liquidity requirement, to accommodate liquidity traders without allowing information traders too much profit. It is buttressed by assumption (9): if information traders could deal several times a day, this would allow them to circumvent assumption (8) and increase q. These assumptions allow the model market maker to minimize Q and make it exogenous.

These assumptions prevent adverse selection in this model. Yet in practice, a wide price spread would be likely to cause some liquidity traders to leave a financial market. Yet as long as this remained within the value spread, all information traders would remain in the pool. In terms of the single-size market analysed here, this would lead to an increase in the parameter Q describing the mix of clients in the pool. This in turn would lead to a widening of the price spread, leading to a further deterioration in the mix, and so on. *In extremis*, if all liquidity traders are forced out of the market, trade vanishes. This helps to explain why it is hard to establish dealership markets in small company securities when public information is sparse and insiders have a great advantage.

Easley and O'Hara allow clients to trade in one of two sizes: either large or small. If there are sufficient liquidity traders who need to trade in large size, a separating equilibrium occurs in which informed clients trade 'large' with them, facing a commensurately wide price spread, while the small-liquidity traders have the small-trade market to themselves. There is no reason for the dealer to charge them a price spread in this situation, since all of the informed agents find it more profitable to take advantage of the bigger trades possible in the other market. However, a mixed equilibrium is also possible, in which some informed clients find it more profitable to pool with the uninformed clients, meaning that a narrow spread opens up in the small trade market. This parallel market model helps us to understand the operation of the 'upstairs' or 'block' trade systems used for conducting large trades off-market in New York and London. These are usually settled at prices which depart from the prices quoted for trades of normal size. Inventory and risk position costs also help to explain the divergence between price quotes and block trade prices.

EXERCISES

The King and Roell (1990) model

Question 1. Risk-neutral market makers quote bid and ask prices (P^a and P^b) at which they stand ready to buy a fixed number (n) of shares in an electricity distributor. It is rumoured that a takeover bid is imminent, which will push the price to $V^h = £11$ if it is announced. Market makers think this bid has a 50 per cent chance of emerging the next day, but that the share price will fall to $V^l = £7$ if it does not.

(a) What is the value of their current best estimate (m)?

$m = (V^h = V^l)/2 = £9.$

(b) Company insiders know whether it will be announced and the probability that a market maker trades with such an insider (rather than an uninformed investor) is fixed at $q = 0.05$. Uninformed buyers and sellers are evenly matched. Focusing on the ask side, and assuming that $P^a > m$ is given, what is the probability and the expected gain or loss of dealing with (i) inside (ii) uninformed buyers?

This table shows these probabilities and gains:

| | Market maker encounters with: | |
	(a) Probability	(b) E (gain)
Insider	$q = 0.05$	
(i) Insider who buys at P^a	$q/2 = 0.025$	$P^a - V^h = P^a - 11$
Uninformed agent	$1 - q = 0.95$	
(ii) Uninformed buyer	$(1 - q)/2 = 0.475$	$(P^a - m) = (P^a - 9)$

(c) Determine the values of P^a and P^b for costless competitive equilibrium. How does the spread between them depend upon Q and the general degree of uncertainty $(V^h - V^l)$?

Taking the probability-weighted average on the ask/offer side using the table:
$$E(gain) = a(i) \times b(i) + a(ii) \times b(ii) = 0.025 \times (P^a - 11) + 0.475 \times (P^a - 9)$$
$$= 0 \text{ in competitive equilibrium.}$$

So (multiplying by 2 and taking price to the left-hand side):
$$P^a = 0.05 \times 11 + 0.95 \times 9$$
$$= 0.55 + 8.55$$
$$= 910p.$$

Similarly, using the same approach for the bid/buy side (ii) of the table we get:
$$P^b = V^l(1 + q)/2 + V^h(1 - q)/2 = m - 1/2Q(V^h - V^l)$$
$$= 890p.$$

Algebraically, the spread is $P^a - P^b = Q(V^h - V^l)$. So we see that it increases with both the weight of insider dealers q and the general degree of uncertainty $(V^h - V^l)$.

(d) Why would an increase in n be likely to increase the spread? What are the costs and benefits of rules which specify that those who quote prices have to be prepared to trade up to certain quantities at those prices? (University of London, Faculty of Economics, B.Sc. (Econ) Examination, 3rd Year, 1997)

Insiders can see sure profits and will want to trade up to the maximum size they can. In practice this will be limited by either the largest liquidity trade size (since insiders must mimic liquidity traders) or the stock exchange limit (if this is smaller). Uninformed transactions will be driven by the needs of trade, which are finite, typically small. So by restricting the size of the maximum order n, dealers can bias the sample of trades in their favour, cutting back on the size of inside trades while keeping the size of uninformed trades below the maximum unchanged. Allowing n to increase will have the opposite effect. It is hard to model this formally in this model, but the effect will be similar to an increase in q, tending to raise the spread.

Market makers thus have an incentive to reduce their trade size and it is important for the stock exchange authorities to ensure that this does not fall below the size of a normal liquidity trade, damaging the liquidity of the market.

Measuring liquidity

Question 2. P^a is the ask price quoted by a stock or bond trader, P^b is the bid price, s is the minimum amount the trader must be prepared to trade at the quoted bid or ask, P is the average of the bid and ask, σ_P^2 is the variance of P over a trading day, and T is the average amount traded on a typical trading day.

(a) Assess the pros and cons of using the following indicators as measures of 'liquidity':

(i) $P^a - P^b$

(ii) $(P^a - P^b)/(P^a + P^b)$

(iii) $(P^a - P^b)/\sigma_P^2$

(iv) $(P^a - P^b)/s$

(v) $(P^a - P^b)/s.\sigma_P^2$

(vi) $(P^a - P^b)/T.\sigma_P^2$

(i) $P^a - P^b$

Basic measure of spread. Fails to allow for the riskiness of a security, which is a major factor in demand for liquidity/immediacy by the investor and inventory cost of the market maker.

(ii) $(P^a - P^b)/(P^a + P^b)$

Better, because it expresses spread as a percentage, but still deficient.

(iii) $(P^a - P^b)/\sigma_P^2$

Variance offers a reasonable measure of the riskiness of a security, which is a major factor in demand for liquidity/immediacy by the investor and inventory cost of the market maker. Deflating by variance gives a much better measure, since it allows the spread to increase with risk. But it does not allow for the likelihood of insiders and other information traders, which is a major influence on the spread in a competitive market.

(iv) $(P^a - P^b)/s$

Deflating by the maximum trade limit allows the spread to increase with the average trade. This is appropriate, because a liquid market is characterized by a narrow spread and a large limit.

(v) $(P^a - P^b)/s.\sigma_P^2$

Combines the advantages of (iii) and (iv).

(vi) $(P^a - P^b)/T.\sigma_P^2$

High average turnover should indicate that information trades are low relative to liquidity trades. There is no reason to allow spread to increase with turnover, quite the opposite. We prefer (v).

(b) Can you suggest any other factors which might be taken into account in this assessment? (University of London, Faculty of Economics, B.Sc. (Econ.) Financial Economics, Easter Problem Set, 1999)

None of these statistics takes into account the likelihood of informed trade. This is likely to be high in the case of small companies with poor disclosure. It might be possible to make some allowance for size and measures of news flow, but this would be difficult.

5 Information Revelation, Transparency and Insider Regulation

The Copeland and Galai (1983) model described in the previous chapter offers a simple introduction to market microstructure theory. But as it stands it is a static specification: it rules out dynamic learning effects which are likely to be important in practice. Prices are fixed throughout the trading day, irrespective of the order flow.

However, as orders accumulate, the market maker is in a position to learn from the balance of her inventory whether insiders are at work and if so, whether they reckon that prices are going to rise or fall. That is simply because, if there are no insiders, then she would just get un-informed orders which she would expect to balance out to zero. If there are inside buyers in the market, then the market maker will tend to lose stock and experience falling inventory. She builds inventory if insiders are selling.

Early microstructure models such as Ho and Stoll (1981) assumed that market makers were risk averse and would react to an inventory accu-mulation by raising prices in order to lose inventory. That is certainly possible, helping to account for the range of prices seen on dealing screens. However, the information-based models which we are analysing abstract from such effects and focus upon the signal of value provided by trade flows and inventory movements.

In this respect, the Copeland–Galai information structure offers a good way of describing *initial* expectations and price-setting behavior in deal-ership markets. But these prices are not administered prices: inventory changes would probably lead dealers to revise prices quickly in line with trade flows. Indeed, if the market is transparent in the sense that trades can be observed by clients, then they too can revise their expectations appropriately, meaning that the dealer will lose money if her prices do not change. This is the essential insight of the Glosten and Milgrom (1985) paper. The basic structure of their model is the same as that developed here, except that they look at a sequence of trade prices assuming opti-mal learning by the market maker. This chapter develops a simplified ver-sion of their model and employs this to consider the regulation of insider trading and market transparency.

5.1. The Glosten and Milgrom (1985) model

Glosten and Milgrom approach the pricing problem from the perspective of Bayesian statistical theory. However, because the competitive breakeven price is the same as the appropriate conditional expectation under the simplifying conditions used in Section 4.6, the nature of the Bayesian learning process can be seen directly from the static price equations (4.4) and (4.5). In Bayesian language, the initial expectation μ is the 'prior expectation' and p the 'prior probability' of a high value outcome. We now denote these initial values as μ_1 and p_1 to indicate that they are valid for the first trade. (More realistically, in a fast market, these values might be valid for a set of trades, which take place before the dealer has a chance to revise prices.)

Now recall that the market maker sets the initial selling price P^a at a level which leaves her expecting to break if a sale takes place. But this is just another way of saying that this price is set in line with the new expectation she would have if she were actually to experience a sale. So to use Bayes's terminology, P^a is the 'posterior expectation' conditional upon finding a buyer, and by the same argument, P^b is the posterior expectation conditional upon meeting a seller.

Once the first trade is conducted, a rational market maker will reset these prices to take account of the posterior probabilities, and the trading process will move into the next round. The expectation μ_2 is then set in line with P^a if the first client is a buyer, or P^b if it is a seller. Assuming that V^h, V^l do not shift, the new probability value p_2 follows by inverting (4.1) to get:

$$p_2 = (\mu_2 - V^l)/(V^h - V^l) \tag{5.1}$$

where $\mu_2 = P^a$ or P^b.

To take a simple example, suppose that $p_1 = 1/2$. If the first client buys then we set $\mu_2 = P^a$. We have already seen (4.6) that in this simple case $P^a = \mu + q(V^h - V^l)/2$. This is shown alongside the bid in Figure 5.1. Substituting this μ_2 into (5.1) and simplifying gives: $p_2 = 1/2 + q/2 = p_1 + q/2$. In words: the dealer revises up the probability of another sale by an amount which is half the share of informed clients in the total q. If, on the other hand, the first client sells, she revises p down by this amount. If there is a large client pool, the value of q will not change after the first trade. The new price quotes then follow in the same way as before: we simply replace p in (4.4) and (4.5) by the appropriate value of p_2.

The simple case $p_1 = 1/2$ is illustrated in Figure 5.1. The market maker starts at zero with the simple arithmetic average expectation μ. Then she

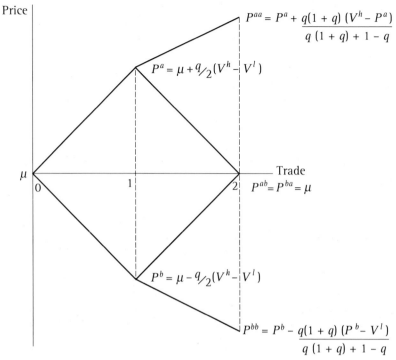

Figure 5.1 Bayesian learning by the market

trades at P^a or P^b. In the first case she resets prices straddling $\mu_2 = P^a$ to get the second trade prices P^{aa} and P^{ab} as shown by the formulae in the figure. Alternatively, with $\mu_2 = P^b$ she calculates P^{ba} and P^{bb}. Interestingly, in this simple case we get $P^{ba} = P^{ab} = \mu$. This is because in both cases she makes one purchase and one sale of stock, with a neutral effect on expectations (and inventory). The spread narrows for the second trade, however, because the other two cases contain unambiguous bullish or bearish signals. Exercise 1 provides a numerical illustration.

5.2. Price dynamics

Providing that no new information or other disturbances occur, Glosten and Milgrom show that this process will iterate forward until the price converges on the true value and the spread disappears. Consequently, assumption (2) (Section 4.6) can be discarded: informed trade will quickly push prices into line with fundamentals even if these are not disclosed at the end of the day. Moreover, this washes away the information asymmetry and with it the price spread. In our Bernouilli version of the model, this happens because these depend upon the Bernoulli variance term $p(1 - p)$ discussed in the previous chapter, and this shrinks to zero as p moves towards 0 or 1.

This model converges upon an equilibrium in which the market is perfectly efficient and prices reflect the informed expectation—so we get the best of both worlds. In the short run, however, the spread and the speed of convergence are both positively related to the amount of insider dealing, represented by q.

Exercise 2 describes a computer program which uses a random number generator to simulate this updating process. Figure 5.2 shows a typical set of bid and ask prices generated by this program when the insiders know that a bid is imminent at £11. Market makers initially think this bid has a 50 per cent chance of emerging, but that the share price will fall to £7 if it does not. Their prior is thus £9. There is a 10 per cent probability that a market maker trades with such an insider rather than an uninformed investor ($q = 0.1$). Uninformed buyers and sellers are evenly matched.

This chart shows that the spread is fairly large to start with and the price gets buffeted up and down randomly, like the price of an actively traded stock. As it happens an (uniformed) sell order is drawn first, pushing the price down to P^b, and a buy order second, generating $P^{ba} = \mu = £9$. Then we get two sells and two buys, leaving us at £9 again. After one more client sale, a sequence of purchases starts to push prices up to the true value. After around 100 trades, the preponderance of informed purchases asserts itself, the price converges on £11, and the spread disappears. In practice, things are generally much more complicated. Investors trade on differential information about several eventualities. Periods of volatility (like the first part of the chart) are mixed with periods of relative certainty (like the middle section).

5.3. Information revelation

In this model, informed clients gradually reveal their information by trading. As the figure shows, the cumulative effect of this is to move prices towards the true value, reducing the potential gains from subsequent trades. In some situations, if he had exclusive information for example, this leakage could cause an insider to behave strategically, restricting his trade and hence the release of information. For example, Kyle (1985,

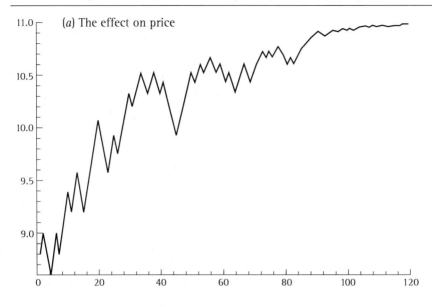

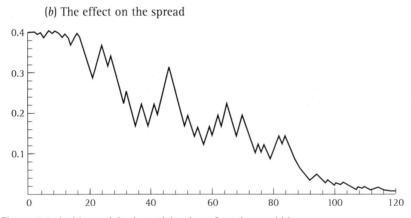

Figure 5.2 Insider activity in anticipation of a takeover bid

1989) develops a dynamic model in which there is a single inside trader. He acts as an information monopolist and finds it optimal to reveal information slowly over time. The model of Bernhard, Hollifield, and Hughson (1995) is similar.

However, in the present context, the all or nothing nature of the client's trade option means that he can only withhold information by not trading, forgoing a sure profit. If there are many others with the same information, then this will eventually emerge from their trades, irrespective of whether or not he trades. There is no reason to behave strategically in this model. Nevertheless, it still takes time for trade to fully reveal this inside information.

This dynamic version of the model offers a reasonable approximation to the operation of a market trading system such as the NYSE, NASDAQ, SEAQ, and SETS mechanisms. In these markets dealers supply price quotes (valid up to a trade size limit) or in some cases price-contingent limit orders. These are in principle revised as trades are observed, in line with conditional expectations. The size limit affords a degree of protection to dealers and other uninformed participants, because restricting the size of the limit order should have the effect of cutting back on the size of inside trades while keeping the size of uninformed trades below the maximum unchanged (Exercise 1).

5.4. Should insider dealing be prohibited?

This theoretical model serves to focus the long-standing debate about insider dealing. It views the market trading process as a kind of game in which insiders deal at the expense of uninformed investors, widening spreads, particularly when there are extreme events like takeovers in the offing. This makes it particularly difficult to establish and maintain markets in small company shares, as the experience of the London Stock Exchange in this arena testifies. Spreads are significant even in the case of large companies, weakening both primary and secondary market activity, raising the cost of capital and depressing investment (Manove 1989).

However, one of the main functions of a financial market is to disseminate knowledge. Information traders play a key role in this process, particularly in the case of small companies and takeovers. Their trades push security prices towards their true value, helping to make the financial markets and economic systems efficient and to discipline unsuccessful managers. Manne (1966) originated this line of argument, which has been developed by Leland (1992).

The microstructure model reveals a tension between market efficiency and the informativeness of prices. In the static specification of the previous chapter, market efficiency can be achieved simply by outlawing insiders, eliminating the spread and maximizing liquidity. However, prices then reflect the *uninformed* expectation rather than the true value. Trading takes place at false prices. More worrying, the market provides false signals to the rest of the economy, possibly leading to resource misallocation. These distortions may even be apparent at the macroeconomic level: for example the overvaluation of the Japanese equity market in the 1980s led to overinvestment.

The dynamic version of the model used in this chapter shows insiders in a more favourable light. It suggests that if market makers and other agents learn from trades, prices become highly informative and the effect on spreads is largely transitory. But even in this specification, with its once and for all change in the informed information endowment, there is a short-run trade-off: the greater the weight of informed trading the wider the spread but the faster the convergence to long-run equilibrium. There is a single market maker in our mathematical model. In practice, there are likely to be many dealers, all observing different trades, and in this situation prices may not be informative of trades. In this case it is important to ensure that transactions are reported and published speedily.

The point which a regulator selects upon this trade-off curve must obviously depend upon the relative costs and dynamics of spreads and false prices; that is, market and price efficiency. If the asymmetry is likely to be temporary, as in the case of a takeover bid for example, then there is a cast-iron case for clamping down on insider trading and the misallocation which such activity leads to through the spread. Trade at false prices will occur until the bid is announced, and sellers will come to regret their actions, but that is the extent of the problem. However, more systematic mispricing, owing to a market misperception of the fundamentals for example, will not be resolved quickly and may have serious effects on investment and management motivation. It is important to discriminate between these cases and to regard insider dealing of the second kind less unfavourably.

5.5. Director share dealings

Share dealings by managers and employees of small companies play an important role in ensuring that their share prices do not get too far out of line with fundamentals. This practice is governed by disclosure rules which help to prevent abuse. (The British rules are described in Sections 5.6 and 5.7.) These rules have the important side effect of bringing these informed deals into the open, allowing them to act as a signal to outside investors (Gregory, Matatko, and Tonks 1994). These provisions are reinforced by the prohibition of dealing on 'unpublished price sensitive information'.

Even the advocates of the *laissez-faire* approach to insider trading like Manne (1966), Carlton, Fischel, and Fischel (1983), and Dye (1984) are only prepared to defend company insiders who deal on the basis of *published* information, taking advantage of their superior understanding of the organization and its management to make profits. These papers argue that insider trading provides an optimal form of remuneration for managers. This argument is, however, a controversial one. In particular, Fischer (1992) shows that this form of remuneration is suboptimal when there are agency costs. (The latter are discussed in the next chapter.)

In this respect, our microstructure model may again be misleading. It assumes that the true value of the security is to be revealed imminently (4.6 (2)). This is perhaps a realistic way to handle a bid situation. However, such events are infrequent. In practice, bids are only likely if a share price moves to a substantial discount to fundamental value (for the reasons discussed in Chapter 7). Bids do not stop the price moving to a premium. Moreover, bidders, like other outside investors, may not know what the true value of the company is. Arguably, in the case of a small company, only its employees, directors, and associates can judge that. Allowing them to trade actively can offer a better way of avoiding systematic mispricing than the takeover process. It is generally recognized that directors should be encouraged to hold their company's shares (and options on these) as a performance incentive and there is a strong case for allowing company insiders to trade openly: with a high level of informational disclosure.

It is also important to bear in mind that this model is still based on the assumption that information endowments are fixed. This situation is epitomized by the inside trader who finds out about a bid in conversation. We must be careful to distinguish information traders like fund managers, company analysts, and private investors who devote valuable resources to acquiring and analysing public financial information in order to get an advantage. In this case, information is an endogenous factor. The analytics and the arguments become more complex and are set out in the next chapter. Anticipating these arguments, it is important to note the paradoxical result that insider dealers can actually make prices less informative when information is endogenous. Fishman and Hagerty (1992) show that competition from insiders can discourage security research by other investors, making prices less informative.

Such arguments should be considered objectively, without being blinded by the simplicity of mathematical models, or the bad name which insiders, 'smart traders', 'spiv clients', and their like have in the financial markets. Market makers have a natural interest in eliminating informed trading activity, even when there may be an economic case for allowing it. Microstructure theorists assume that the market is cost-free and competitive and that fundamental value is accurately revealed at the end of every trading session. In this framework insiders just cause a misallocation of resources by forcing market makers to impose a spread which discourages liquidity traders. But in fact few market making organizations have any conception of forward planning or even cost control. They are largely responsible for the size of the spread. There is also an element of hypocrisy in calls from finance ministers and officials for insider regulation, when stamp taxes and other levies have precisely the same effect, without any of the informational benefits.

Having said that, it would be equally naïve to swing to the opposite end of the argument and accept the argument of Henry Manne (1966) that insider dealing is a 'victimless crime' and should not be discouraged. Manne argues that an inside buyer pushes up the price of a security and ensures that the seller gets a better price than he otherwise would. However, this argument is specious, because the seller would otherwise have sold to another uninformed trader, who would eventually profit instead of the insider. The fact is that uninformed traders as a group lose out to the informed.

5.6. Insider regulation in practice

The old adage that insider trading has 'victims but no plaintiffs' is nevertheless accurate, and this is the basic reason why the criminal rather than civil law has until now been used to deal with insiders in Britain. In contrast, the US courts have considered such insider trades to be a misappropriation of property rights and have issued orders requiring the profits to be surrendered. The Securities and Exchange Commission (SEC) has the power to bring a civil suit against insiders, on behalf of the investor community. It can claim restitution of up to three times an insider's profits.

The 1980 Companies Act made insider trading illegal in the UK. The 1985 Companies Act also included important statutory provisions on insider trading, which were consolidated in the 1993 Criminal Justice Act.

These provisions will remain in place once the Labour government's Financial Services and Markets (FSM) Bill is enacted in 2001. Basically, it is a criminal offence for a company insider to use or pass on 'unpublished price sensitive information', and for anyone in receipt of such information to trade upon it prior to publication. Importantly, this does not cover market professionals like analysts exploiting their own research, provided that this is based upon information in the public domain. The UK differs from the USA in this respect: the celebrated Carpenter case in 1980 involved a prison sentence for a US journalist who traded in advance of his own share tips. The LSE does, however, have rules against 'front-running', discussed in the next section.

Until the FSM reform, responsibility for British legislation in this area lay with HM Treasury and cases of insider dealing were referred to the Department of Trade and Industry for investigation. This could be either a criminal investigation or one conducted under section 177 of the Financial Service Act 1986, which was not a criminal investigation. The Department then had the option of simply publishing its findings or proceeding to a criminal trial. An example of an occasion upon which the Department simply published its findings is provided by the 1995 report on Jeffrey Archer MP. He was found to have passed on to a dealer information obtained by his wife as a director of Anglia Television.

The high standard of proof required in a criminal court makes it hard to convict insiders. Moreover, even when prosecutions have been successful, the British courts have been surprisingly lenient. For example, in 1986 Paul Collier, the former chief executive of Morgan Grenfell Securities, who pleaded guilty to insider dealing in connection with the Blue Arrow/Manpower takeover, escaped with a £25,000 fine and a one-year suspended sentence. In contrast, two months later in the USA, David Levine, chief executive of Drexel Burnham Lambert, was convicted of passing on inside information to Ivan Boesky and sent to a federal prison for two years.

The new FSM legislation seeks to improve upon this situation by giving the FSA additional authority to impose fines of restitution under civil law. However, there was an ambiguity under the previous DTI system of investigation which many commentators are concerned may extend to the new system. This ambiguity was exploited by Ernest Saunders, the former chief executive of Guinness, who successfully took the UK to the European Court of Human Rights in 1996. He claimed that the evidence used to convict him of insider dealing in the 1988 Distillers–Guinness case had been obtained under the section 177 rules of investigation and not through a criminal investigation with the right to silence. Although the right to silence was amended in the 1993 Criminal Justice Act, the difference between criminal and civil investigation remains. Many of its critics argue that the FSM legislation effectively gives the FSA the power to inflict criminal law punishments on a lower burden of proof. It remains to be seen how this ambiguity will be resolved in practice.

In addition to these powers, the FSA is now responsible for the enforcement of the LSE's listing rules, which regulate company flotations, capital issues, and admission to the secondary market. As we have established, these place a heavy emphasis upon public disclosure, particularly concerning new issues (Section 4.1). The regulator has a range of sanctions at its disposal for enforcing these rules. At one end is the kind of public reprimand which the Prudential Insurance Company received from the LSE in 1995. (Their chief executive, Mick Newmarsh, sold share options the day before the official DTI report on pensions misselling was to be made public, leading to a significant fall in the share price.) At the other end of the spectrum, the FSA can delist the company's shares, meaning that they can no longer be traded on the LSE. Under the new FSM regime, violations of the listing rules can also result in heavy fines.

5.7. Market transparency

One of the implicit assumptions of the Glosten and Milgrom (1985) model used here is that the market is transparent—that all participants can immediately see the trades taking place. In this case, the competitive structure of the market means that if the market maker did not revise prices in the way predicted by the model, then she would lose money and be replaced by someone who did so. If on the other hand she could restrict the publication of trade information, this would put her at an information advantage to other 'uninformed' participants, including potential market-making rivals. It is important for the stock exchange authorities to prevent this by imposing trade disclosure rules.

More generally, the transparency of a market depends upon the availability of financial information and the speed with which this is reflected in prices. It is one of the factors which can influence the value of a security. A security tends to be neglected and undervalued if investors think that the market is subject to manipulation or arbitrary influences. On the other hand it will fetch a higher price if investors are confident that the market is valuing it in line with the fundamentals. This means that they can free ride to some extent on others' research and avoid trading at false prices, giving them a rational basis for calculation.

For this reason, European governments like those of France and the UK have made great efforts in recent years to make their bond markets more open, more like the US Treasury bond market. They now conduct regular auctions, organize other sales in a much less haphazard way, and release more timely official information and statistics. They have also tried to consolidate stock and coupon payment dates and have ironed out many idiosyncratic tax and other anomalies. This is designed to attract international investors by helping the transparency and liquidity of the market, lowering the cost of debt finance.

In most securities markets there are rules against 'front running' or positioning by brokers ahead of circulars which are likely to move the market. These rules are designed to improve transparency and prevent market makers becoming informed relative to their clients (Pagano and Roell 1992b). But other rules give the market maker the edge. For example, until 1996, London's equity dealers had access to the Inter-Dealer Broker screens, which reveal when someone is trying to lay off a large block trade or other awkward position. Their large institutional clients had to campaign for many years to get access to this system.

Another example concerns the issue of post-trade reporting. In the New York Stock Exchange, the 'ticker tape' reports the prices and quantities involved in trades as they are struck. (It has been disseminating this information for over a century.) This is true of large 'upstairs' trades which are conducted off the floor of the exchange, just as it is true of small retail trades, which are conducted on the floor. In London, until 1996, market makers had 90 minutes to report trades of 3 to 75 times Normal Market Size (NMS), and 5 working days to report larger trades. These exemptions have been tightened up considerably since the introduction of the SETS in 1998 (see Box 4.3).

The LSE used to justify this delay by arguing that unlike New York, where block trades are struck 'upstairs' by matching ultimate buyers and sellers, block trades are usually taken onto the market maker's book in London. This upsets the market maker's inventory position. It leaves her prone to unfavourable and uncertain shifts in price when trade details are published quickly, since it is difficult to gauge the way the market will react to such information. Prices are likely to fall, but that is not the case if traders realize that an institutional or corporate position which has been overhanging the market has been removed.

However, the flaw in this argument is that this provision allows market makers to work the position off by shifting it on to uninformed investors who suffer the loss when the block trade is eventually announced. This is an unsatisfactory arrangement, which allows big institutional investors and their market makers to extricate themselves from awkward positions by passing them on to smaller investors. These disclosure rules have now been tightened up. Market makers have to buy these blocks at bigger price discounts or premia, work the order book, find other counterparties, and try harder to gauge the market impact.

EXERCISES

Question 1. Risk-neutral market makers quote bid and ask prices (P^b and P^a) at which they stand ready to buy a fixed number of shares in a public company. The annual accounts are due to be announced the next morning. Company insiders know whether the results are good or bad. Market makers (and uninformed investors) think there is a 50 per cent chance of 'good' results, meaning a share price of $V^h = 220$p, and a 50 per cent chance of 'bad' results and a price $V^l = 200$p.

(a) What is their prior (i.e. initial) expectation of the next day's price (m)?

$$m = (V^h + V^l)/2 = 210\text{p}.$$

(b) The probability that a market maker trades with an insider (rather than an uninformed investor) is fixed at $q = 0.05$. Uninformed buyers and sellers are evenly matched. Focusing on the ask side, determine (in terms of q, V^h, and $P^a > m$) the probability and the expected gain or loss of (i) a deal with an insider and (ii) an uninformed buyer?

The table shows these probabilities and gains:

	Market maker encounters with:	
	(a) Probability	(b) E (gain)
(i) Insider who buys at P^a	$q/2 = 0.025$	$P^a - V^h = P^a - 220$
(ii) Uninformed buyer	$(1 - q)/2 = 0.475$	$(P^a - m) = (P^a - 210)$

(c) Determine the values of the initial quotes (P^b and P^a) for costless competitive equilibrium.

Taking the probability-weighted average on the ask/offer side using this table:

$$E(\text{gain}) = a(i) \times b(i) + a(ii) \times b(ii) = 0.025 \times (P^a - 220) + 0.475 \times (P^a - 210)$$
$$= 0 \text{ in competitive equilibrium.}$$

So (multiplying by 2 and taking price to the left-hand side):

$$P^a = 0.05 \times 220 + 0.95 \times 210$$
$$= 11 + 199.5$$
$$= 210.5\text{p}.$$

Similarly, using the same approach for the bid/buy side (ii) of the table we get:

$$P^b = V^l(1 + q)/2 + V^h(1 - q)/2 = m - 1/2Q(V^h - V^l)$$
$$= 209.5\text{p}.$$

(d) Suppose the first client happens to be a seller so that a trade takes place at P^b. What is the market makers' posterior expectation of the next day's price? Describe qualitatively what is likely to happen to the bid and ask prices quoted for the next trade. (University of London, Faculty of Economics, B.Sc. (Econ.) Financial Economics, Final Examination, 1998).

The relationship between this zero-profit accounting framework and Bayesian inference means that P^b is the posterior expectation (m_2) if the market maker encounters a seller. Consequently the market maker resets expectations as $m_2 = P^b = 209.5\text{p}$.

Qualitatively, $m = 210$ falls to $m_2 = P^b = 209.5\text{p}$ because the posterior probability of a bad set of accounts has risen. This means that both the bid and ask prices fall for the second trade. It is easy to see that the new ask price is equal to the prior expectation $m = 210$ because that is the expectation conditional upon meeting a seller the first time and a buyer the second time. The information implied by these two trades is neutral and leaves the expectation where it started at $m = 210$.

[The question does not ask for quantitative analysis, but, assuming that nothing else has changed, we can solve for the posterior probability ($= p_2$) using the definition $m_2 = p_2 V^h + (1 - p_2)V^l$. This gives

$$p_2 = (m_2 - V^l)/(V^h - V^l)$$
$$= \tfrac{1}{2} - q/2$$
$$= 0.475,$$

which allows the market maker to recalculate new bid and ask prices straddling m_2 as she does for first trade. This confirms the new ask price of 210p and gives a new bid price of 209.0025p. Note that the spread narrows slightly because of the arrival of information.]

The Glosten and Milgrom model

Question 2. First set up the following code on MAPLE or some similar program (the syntax for MATHEMATICA is very similar). The first four lines dictate V^h, V^l, q, and the starting value for p:

```
> h: = 11:
> l: = 7:
> q: = 0.1:
> p(1) : = 0.5:
```

The next three lines set up the random integer generator to dictate whether the market maker meets an insider (inn = 1), an uninformed buyer (buy = 1), or seller (inn = buy = 0):

```
> x: = rand(1..10):
> z: = proc(x) if x = 1 then 1 else 0 fi end:
> y: = rand(0..1):
```

Now we simulate the sequence of trades and prices:

```
> for n from 1 to 120 do
> inn(n):= z(x()):
> buy(n):= y():
> ask(n):= (h*p(n)*(1 + q)/2 + l*(1 - p(n))*(1 - q)/2)/
(q*p(n) + (1 - q)/2),
> bid(n):= (l*(1 - p(n))*(1 + q)/2 + h*(p(n))*(1 - q)/2)/
(q*(1 - p(n)) + (1 - q)/2),
> sp(n):= ask(n) - bid(n),
> price(n):= inn(n)*ask(n) + (1 - inn(n))*(buy(n)*ask(n)
+ (1 - buy(n))*bid(n)),
> evalf('),
> p(n + 1):= (price(n) - 1)/(h - 1)
> od:
```

The remaining lines generate the output:

```
> sequence:= [seq([i,price(i)],i = 1..120)]:
> plotpoints:= [sequence]:
> plot(plotpoints,style = point),
> sequence:= [seq([i,sp(i)],i = 1..120)]:
> plotpoints:= [sequence]:
> plot(plotpoints,style = point),
> sequence:= [seq([i,ask(i)],i = 1..120)]:
> for n from 1 to 120 do print(n,p(n),inn(n),buy(n),
> bid(n),ask(n),sp(n),p(n)) od,
```

Running this code will generate random price and spread plots similar to those of Figure 5.1 of the text, as well as trade details.

(a) Why does the price sometimes fall and the spread increase (e.g. between trades 40 and 50 in Figures 5.1(a) and 5.1(b) in the text)? Examine the trade data and the cumulative mix of buy/sell orders to see what causes this effect. How many inside trades do you find in your samples?

(b) Now try varying the parameters h, l, and q. What effect do these parameters have on the rate of convergence (the number of trades usually necessary to get close to $p = \pounds 11$). Then try changing the starting value $p(1)$.

(c) What happens if insiders know that a bid will not materialize? How can that be simulated?

Insider dealing

Question 3. Is there anything wrong with so-called insider dealing? (University of London, Faculty of Economics, B.Sc. (Econ.) Financial Economics, Final Examination, 1996).

Question 4. Consider the *economic* implications of allowing people to deal in the shares of Target Television Plc in the following situations:

(a) Target's CEO is unaware of any bid or other situation, but buys shares thinking that Target is undervalued by the market.

(b) Target's Finance Director sees the bad trading account prior to publication and sells shares.

(c) A city analyst thinks Target's shares are overvalued by the market, sells shares, and puts out a sell recommendation.

(d) The MD of Predator Plc is planning a bid for Target and buys shares in the latter.

(e) Associates of Predator's chairman buy Target shares as part of a 'concert party' to support the bid.

(f) The market-making arm of Predator's merchant bank buys call options on similar television companies.

(g) Predator's merchant bank buys shares in Target to support the bid.

(h) An employee of Predator finds out about the bid and buys shares in Target.

(i) Target's CEO is aware of the bid, buys shares, and gets his wife's friend to do the same.

(j) A waiter overhears talk of the bid and buys shares in Target.

(k) A best-selling author learns of the bid from his wife (who is a non-executive director) and gets a friend to buy Target shares.

Question 5. 'Company directors are obviously insiders and so should be banned from dealing in their company's shares. Any shares which they hold should be managed at arm's length by a trustee.' Do you agree? (Birkbeck College, London, Postgraduate Certificate in Finance, Final Examination, 1998).

6. Security Research and Regulation

Previous chapters assumed that information endowments were fixed exogenously. In Chapter 5 for example some investors were endowed with superior information, and others learned of through trading activity. This is a reasonable way to approach the problem of insider dealing, since most insiders obtain their information advantage through a random rather than a research process. This chapter investigates the role of security research—the endogenous information case. The analysis follows the seminal paper by Grossman and Stiglitz (1980). They prove that when research is costly it is impossible for capital market prices to be 'informationally efficient'.

The model of the previous chapter is modified by relaxing assumption (4) and showing how the situation changes when clients can improve the precision of their information by undertaking costly research. This modification allows a series of important questions to be addressed. Does security research play any socially useful role? Are there reasons for treating security analysts, financial journalists, and private researchers any differently from company directors or other insiders? Should we allow the researcher to benefit from trading activity or are there other ways in which this activity can be rewarded?

In this version of the model, all traders start with the same information, but can find out what the end of period value is immediately by paying a lump sum research cost: $c > 0$. I maintain assumption (9) so that clients who have undertaken research can only trade once in this system. The market makers maintain this rule, together with the unit trade size restriction since they know that liquidity traders want to trade only one unit of stock. Anyone wanting to trade in larger size (or, equivalently, more than once) must therefore be an insider.

6.1. Research-free equilibrium

This specification makes the proportion of information traders (q) endogenous. However, if the market is transparent and everyone knows the scale of research activity, then q is observable and the algebra of the previous chapter remains intact. We just have to solve simultaneously for the value of q. To do this we put ourselves in the shoes of an uninformed agent without any liquidity requirement and ask whether research is likely to be profitable. This depends upon the cost c, the likelihood of different research findings, and the associated trading gains.

Assume initially that all traders are 'uninformed'. The market maker cannot become informed. Trading begins with the uninformed prior probability of a high value outcome (V^h) equal to p as in Copeland and Galai. (This probability may be informed by research and trading activity in earlier periods.) If research reliably reveals the true state, then it will show a researcher V^h with the same probability: p. Our researcher would then buy at P^a and sell at the end of the day for V^h. The net gain is $(V^h - P^a)$. Similarly, research will reveal V^l, with probability $(1 - p)$ and result in a net trading gain of $(P^b - V^l)$. Taking the probability weighted average gain gives the expected gain: $p(V^h - P^a) + (1 - p)(P^b - V^l)$.

If there are no research or trading delays our researcher compares this expected gain with the cost c when deciding whether to become informed or not.[1] They do not undertake research if

$$c \geq p(V^h - P^a) + (1 - p)(P^b - V^l). \tag{6.1}$$

Several market outcomes are possible if information is endogenous. The first is an outcome in which research is too costly to undertake profitably. When there is some liquidity trade then $q = 0$. In this case the spread disappears (since there are no informed traders and the market is contestable) and trivially:

$$P = P^a = P^b = pV^h + (1 - p)V^l. \tag{6.2}$$

Using this to eliminate P^a and P^b allows (6.1) to be rewritten as:

$$x = c/(V^h - V^l) \geq 2p(1 - p), \tag{6.3}$$

where x is a normalized research cost or 'spread'. This is the key parameter in this version of the model. The boundary of this relationship, the cost spread at which investors are indifferent to undertaking research, is described by a quadratic function of p. This is shown in Figure 6.1.

If the cost–probability combination lies outside the area shaded in the figure, we have a research-free equilibrium. As in the Copeland–Galai model with $q = 0$, the market is efficient, but price equals the uninformed expectation. This price and probability configu-

---

[1] In practice the time lags could reduce the expected gain significantly: trading activity by other researchers who are nimble or lucky enough to trade more quickly could push prices towards fundamental values before our researcher had traded. However, we do know that no one will undertake research if the market maker sets prices so that (6.1) holds.

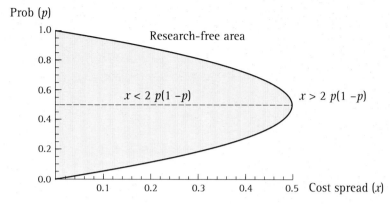

Figure 6.1 Is security research profitable?

ration persists until V is revealed to everyone at the end of the day. The market is then efficient, but the informativeness of prices depends upon the amount of informed trade which has taken place before prices attain this equilibrium.

If we set (6.3) to an equality and solve for the breakeven research cost we see that this is proportional to the value spread times the Bernoulli variance $p(1 - p)$: $c = 2p(1 - p)(V^h - V^l)$. The Bernoulli variance indicates the uncertainty of the uninformed expectation, which is maximized at $p = 1/2$ (Exercise 1 gives a numerical example of this effect). Substituting this value of p into (6.3) shows that if

$$x = c/(V^h - V^l) \geq 1/2 \tag{6.4}$$

then (6.3) will hold for all possible values of p. In other words, it will never be profitable to undertake research if the research cost is more than half of the value spread.

6.2. Endogenous research trading

In the second kind of outcome, the cost inequality (6.1) is reversed and research is profitable for those who can trade at these prices. In terms of Figure 6.1, the (p, x) combination lies within the shaded area. If there is some liquidity trade to mix with then $0<q<1$. In order to abstract from research gestation and trading delays I now adopt a stylized trading structure. The trading day is divided into trading rounds or stages as in the Glosten–Milgrom model of the previous chapter. At the beginning of each round, a batch of clients is chosen at random and allowed to enter the market. Everyone starts with the same prior probability p.

A small fraction l of clients in this pool have liquidity trades to make. Since this is their only opportunity to trade (assumption (9)) they all become liquidity traders. Some of the others see that (6.1) does not hold and so they begin to undertake research and become informed. The rest remain uninformed and do not trade. I assume for simplicity that researchers cannot be identified individually but drive up the price of scarce research inputs (like analyst's pay) and thus reveal the total amount of research and q as in the model of the previous chapter. Hence in this model, $q \in [0, 1-l]$ is observable and endogenous.

Since the market is contestable, researchers know that prices will be set in line with (4.4) and (4.5), which it is convenient to rewrite as:

$$V^h - P^a = (1-p)(1-q)(V^h - V^l)/(2pq + 1 - q),$$

$$V^l - P^b = p(1-q)(V^h - V^l)/(2(1-p)q + 1 - q).$$

They also know that q will stop increasing when (6.1) holds as an equality

$$c = p(V^h - P^a) + (1-p)(P^b - V^l) \tag{6.5}$$

and research activity ceases. Thus they can find the equilibrium values of P^a, P^b, and Q for each round by solving these three equations simultaneously. Once these values are attained, research stops, trades are executed, and this batch of clients leaves the market, consistent with assumption (9). Then a new round of trading begins.

We analyse this model in the same sequential way as we did the one of the last chapter. First we look at what happens in a single trading round with a given p. The difference is that q is now endogenous. Then we look at how research-driven trades (represented by q) inform expectations and determine p (and q) in subsequent trading rounds. As in the last chapter, this drives p towards 0 or 1 (i.e. it drives prices towards V^h or V^l). However, in this case probabilities and prices never reach the Glosten–Milgrom full-information solution. That is because research stops when prices reach the research-free boundary shown in Figure 6.1. And with $q = 0$, that is the end of the story. Later trading rounds simply satisfy liquidity trades in the research-free equilibrium analysed in the previous section.

Mathematically, we proceed as follows. Substituting the price equations into (6.5) gives a quadratic equation for the level of research q:

$$0 = q^2(2p-1)^2x + q\{2p(p-1)\} + [2p(1-p)-x]. \tag{6.6}$$

Solutions to this equation which are in the range $q \in [0, 1-l]$ represent endogenous research equilibria. Remember, q represents the share of informed traders and we use it here as an indicator of research activity.

Some special cases are apparent. Note that if (6.3) holds as an equality, then the term in square brackets in (6.6) disappears and the solution[2] is $q = 0$. This configuration puts the system on the boundary of the research-free equilibrium, with the implications discussed in the previous section. If, on the other hand, research is costless, $c = x = 0$, the first term vanishes leaving $0 = (1-q)[2p(1-p)]$. This has a solution $q = 1$. However, since the maximum value of Q is $1-l$, the solution is that all of those without liquidity demands become informed traders' and the system moves to the boundary $q = 1-l$.[3,4] The baseline case $p = 1/2$ is also special. In this case the first term of (6.6) vanishes and the quadratic reduces to a simple proportional relationship between the share of liquidity traders $(1-q)$ and the relative research cost x: $(1-q) = x/2$.

Excluding these special cases, the general solution[5] to (6.6) is:

$$q(x,p) = \frac{1}{2} [n(x,p) - \sqrt{n(x,p)^2 - m(x,p)}],$$

$$\text{where: } n(x,p) = 2p(1 - p)/(2p - 1)^2 x > 0,$$
$$m(x,p) = 4[2p(1 - p)/x - 1]/(2p - 1)^2 > 0$$
$$0 < x < 2p(1 - p), \ 0 \le p < 1/2 \text{ or } 1/2 < p \le 1.$$

Figure 6.2 shows the graph of this relationship. This is symmetric in p around $p = 1/2$. The base of this diagram is the x,p plane shown in Figure 6.1. The height of the three-dimensional structure shows the share of research trading in (q) any trading round as a function of the relative cost (x) and the prior probability (p) given by previous trading history. The

---

[2] There is another solution $(q = (2p - 1)^{-2} > 1)$ but this is irrelevant since values of q that exceed unity are meaningless.

[3] Note that if the number of potentially informed agents is unrestricted $l = 0$ and $q = 1$. As in the Copeland–Galai model, the market disappears. We get the result that although research is costless, nobody undertakes it since they cannot trade.

[4] Substituting this into (6.6) shows that this situation emerges more generally if $c \in [0, 2lp(1-p)(V^h - V^l)/[1 - (1-l)(2p-1)^2]]$.

[5] The coefficient shown in the braces is negative and the intercept (in square brackets) is non-negative because (6.3) does not hold. This means that the two roots are both positive. However, the larger root is always greater than unity and thus irregular. (This may be seen by rewriting (6.6) as a quadratic in $(1 - q)$. The intercept term becomes $c[(2p - 1)^2 - 1]$. Since this is negative, one root is positive (i.e. $q < 1$) and the other negative (i.e. $q > 1$).) Eliminating the irregular root gives the solution shown.

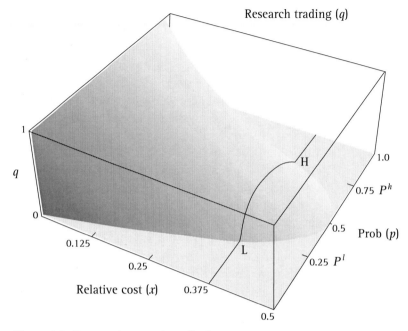

Figure 6.2 How much research trading?

zero contour of this structure, where $q = 0$ and there is no research trading, is the boundary between the research and research-free areas shown in Figure 6.1.

As we would expect, the amount of research-driven trade in any trading round is a decreasing function of the research cost. Indeed, for very-low-cost parameters, research trades dominate the market, almost irrespective of the prior. With $x = 0.25$, however, the maximum value of q is $1/2$, which occurs when $p = 1/2$. As we have established, when $x = 0.5$, no research ever takes place.

This endogenous research situation evolves dynamically because the research and trade executed by each batch of clients gives everyone more precise information. This moves p in the next round, just as it did in the model of the last chapter. This dynamic effect can be modelled in the way indicated in Exercise 4. As precision increases, q falls, the spread narrows, and p is pushed towards one of the boundary values shown in Figure 6.1. However in this case, research activity is costly and informed trading ceases altogether at the boundary. So prices do not become fully revealing as they do in the Golsten–Milgrom model.

Equating the two sides of (6.3) and solving for the boundary proba-bilities gives two roots p^h, p^l, defined respectively as the high and low solutions:

$$p = \frac{1}{2} \pm \frac{1}{2} \sqrt{1 - 2x}, \qquad \text{for } x \leq 1/2. \tag{6.7}$$

We see that $1 > p^h > \frac{1}{2} > p^l > 0$. Substituting into (6.2) yields the associated boundary prices P^h and P^l (not to be confused with P^a and P^b):

$$P = \frac{1}{2} [(V^h + V^l) \pm \sqrt{(V^h - V^l)^2 - 2c(V^h - V^l)}]. \tag{6.8}$$

These four boundary values depend upon the cost/value spread ratio. As x increases towards $1/2$ they converge upon the mid-point values $p = 1/2$, $P = (V^h = V^l)/2$. In other words, only values close to the base-line case $p = 1/2$ generate any research. On the other hand, the range widens out to $[V^h, V^l]$ as x becomes very small and p converges on either 0 or 1. Figure 6.2 shows the relationship between the probability boundaries $p^h = 0.75$, $p^l = 0.25$ with cost/value indicator $x = 0.375$. The price boundaries have the same quadratic shape but are scaled up by $V^h - V^l$.

If the initial probability lies within the range shown in the figures, then endogenous research is undertaken until it pushes the system to one of the research-free boundaries. In the case of Figure 6.2, with $x = 0.375$, research-driven trade will drive the system randomly along the arc LH until the zero contour is reached. Whether p^h or p^l is attained will prima-rily depend upon whether researchers observe V^h or V^l, since this deter-mines the research-driven drift. However, random liquidity trades could push the system to the 'wrong' boundary by accident. That is why even in equilibrium, prices are noisy or inaccurate signals in this version of the model.

For example, suppose that as in the basic numerical example everyone knows that nature selects $V^h = £11$ and $V^l = £7$ with equal probability. Their prior expectation is again $\mu = 9$. Also assume that $c = £1.50$ so that $x = 0.375$ still. Substituting this into (6.7) and (6.2) we see that the mar-ket will eventually settle down at either $P^h = £10$ and $p^h = 3/4$, or $P^l = £8$ and $p^l = 1/4$. With $P = 10$ we can be fairly (75 per cent) sure that a bid is imminent, but this is not certain. That is because even if insiders find that a bid is not going to be forthcoming, there is still a (25 per cent) chance that positive liquidity trades will push the price up to the high boundary $P = 10$ before research activity ceases.

6.3. The impossibility of informationally efficient prices

Grossman and Stiglitz (1980) analyse a static mean variance market equilibrium model with endogenous research. They develop the concept of an informationally efficient price which:

1. equals the informed expectation, with
2. a socially optimal level of research activity.

The second criterion is obviously redundant in the exogenous information case analysed in the model of the previous chapter. Since prices converge upon the informed expectation it meets the first criterion and is thus informationally efficient. However, Grossman and Stiglitz show that if research is costly, capital markets cannot be informationally efficient.

First, suppose that there is no 'noise' or liquidity trade: people would buy and sell securities only if they did some piece of research which revealed mispricing. Then, as we have seen, $q = 1$, and the market maker would move the price against them until no trade took place. In this case there would be no research activity and indeed no market. If, on the other hand, there is a mix of liquidity- and research-driven trades which cannot be distinguished, prices will reflect both noise and fundamentals, which is not consistent with criterion (1). Prices convey too little information. Either way, prices are not informationally efficient.

In the dynamic specification of the previous section, research is also endogenous. The structure differs from that used by the Grossman–Stiglitz model, but we get the same result. Research activity stops before bid and ask prices approach the informed expectation because at some critical point the expected gain falls back into line with the research cost. This model also fails on the first criterion.

6.4. Does security research play a useful role in the economy?

Financial economists take it as axiomatic that financial research and efficient prices play an important role in resource allocation, yet few have developed theoretical models with this property. Nevertheless, Bresnahan, Milgrom, and Paul (1992) and Dow and Rahi (1996) offer theoretical models in which security research helps inform prices and the physical investment decision. In a slightly different vein, Holmstrom and Tirole (1993) analyse the effect which this has on managerial incentives. Financial research is socially useful in all of these models.

The previous chapter considered various ways in which company insiders could influence share prices and make them more informative to outsiders. The main justification put forward for allowing this activity was that it tended to reduce mispricing. It might thereby lead to better remuneration and other management decisions. However, this is a weak argument, because these decisions could be taken by company insiders irrespective of the behaviour of the share price, since they are supposed to know what the true value of the firm was.

In this chapter it is assumed that even company insiders do not know the true value of the firm (unless they engage in research). This is realistic because, although they may know a great deal about their own company, insiders may not know much about outside influences: the macroeconomic situation, the beta risk factors built into share prices, and so on. It is the job of the security analyst to combine these company-specific and macro factors and provide an objective assessment of management ability and share value. If they do this well, then the company and the economy benefit from better-informed decisions. In this case outsiders signal value to inside decision takers rather than the reverse.

This effect can be illustrated using the mathematical model. Suppose for example that the model company has the opportunity to double its capital stock (financed by new shares) at a cost of C per original share (where $V^h > C > V^l$). For simplicity assume that everything can be scaled up by a factor of two (but no more) leaving the fundamental value per share at V^h or V^l. The problem is that nobody knows which of these values is the relevant one. Initially, they know only that nature selects them with equal probability. The prior expectation of value is then $\mu = (V^h + V^l)/2$.

Now suppose that the investment is irreversible and has to be made before the uncertainty is resolved at the end of the trading period. If there is no security research the company goes ahead with the investment and share issue 'blind' if $C < \mu$, but not otherwise. This would lead to *ex post* losses through over-investment if $C < \mu$ but the true value was $V = V^l$. On the other hand, it leads to a missed profit opportunity if $V = V^h > C > \mu$. If informed trading pushes the market price P to the true value of V before the investment decision has to be taken, then the company can pick up the gains and avoid the losses. If $P > C$ it invests, financing this with a rights issue. The shareholders gain $V^h - C$ per share. Otherwise the company does not proceed with the expansion. The *ex ante* expected gain is $(V^h - C)/2 > \mu - C$ per share.

Research costs will prevent the market price from fully revealing the true value. However, unless (6.4) holds, research will push the share price to $P = P^h$ or P^l, which is a better estimate than the prior μ. Suppose initially that the company management cannot find the true value of V itself. Then they go ahead with the investment if $C < P$. The company only loses if $V = V^l < C < P$. Similarly, it only misses a profitable opportunity if $V = V^h > C > P$. Suppose for example that $V^h = 1$, $V^l = 0$, $x = c = 0.375$. Recall from Section 6.2 that in this case the dynamic security market provides noisy signals which stop at either $p^h = 0.75$ or $p^l = 0.25$. (6.7) gives the same values for the boundary prices. Suppose also that $C = 0.4$. If the management decide 'blind', they proceed with the investment, resulting in an unconditional expected gain of $\mu - C = 0.5 - 0.4 = 0.1$. However, there is a 50 per cent probability that the market will show $P = 0.25$ and tell them not to proceed. The conditional expected gain is then zero. The other half of the time it will show $P = 0.75$ and tell management to expand, with a conditional expected profit of $0.75 - 0.4 = 0.35$. Thus the market-based decision rule gives the unconditional expected gain of $0.35/2 = 0.175$. This exceeds the return under the uninformed rule by 7.5 per cent, which is the expected loss with $P = 0.25$ weighted by $1/2$. Exercise 3 looks at another example.

Suppose now that the management is just as good at research as the analysts. Is it worth them paying $c = 0.375$ in order to get a better informed decision? If so, the market signal is irrelevant. Suppose that as it happens they observe $P = 0.75$. If they pay c then they will expect research to reveal $V = 1$ (so that they proceed) with probability 0.75 and see $V = 0$ (and not proceed) otherwise. The fully informed expected gain is then $0.75(1 - 0.4) = 0.45$. But this is only 0.1 better than the partially informed gain of 0.35. Since this is less than $c = 0.375$, they do not undertake research. If $P = 0.25$, the gain from becoming informed is even less, just 0.15. It can be shown that in this model, when prices are in research-free equilibrium and management are only as good at research as the analysts, then it is never optimal for them to undertake it. The best that they can do is to allow themselves to be guided by the market.

6.5. Research cost duplication

The Grossman and Stiglitz (1980) specification has a research cost structure which is similar to the one assumed in our model. Both models assume that an uninformed participant must pay a lump sum charge of c

in order to observe informed values which are exclusive, only communicated indirectly by trade. It is reasonable to make this assumption in the case of securities research, since this yields valuable proprietary information. It is in the researcher's interest to keep these results secret since communicating them to others would reduce trading profits.

Trading activity partially discloses underlying value in these microstructure models, but only after several uninformed investors have had to pay the research fee. There is duplication which is socially wasteful. While there may be some debate about the usefulness of informationally efficient prices as a way of informing management decisions, it is clearly wasteful for several researchers to pay for the same information. From a social perspective, it is optimal for one researcher to find out what the true value of the security is and to publish this in a credible way. These models determine q, which is the share of informed trade. This means that the level of wasteful duplication increases with the size of the market, which makes it extremely important to ensure transparency in large, heavily traded markets.

These observations reflect a general problem with knowledge-based industries. Knowledge is a standard public good—my knowing something does not prevent others from knowing it. The social first-best optimum is one in which information is not exclusive but is freely available. Yet if the acquisition of information is costly, there needs to be a reward to encourage this. *Ex ante*, exclusivity is necessary to reward research, while *ex post*, knowledge should be non-exclusive.

In the scientific area knowledge acquisition is regulated through the patent system. This provides a second-best solution, which usually works quite well. A patent gives a successful researcher exclusive rights to use or licence their results for a limited period. This gives them the chance to recoup their research costs. After that, the patent expires and the information becomes a free good.

This solution depends upon the ability of the researcher and the regulator to monitor the use of the results during the patent period, which is practically impossible in the area of financial research. Instead, one solution is for investors to conduct their own decentralized research 'in-house' and recoup the cost from informed trading. But as in the microstructure models, this leads to market and price inefficiencies, as well as a high level of duplication.

There is a strong economic argument for centralizing this research effort in order to avoid duplication. However, the theoretical model suggests that this would be difficult. Suppose for example we relax our initial assumption and allow the market maker to observe V. She would then have to reset prices appropriately, to try to recoup the cost. But as soon as trades and prices deviated from those described by the Bayesian learning model, other market makers would be able to see what had happened. They could then move in and eliminate the spread, leaving the original dealer with a loss of c. Of course she could perhaps try to recoup this instead by closing down and trading with a new market maker, but that would just make her a client.

In practice things are not quite so bad. First, decentralized research is not entirely wasteful, since different researchers are likely to come up with slightly different findings, which are then pooled by the market price. It is an oversimplification to assume that they all make the same observation. Second, the market is not completely open or contestable. In practice the costs of centralized broker research can usually be recouped through commissions. Clients usually direct their commissions to the brokers who supply them with the best research. The costs of company research can be reduced if companies develop relationships with brokers and allow analysts to visit their establishments. Synergies between the primary and secondary markets also allow costs to be reduced. For example, market-making units employ industry analysts who can also advise the corporate finance department about new issues in their area.

6.6. Revelation in complete financial markets, Hirshleifer (1971)

The Grossman and Stiglitz (1980) paper is based on a one-period model. Consequently, prices reflect both informed and liquidity trades and do not disclose underlying value. This means that they are not fully revealing. In contrast, the dynamic dealer model developed in the previous chapter is fully revealing in equilibrium. Hirshleifer (1971) argues that there are instances in which fully revealing prices can convey too much information too quickly, preventing efficient risk-sharing.

A financial system is fully revealing if it is complete in the sense that the dimensions of the market (or the number of independent securities traded) equals the dimension of uncertainty (the number of random state variables affecting it). Recall from Chapters 1 and 3 that, in this situation, individuals can in principle achieve full insurance by taking out positions in these securities (Exercise 5 gives a numerical example). Arguably, much of the trading activity seen in futures and other financial markets represents hedging activity of this sort, even though these markets are incomplete. However, Hirshleifer shows that if security prices can move before individuals can insure, then these hedging gains are lost. In this case, prices are too revealing, causing misallocation.

Hedging behaviour and insurance does not play any role in the dealer model developed in these chapters, because for simplicity these are based on the assumption of risk neutrality. However, the model of the previous chapter can be used to illustrate the problem. Imagine for example that there is an industrial dispute in Chile and the market begins to worry about a copper strike there. Consider the market in a copper future (or equivalently shares in a copper mining company). An announcement is to be made at the end of the trading day. If the strike goes ahead, then the price of the copper future (or mining share) will rise to V^h. Otherwise it will fall back to V^l. The initial odds are thought to be 50–50.

If the strike goes ahead, this will hurt industrial consumers. If they are risk averse, they buy copper futures (or shares) as an insurance against a strike. Rival copper producers would, however, gain from a strike and (if risk averse) sell futures to insure against the 'no-strike' outcome. Both parties gain *ex ante* from risk sharing. However, suppose that insiders who are involved in the negotiations know for sure either that the strike is going ahead (or that the dispute is going to be settled without one). If they can buy (sell) futures to profit from this, the price will quickly go up (down) to the strike (no strike) price, since there are no research costs. This will prevent anyone from insuring. In this case a rapid price adjustment precipitates a suboptimal outcome. A numerical example of this effect is set out as Exercise 6.

6.7. Security research and the financial analyst

The market microstructure literature provides a very useful framework for thinking about the regulation of information in securities markets. It tells us that, on the one hand, transparency leads to low spreads and liquid markets and makes prices very revealing while, on the other, it discourages security research that can inform important decisions. This trade-off is the essence of the Grossman–Stiglitz theorem.

The point which we choose on this trade-off curve depends upon the respective value which we place on liquidity and financial research. Normally, it is reasonable to suppose that markets provide too little knowledge, because research is a costly public good. However, in the case of financial research the private returns are potentially very large and the social return is questionable. This is a reason for thinking that the former exceed the latter. If this is the case, financial research is overprovided and should be discouraged by making the market as transparent as possible. On the other hand, if, as the example of Section 6.2 suggests, financial knowledge acquisition sends valuable signals to decision takers, we might want to find some mechanism for rewarding it.

At the macroeconomic level, stock market prices and the yield curve are important leading economic indicators, closely watched by economic forecasters and advisers in government, banking, and commercial organizations. These indicators feature prominently in Alan Greenspan's speeches and the deliberations of the Federal Reserve Board's Open Market Committee, which decides interest rates. Similarly, in the UK, they feature prominently in the minutes of the Monetary Policy Committee of the Bank of England. They influence financial and commercial decisions right down to the household level. In ensuring that economic data and analysis are properly reflected in these signals, the economist on the City trading floor arguably plays an important role.

The evidence suggests that financial sector economists produce good forecasts. In the case of quarterly national income forecasts, they do at least as well as the large econometric-model-based teams at the LBS and elsewhere (Baimbridge and Whyman 1997). Blue chip forecasts on Wall Street also have a reasonable track record (Cowles 1933; Batchelor and Dua 1990, 1991).

Similarly, company share prices help inform corporate decisions and allocate capital between different firms and activities. Senior company managers keep a keen eye on the share price, not just because this influences their remuneration, but because it provides a critical assessment of their performance. As the next chapter argues, failure in this respect can leave them prone to takeover by other companies, putting their jobs on the line. Executives of large companies spend a lot of time cultivating contacts in the City, keeping sector analysts abreast of their thinking on strategic issues, in a way which is not possible with small, decentralized shareholders. The relationship between the share price and company earnings indicates the rate of return which shareholders require of the company, and the treasurer's job is to ensure that new investment projects meet hurdle rates which are set in line with this return.

A great deal of academic research has been conducted on the accuracy of company analysts' forecasts. This divides into two separate but related types: studies of analysts' company earning projections and studies of their buy/sell recommendations. Analysts do not seem to perform well in the first type of test but do surprisingly well in the second.

The first strand of this literature usually finds evidence of 'excess dispersion' or exaggeration in cross-section earnings forecasts: companies with good (bad) earnings prospects tend to undershoot (exceed) the forecast. De Bondt and Thaler (1990) give evidence for the USA, and Bulkley and Harris (1995) for the UK. If this is the case, rational investors would discount such forecasts, and not take them literally. Indeed, this effect is sometimes so extreme that investors would be better off relying on the average market prediction than the individual company projection (Bulkley and Harris 1995). This could be because analysts are tempted to exaggerate their predications to generate trades for their firms. However, earnings outturns and 'surprises' calculated relative to these forecasts move the market, suggesting that investors do take them seriously (Brown *et al.* 1995). Curiously, Batchelor and Dua (1990) find evidence of the opposite effect—consensus seeking—among their colleagues on the economics desk.

Despite early evidence to the contrary (Bidwell 1977), it now seems that company analysts' share tips are valuable indicators. (For the USA see Groth *et al.* (1978), Givoly and Lakonishok (1979), Stickel (1992, 1993), and Elton (1986), and for the UK Dimson and Marsh (1984) and Dimson and Fraletti (1986).) Importantly, these studies carefully distinguish the announcement effect, which only the tipster can trade upon, from the longer-term effect. Surprisingly, the last of these studies showed that investors could make significant profits by trading some time after publication of the tip (as do the studies by Lloyd-Davies *et al.* 1978; Liu *et al.* 1990; Bjerring *et al.* 1983) and study the value of these tips to a firm's clients, before they are published in the press. A detailed study by Womack (1996) suggests that analysts display both stock selection and timing skills.

Nevertheless, investor surveys such as those conducted by Greenwich Associates and the *Institutional Investor* magazine often report their clients as saying that the New York and London markets are 'over-researched' or 'overbrokered'. In particular, the 1996 Extel report documented widespread dissatisfaction with the quality of stockbroker research in London, indicating a high level of research overcapacity and duplication. A normal reaction in this situation would be for institutional investors to prune their dealing lists and concentrate their business with a smaller number of larger firms. This sort of finding might also prompt the regulators to look again at the balance being struck between market maker's profits, the number of firms in the industry and the transparency of the market.

6.8. Strategic research versus security analysis

The Hirshleifer (1971) paper suggests that there may be occasions when the early release of information is damaging and should be delayed. However, in practice, financial futures markets offer a high degree of 'immediacy', allowing companies and even individuals better to hedge their exposures on an almost continuous and comprehensive basis. In view of this, it is unlikely that announcement delays allow liquidity traders to hedge their risk positions. It seems more likely that they just allow time for information traders to benefit. Reflecting this, most economists are inclined to favour the early resolution of uncertainty through fast publication and wide dissemination of financial information.

It is important to distinguish at this stage between financial and commercial knowledge acquisition. Even if financial research is over-privileged and is discouraged by making the capital market as open as possible, there are reasons for treating strategic information on things like research and development differently. Take the case for example of research by a drug company. This sort of information is likely to be strategic in the sense that the company does not want its commercial rivals to know which line of research it is pursuing, or what the results are like, at least until this is well advanced. Otherwise their rivals can take a free ride, with a good chance of obtaining useful patents which might otherwise fall to the original research team.

There is a risk that making the capital market more transparent would bring this sort of strategic information out into the open, reducing its value to the firms undertaking it and hence the general level of research and development spending in the economy. However, this risk can be minimized in a variety of ways. First, we should distinguish between financial information, which arguably should be published in a timely manner, and commercial information, which could remain confidential for a time. Second, there are a variety of ways in which senior executives can credibly signal the commercial value of the company's research and development portfolio and future earnings potential without giving away any trade secrets (Bhattacharya 1979, 1980; Ross 1977) . Increases in dividends and debt, both of which can be financed out of buoyant future cashflows, are credible ways of indicating that there are development projects with good prospects, as are equity investments by management and inside investors.

Yet all of these signalling devices have their drawbacks in practice. Dividends act as a drain on current cashflows, which may already be tight for a small company with new products to develop. The managers and employees of these companies may also be short of cash, or feel that they are already heavily exposed to the firm through their jobs. Public debt issues have to be accompanied by the release of financial and other relevant commercial information, which may reveal the nature of the project to rivals in the product market (Bhattacharya and Ritter 1983; Gertner, Gibbons, and Scharfstein 1988).

Yet this is not the case with a bank loan, which is cloaked by a confidential banking relationship and well suited to project finance. Moreover, by consolidating project finance and dealing with a single institution or syndicate manager this device avoids the duplication of monitoring and research effort by multiple investors. We take up this idea again in Chapter 8.

6.9. Secondary market regulation

In practice, the regulator has three main concerns in overseeing these markets. The first is the control and compartmentalization of information within securities houses themselves. I have already mentioned the ban on front running within a market-making division. Similar barriers, known as 'Chinese walls', are in place to inhibit communications about takeover targets and the like between different departments, which will typically include fund management, market making, and corporate finance in an integrated firm.

The second concern is the financial viability of secondary market makers and their parents, and in particular counterparty risk to a firm's clients in the event of failure. As Nick Leeson demonstrated at Barings Bank in February 1995, these market-making divisions are exposed to immense risks and quite capable of bringing down a major institution. Margin requirements on futures and options exchanges go some way to alleviating counterparty risks, but this still leaves a lot of financial transactions which are not exchange mediated and would be at risk if a major market maker failed.

To minimize these risks, the regulator has to see that these firms are adequately capitalized and that proper risk-control systems are in place.

In the UK the separate divisions must be set up as separate companies, with dedicated capital, on the view that compartmentalization will allow one division to fail without sinking the whole ship. However, the Leeson affair throws all of these theories into question.

Finally, regulators are always keen to maintain the reputation of the industry and lay down minimum standards for its member firms and operatives. The British SFA, being a self-regulating organization, was particularly keen on this, laying down stringent rules governing the qualification and behaviour of finance professionals. It set strict entry requirements (including examinations) and rules of conduct for traders, registered representatives, and directors of member companies, which have been adopted by its successor, the FSA.

These rules strictly regulate informed trading by securities houses and their employees. The onus is placed upon the member firms themselves, who employ compliance officers to police the regulations internally. Personal account ('p/a') trading must be conducted in-house or at least reported automatically to the compliance officer. These rules prohibit personal account trading by stockbroker analysts and traders on the basis of information or analysis which is not in the public domain. Front running of research by analysts—communicating the results to in-house traders or select clients in advance of publication—is also prohibited (Pagano and Roell 1993). Sanctions open to the SFA include fines and 'deregistration', which effectively bars market professionals from working in the City, either for a time or permanently.

EXERCISES

The value of information

Question 1. With reference to the model of Chapter 4, Question 1, what is the maximum you would be prepared to pay as an uninformed investor to become informed? Does this seem high? Comment on your result.

This cost is given by setting (6.1) to equality and substituting the relevant values:

$$c = p(V^h - P^a) + (1 - p)(P^b - V^l) = 0.5[(11 - 9.1) + (8.9 - 7)] = £1.90.$$

The breakeven value is always proportional to the spread, which is large in this case, helping to explain the high value. It is maximized at $p = 1/2$, the value used here, reflecting the uncertainty of the uninformed expectation.

Security research

Question 2. Assume that in the model of Section 10.2 $V^h = £1$, $V^l = 0$, $c = 0.15/32$.

(a) Calculate p^h and p^l.

(b) Is it worth researching when (i) $P = 37.5$ pence, (ii) $P = 62.5$ pence?

(c) Now suppose that their inside knowledge reduces the research cost for management. If nothing else changes, what is the maximum cost they would pay for research?

> Substituting these values into (6.7) gives values of $p^h = 0.625$ pence and $p^l = 0.375$ pence. Using (6.9), $P^h = 62.5$ pence and $P^l = 37.5$ pence and we see that it is not worth investing in either case (i) or (ii).

Informing the investment decision

Question 3. Assume that in the model of Section 6.4 $V^h = £1$, $V^l = 0$, but now $c = 15/32$ and $C = 0.45$.

(a) Is it worthwhile for management to invest in the absence of a share price signal?

> The expected profit from investing blind is $0.05 = 0.5 - 0.45$, so this is worthwhile.

(b) If the market signal is (i) $P^* = P^h = p^h = £0.625$ what is the correct investment decision? (ii) What if $P^* = P^l = p^l = £0.375$?

> The market tells management to invest in case (i) with an expected gain of $£0.175 = 0.625 - 0.45$, but not to invest in case (ii).

(c) What is the maximum price you would be prepared to pay for a share in this company before the market opens?

> The existing capital is locked in and worth £0.50 per share. To this we add the ex ante gain from the conditional investment described in (b). This is an expected gain of £0.0875 (£0.175 times the *ex ante* probability of 0.5). I would thus be prepared to pay up to 58.75 pence a share.

Endogenous research trading dynamics

Question 4. Endogenize q by replacing the do loop in Chapter 5 Question 2 by:

```
> for n from 1 to 40 do
>.q:=(p(n)*(1-p(n))/(x*(2*p(n)-1)^2))^2+(1-2*p(n)*(1-p(n))/
(x*(2*p(n)-1)^2)^0.5;
> u:=rand(1..round(subs(v =1/q, v))):
inn(n):=z(u()); ask(n):=(h*p(n)*(1+q)/2+l*(1-p(n))*(1-q)/2)/
(q*p(n)+(1-q)/2);
bid(n):=(l*(1-p(n))*(1+q)/2+h*(p(n))*(1-q)/2)/(q*(1-p(n))+(1-q)/2);
buy(n):=y();
sp(n):=ask(n)-bid(n); price(n):=inn(n)*ask(n)+(1-inn(n))*(buy(n)
*ask(n)+(1-buy(n))*bid(n)); p(n+1):=(price(n)-l)/(h-l); od:
```

You will also need to drop the line setting q and reset the prior $p(1)$ at some figure other than 0.5, say 0.45.

(a) First set $x = 0.375$ as in the example discussed above. How long does it typically take p to reach the boundary value of £10? Does it ever reach the other boundary in your sample? On what percentage of occasions? How does this compare with the theoretical percentage?

(b) Now set $x = 0.45$. How does this affect the typical result? Why?

(c) The price spreads tend to erode much faster than in Question 2 in Chapter 5. Why?

(d) What happens if insiders find that a bid will not materialize? How can that be simulated?

Hedging in complete futures markets

Question 5. You own a well which produces 40 barrels of crude oil a day. Production costs are negligible. Suppose that this can be converted into 20 (100 litre) units of kerosene and 20 units of fuel oil at negligible cost. Spot price scenarios are as in Question 2 of Chapter 3 (Tables Q2.1 and Q2.2). Recall that they depend upon two uncertainties, the Middle East situation and the severity of the next winter. Suppose now that the futures market agrees with your evaluation of a crisis probability of $l = 0.2$ and a harsh winter probability of $q = 0.5$. This generates futures prices of $26 for kerosene and $11.8 for fuel oil.

You do not hold any futures initially. Your *ex post* utility (U) is described by the natural logarithm of daily consumption, which is equal to *ex post* sales revenue plus any profits from futures positions taken out in the meantime (R):

$$U = \ln(R). \tag{6.10}$$

You do not speculate but only sell your production either *ex ante* at these futures prices or *ex post* in the spot markets (Tables Q2.1 and Q2.2). Let K and F represent the effective spot or future prices at which production is sold, whichever is appropriate. Then $R = 20 \times K + 20 \times F$ and we can write *ex post* utility as

$$U = \ln(20 \times (K + F)) = \ln(20) + \ln(K + F) = 3 + \ln(K + F). \tag{6.11}$$

(a) What is the utility level achieved by selling all of your future production at the futures prices shown for scenario 4?

> In this case sales revenues are known with certainty. Substitute the given futures prices of $F = 11.8$ and $K = 26$ to get
>
> $U = 3 + \ln(37.8) = 6.6323.$

(b) Now assume that there are no futures markets: you have to sell your oil products on the future spot market at the *ex post* prices shown in Tables Q2.1 and Q2.2. Expected utility (EU) is described as the probability-weighted average of *ex post* utilities of the spot revenues in these four *ex post* scenarios:

$$EU = 3 + (1 - l)(1 - q)\ln(20 + 10) + l(1 - q)\ln(40 + 14) + q(1 - l)\ln(24 + 12) + lq\ln(44 + 16).$$

(i) What is your expected utility in this situation?

Substituting the given probabilities $l = 0.2$, $q = 0.5$ into *EU* and evaluating gives

$$EU = 3 + 0.4\ln(30) + 0.1\ln(54) + 0.4\ln(36) + 0.1\ln(60) = 6.6021.$$

(ii) How does this compare with your answer to (a)?

This expected utility level is less than the utility level of 6.6323 obtained by selling products forward: access to complete futures markets increases your expected utility. Technically, this happens because your logarithmic utility function is strictly concave, and the expected value $E[U(X)]$ of a strictly concave function $U(X)$ of a random variable X is less than the function $U(E[X])$ of the expected value of this variable $E[X]$ (see the discussion of Chapter 9).

The Hirshleifer (1971) effect

Question 6. The basic spot price scenarios are again as in Tables Q2.1 and Q2.2 of Question 2 in Chapter 3, and production data as in the previous question. The futures markets are open and initially agree with your evaluation of *l* and *q*, generating scenario 4 of the following *ex ante* scenario table:

	Scenario:		
	4	5	6
K	26	42	22
F	11.8	15	11
l	0.2	1	0
q	0.5	0.5	0.5

Table Q4

(a) Now assume that the futures prices shift from those shown in scenario 4 to those shown in scenario 5.

(i) What does this tell you about secret negotiations which are under way to resolve the crisis?

Scenario 5 prices reflect a 100 per cent probability of a crisis. So the shift in the futures market reveals that the talks have broken down and that a significant number of traders are aware of this and have forced prices up accordingly, removing any trading profit opportunity.

(ii) What is your expected utility now?

The only remaining uncertainty concerns the severity of the winter. However, this can be hedged away by selling forward at the new scenario 5 futures prices. Substituting these prices into the *ex post* utility function gives the new utility level $U = 3 + \ln(42 + 15) = 7.0440$. The high level of product prices means that this utility level is higher than in the other scenarios. Note that this gives a higher level of utility than would be expected by waiting until the winter weather situation is known and then selling into the spot markets at the prices shown in Tables Q2.1 and Q2.2.

(b) Suppose instead that futures prices shift from scenario 4 to scenario 6. What does this (i) reveal about the negotiations, (ii) do to your expected utility?

(i) This reveals a 0 per cent probability of a crisis and tells us that the talks have been successful.

(ii) Unfortunately for producers, this reduces the level of utility. Substituting these prices into the *ex post* utility function gives $U = 3 + \ln(22 + 11) = 6.4965$. Again, this is the best you can do. Planning to sell into the spot market further reduces the level of expected utility.

(c) Suppose that the markets closed on Friday for the weekend when no one was worried about the Middle East risk ($l = 0$, $q = 0.5$). You have not hedged. A potential crisis situation suddenly looms up in the Middle East and negotiations to resolve this are under way. These have a 20 per cent chance of success. If these are successful, then $l = 0$, $q = 0.5$, otherwise $l = 1$, $q = 0.5$. What is your expected utility assuming (i) that the situation remains uncertain on Monday and you hedge by selling at the prices shown in scenario 4, and (ii) that at the open on Monday, prices will move directly to scenario 5 with probability 0.8 or scenario 6 with probability 0.2 (because some traders will know the outcome of the negotiations)?

(i) From (a) we know that the scenario 4 prices generate a utility level of $U = 6.6323$.

(ii) Weighting up the two utilities derived at (c) and (d) gives the average value: $EU = 0.2 \times 7.0440 + 0.8 \times 6.4965 = 6.6060$. This is less than the value obtained (d(i)) if the uncertainty remains on Monday morning, allowing you to hedge.

(d) Does this illustrate the Hirshleifer (1971) effect?

This is an example of the Hirshleifer result that the early resolution of uncertainty reduces expected utility. This paradoxical result is explained by the fact that early resolution means that traders do not have time to hedge.

7. The Equity Market and Managerial Efficiency

The analyses of the last three chapters were based upon the assumption that a company's fundamental value is not influenced by its share price. However, as the first chapter argued, the value of a company depends critically upon the efficiency of its management, which can be influenced by the behaviour of its share price. This chapter investigates ways in which the stock market can influence corporate efficiency.

As the name suggests, a 'share' or equity represents a fraction of a company's value and a claim to a share of the dividend. However, following the discussion of the introduction, this chapter views an equity as a contract in which the management agrees to work for shareholders to maximize profits and dividends. This sets up a potential moral hazard problem, because management has to put in effort to secure shareholder returns and may want to maximize private benefits or 'perks' rather than dividends.

One solution to this moral hazard problem is for shareholders to monitor managers, as discussed in the first section of this chapter. However, in practice it is normally more cost-effective to motivate management using incentive mechanisms (Section 7.2). These inducements usually take the form of remuneration packages that are geared to stock price performance. However, this precipitates a secondary problem, because it gives managers an incentive to exaggerate earnings prospects in order to give the share price and their remuneration an artificial boost (Section 7.3).

The stock price also influences managerial efficiency through the takeover mechanism—poor performance reflected in a low share price can mean that the company and its management fall prey to a takeover. Ultimately, this takeover discipline provides a backstop, helping to ensure that executives maximize shareholder value when other methods fail. This is essentially the view of Manne (1965) and those of the neoclassical *value maximization* school. They argue that the objective of a firm involved in an acquisition is simply the maximization of shareholder value. Takeovers may facilitate this through synergies, cost savings, or increased monopoly power. On this view, an inefficient incumbent management will simply be replaced by a more efficient one, to the benefit of shareholders.

In this sense the takeover mechanism is part of the 'market for corporate control', in which different managerial teams compete for control of the company's resources.

However, as Mueller (1969) and others of the managerial or *growth maximization* school argue, managers may be interested in private benefits like prestige rather than shareholder value. Shleifer and Vishny (1988) provide an interesting analysis of these benefits. Because managerial benefits are more closely linked to the size of the firm than its share price, this may mean that acquisitions are driven by a policy of growth maximization which is pursued to the detriment of shareholders. This objective may also be facilitated by an active takeover market.

Even if there are no private managerial benefits and there is full information, the takeover discipline is an imperfect one. The seminal paper by Grossman and Hart (1980) shows that under these conditions, a free rider problem will frustrate takeovers when there is a diffuse shareholder register (Section 7.4). Subsequent papers (Section 7.7) show that large shareholders facilitate takeovers, but that managerial benefits and asymmetric information have the opposite effect. Takeovers are often frustrated by anti-trust legislation and political lobbying, as Shleifer and Vishny (1997) note. Uncertainty about the reaction of public opinion and the competition authorities is a factor even in the USA and the UK. Finally, as Shleifer and Summers (1989) argue, the threat of takeover can disrupt contractual relations and lead to short-termism (Section 7.8).

The focus of this chapter is unashamedly Anglo-American, since merger and acquisition activity is much more important in the USA and the UK than in other economies. In the USA the value of company takeovers in 1998 was over 20 per cent of GDP and the UK figure was only just below this level. In contrast, this figure was less than 1 per cent in Germany, France, Italy, and Japan. Moreover, hostile takeovers have until recently been relatively rare in continental Europe and elsewhere. Merger activity in Canada, Australia, and New Zealand is significant, but not as high as it is in the USA and UK.

The USA and the UK are unique (even among the Anglo-Saxon group) in having diffuse shareholder registers (La Porta *et al.* 1998: table 7). This may in part reflect the relative size of these economies and their constituent companies, many of which are large multinationals. La Porta and others argue that the preponderance of small shareholders is also a consequence of a legal framework that allows small investors to exert effective control over management. In the USA legal restrictions on large holdings and exercise of control rights by banks and other institutions discourage shareholder concentration and intervention. It is likely that the tight stake disclosure rules in force in the USA and the UK have a similar effect. In practice, corporate raiders have to find ways of circumventing these rules if they are to be successful. Dealing rings and other ways around the rules are discussed in Section 7.9. At the height of the 1980s takeover boom these rings were operating on a transatlantic basis, which reflected the increasing integration of the Anglo-American capital market.

The takeover phenomenon raises questions which are of critical importance for both competition policy and capital market regulation in the Anglo-American systems (Section 7.10). Do mergers and acquisitions lead to the abuse of product market power or do they secure efficiency gains? Do they encourage insider dealing and lead to capital market corruption? Does the threat of takeover motivate management or lead to short-termism? Is there a better mechanism for disciplining managers and making them more accountable to shareholders? The correlation between the post-war trends in corporate governance, takeover activity, and macro-economic performance makes these key issues for policymakers.

7.1. Moral hazard and the problem of management monitoring

The previous chapter showed that, despite the openness of the secondary capital market and the free rider problem, private investors do have an incentive to undertake company research. Similarly, they have an incentive to mitigate the effect of adverse selection in the primary issue market by screening initial offerings. In both cases, research and screening activity is usually driven by the prospect of quick capital gains. Indeed, because there is likely to be cost duplication such research may be over-provided by the market.

However, there is little incentive for small investors to monitor and influence company executives. Monitoring is a semi-permanent activity, while screening exercises are essentially once and for all. Scrutinizing the behaviour of executives on an ongoing basis is likely to be much more difficult than security research. Investors can attend the AGM and analysts can go on company visits, but these opportunities are necessarily limited. Managers usually consider any further monitoring effort to be intrusive.

The free-rider problem is more serious in the case of monitoring, intervention, and takeover activity than in the case of security research. Because the security researcher is the first in the market, he is likely to make larger gains than the free riders who follow, compensating him for the cost. However, when an investor monitors management, all shareholders benefit (in proportion to their holdings). The same is true of active intervention in management and takeover bids. Since the benefits are spread across the shareholder register, it will not pay anyone to undertake such activity if shareholdings are diffuse (Grossman and Hart 1980; Diamond 1984; Shleifer and Vishny 1986). If small shareholders suspect that there is a management problem, they typically sell their shares and try to find a company that is better managed.

Monitoring and intervention may be worthwhile for large investors. However, in this case there is a coordination problem. On the one hand, if they all monitor, then this will lead to duplication. On the other, there is a temptation to save money and free ride on monitoring efforts by other large investors. Consequently, no one can be sure that anyone is monitoring. One solution to this coordination problem is for small investors to delegate the task of scrutinizing the administration of a company to a *single* large investor. This is the situation analysed by the Shleifer and Vishny (1986) model discussed in Section 7.8, which considers the problems associated with the takeover process when there are large investors.

Ownership concentration has other drawbacks. Obviously, these shareholders can be expected to act in their own interests and not those of the small shareholders (Shleifer and Vishny 1997). Moreover, shareholder activism–intervention in the management of a company–is usually an expensive and unrewarding task. Although some large institutional investors have become quite active in recent years, the openness of the capital market means that shareholder activism is still rare. Stake disclosure rules force such intervention into the public arena, often with dire short-term consequences for the share price. Indeed, intervention can make an investor an insider in an informational sense, which precludes trading activity. For example, intervention by British pension funds during the crisis at British Biotech in 1998 made them insiders, prevented them from selling, and resulted in large losses. This constraint is a deterrent to institutional involvement with company management.

The next chapter considers an important variant of this delegation solution in which small investors effectively hand over the monitoring and intervention role to a large *non-equity* investor like a bank which can act behind the scenes on a confidential basis. In some continental systems, equity investors also delegate their control rights to banks. In Germany, for example, shareholders cannot vote at company meetings like the AGM unless they are present. They often lodge their shares at their bank, which then 'borrows' the voting rights. The deposit contract may also be seen as a mechanism through which investors delegate their control rights (and duties) to a bank. This chapter considers takeovers, which as Shleifer and Vishny (1997) note can 'be viewed as rapid-fire mechanisms for ownership concentration'.

7.2. Delegation and the problem of principal and agent

If it is impractical for investors to actively scrutinize management, the alternative is to provide financial incentives for good performance. Recall from Chapter 1 that this situation is analysed as a principal–agent problem. In this case, the shareholder is the principal and the manager of the firm is the agent, contracted to work on behalf of the shareholder. The term principal–agent problem is originally due to Ross (1973). This model has provided important insights into the working of a range of markets subject to asymmetric information, including product and factor as well as financial markets.

Many different principal–agent problems arise in the financial markets This chapter looks at the case of shareholders who delegate the management of a company to a board of directors, while the next looks at the way in which depositors effectively delegate the management of their assets to a bank and its shareholders. I believe that the shape of the financial system is strongly influenced by the relative effectiveness with which the legal, accounting, and regulatory systems resolve these two principal–agent problems.

A principal–agent situation arises when it is efficient for the principal to delegate the power of decision to the agent. This is usually because the agent has skills or information which the principal lacks, in the case of a doctor or lawyer for example. But it might be because the principal finds it difficult to become actively involved in the decision-taking process. For example, if someone was absent for a prolonged period, they might grant someone else power of attorney: discretion to take decisions upon their behalf. The equity contract can be struck for both of these reasons.

Delegation is facilitated by laws (such as the right of shareholders to vote by proxy at company meetings like the AGM) which allow small shareholders collectively to retain overall control of a company and ensure that it is being run for their benefit and not the managers'. La Porta *et al.* (1997, 1998) find that proxy voting rules and the like are an important feature of the Anglo-Saxon model, helping to explain the diffuse shareholdings seen in these systems. In contrast, shareholdings in Europe tend to be much more concentrated. Many of these countries do not have proxy voting rights. Stake disclosure rules are also less common than in the Anglo-American systems, allowing monitoring and intervention by banks and other large investors to take place behind the scenes.

The principal–agent literature analyses the way in which the principal can design a contract to motivate the agent to act in the principal's interest. It is assumed that the agent's actions cannot be effectively measured by monitoring or inferred from observable variables like the outcome. The point is that the agent will pursue their own interests and these may not coincide with those of the principal. So the principal has to provide financial incentives that align the agent's interest with their own.

The principal will try to design a contract that minimizes the total delegation or agency cost: the cost of incentives and residual misalignment. Monitoring costs may also be included if some monitoring activity is cost-effective. Jensen and Meckling (1976) also include 'bonding costs', which are expenditures incurred by the agent to help assure the principal that they will devotedly work in their interest. At the margin, the costs of incentives (and monitoring and bonding expenditures) must be balanced against the costs of misalignment. In the banking literature, discussed in the next chapter, these agency costs are known as delegation costs.

7.3. Verification and the audit process

A share allows an outsider to participate in the net dividend of a company. Senior managers typically participate through options and other incentive packages. In addition, they enjoy non-pecuniary benefits or 'perks' (Jensen and Mecking 1976). They also have to put in 'effort' to secure a good outcome for the firm, while outside shareholders are usually passive: 'sleeping' partners. Their agenda is likely to differ from that of outside shareholders for all of these reasons.

When monitoring is not effective, shareholders, as principals, can try to overcome the agency problem by devising appropriate remuneration packages. However, there are at least three serious problems with this method. First, although it is important to ensure that shareholders rather than managers design these packages, this is hard to achieve in practice. Corporate pay has been the subject of a great deal of adverse comment on both sides of the Atlantic (see e.g. Crystal 1992). Although boards of directors are meant to represent shareholders' interests, in practice they are invariably dominated by executives. Corporate governance principles state that the remuneration committee is made up of non-executives, but these rules can be side-stepped by cross-membership arrangements. It is revealing that recent UK proposals to give shareholders a veto over remuneration packages at the AGM have been strongly resisted by manager representatives.

The second problem is that equity remuneration and participation contracts are not 'incentive efficient': they do not give managers any incentive to adhere to the basic rules of the game like telling the truth about earnings prospects or the outcome of investment projects (Hurwicz 1972). This makes it very important to make sure that the accounts are audited properly. Even then, results may be inflated by 'creative accounting' to boost share prices, options, and remuneration. As Table 1.1 reminds us, debt contracts are incentive efficient and only have to be audited in bankruptcy. This is perhaps a reason for the finding by La Porta *et al.* (1998) that countries with poor accounting standards usually have weak capital markets.

Finally, even if these devices are effective, they align manager interests with those of shareholders and not those of debtholders.[1] They then set up another agency problem, with the shareholder-managers acting as the agents of bondholders and others who have fixed claims on the firm. This problem is considered in Chapter 10. Jensen and Meckling (1976) argue that at the margin the agency costs of debt finance will be balanced against those of equity and that this will determine the optimal amount of debt leverage. But for now, I assume for simplicity that the firm is financed entirely by equity.

Fortunately, the takeover process offers another way of rewarding or disciplining executives. It is usually regarded as a backstop, one which ensures a reasonable level of efficiency if other methods fail. In principle it establishes a market in managers or a 'market for corporate control' (an expression coined by Henry Manne (1965)). However, there are two major problems with this mechanism. First, as Grossman and Hart (1980) show, there is a free-rider problem which is likely to make hostile takeovers very difficult, leaving shareholders saddled with inefficient management. Secondly, as Shleifer and Summers (1989) argue, takeovers can lead to short-termism by disrupting contractual relationships.

---

[1] If there are a few large shareholders, they can be expected to act in their own interests and not those of the smaller shareholders. Shleifer and Vishny (1997) provide an interesting review of the distortions that can result and the empirical evidence on these effects.

7.4. The takeover mechanism as a management discipline (Grossman and Hart 1980)

Takeover bidders are attracted by firms that can be reorganized to give higher profits, possibly through merger with other enterprises owned by the bidder. Grossman and Hart (1980) provide the basic analysis of this situation assuming that:

1. Shareholders are atomistic: too small to influence the outcome of a bid.
2. All costs and benefits are known to all participants.
3. There are no private non-pecuniary benefits to management.

The last assumption means that there is no asymmetric information in the basic model. However, uncertainty about costs and benefits is introduced later in their paper and is discussed in Section 7.7.

Given the first assumption, the potential bidder can only justify a bid if they believe that the discounted present value of the reorganized firm (V per share) will significantly exceed the costs, including the offer to shareholders (P) and the costs of advisory services ($C > 0$). This gives us our first condition for a successful bid:

Bid viability condition: $V > P + C$. $\qquad$ (7.1)

(All quantities are measured on a per share basis.) The bidder is only entitled to the dividend share that their majority shareholding gives them (with the discounted value of V per share). Moreover, those that remain as minority shareholders after the takeover also get the full benefit (V). Consequently *ex ante*, because shareholders are too small to influence the result of the bid they should not accept bids ($P < V$) lower than the raiders' full valuation. They would obviously not accept $P < Q$, the price they could get in the open market. This gives the second condition:

Bid acceptance condition: $P > \max (V,Q)$. $\qquad$ (7.2)

With $C > 0$, this is inconsistent with (7.1): to be viable, offers must be below the full valuation V, but these would not be acceptable to shareholders and would fail. Since the raider can never justify a bid, shareholders are apparently stuck with the incumbent management and the original market price ($Q < V$). However, this is not an equilibrium if individuals can get P from the raider unconditionally.

This is an example of Nash optimization: in which agents consider only their own interests without considering the aggregate effect of their actions. If a coalition could be assembled to accept a bid $P \in (Q, V)$, this would leave all shareholders better off. Those that accepted would get $P > Q$, while the rest would get $V > Q$. But there would still be a strong temptation for free riders to break out of the coalition to get $V > P$. We now analyse a conditional bid. This gives a unique Nash equilibrium. A two-equilibrium situation is found in Chapter 10 in the context of a bank deposit market.

In practice, US law and the UK takeover 'code' (described in the Box 7.1) allow a 'conditional tender' offer whereby bidders are only obliged to take up shares offered to them if these exceed 50 per cent of the total. In addition, section 209 of the UK Companies Act 1985 allows majority shareholders with 90 per cent or more of the firm's shares to buy out the minority; this is known as the 'buyout rule'.

However, in this situation there is no reason for a small shareholder to accept any offer which is less than the full reorganized value. Consider the example of a bid for a public utility where:

the share price is $Q = £7$ under existing management,
the bidder makes a conditional offer of $P = £9$, because
the company is worth $V = £11$ a share when reorganized, and
the bidder's costs are $C = £1$ per share.

If shareholders are too small to influence the result and do not collude, then this bid will fail and the share price will fall back to $Q = £7$, because it is never in an individual shareholder's interest to accept the bid.

1. If the bid fails then everyone gets the initial market price (of $Q = £7$) and our shareholder is no worse off by not accepting.
2. With a 50 to 90 per cent acceptance rate achieved by the raider, the bid succeeds, in which case our shareholder is better off not to have accepted (getting the full post-reorganization value price ($V = £11$)).
3. If a 90 to 100 per cent acceptance is achieved by the raider, the bid succeeds and our shareholder is no worse off not to have accepted. In this case he is part of the 10 per cent minority. The buyout rule applies and our shareholder is bought out at the same price ($P = £9$) as those who accepted.

Unconditional bids on the other hand are legally possible but are very rare. It is interesting to ask why this is. An unconditional offer is one which does not depend upon an acceptance rate of 50 per cent or more. Such a bid might tempt shareholders to accept the tender price ($P = £9$) just in case the bid fails (and price reverts to $Q = £7$). But raiders are unlikely to make such a bid since failure would leave them as minority shareholders, with incumbent managers in place and with shares worth $Q = £7$, which is less than the tender price $(P = £9)$ they paid.

7.5. Stake disclosure rules and the 'toehold'

One way around the free-rider problem is to allow company raiders to buy shares at a lower price (say T where $Q \leq T \leq V - C$) in the open market without disclosing their presence. This allows them to establish a 'toehold' stake. If they can acquire x per cent of the company this way they can make a profit by offering the full valuation V provided that $(V - T) > C/x$. Compared to the bad Nash outcome with the incumbent management, this represents a Pareto-improvement. The bidder gets the company for some price $P \leq V - C$, the investment bank gets its fee C, some x per cent of shareholders get a price $P > Q$, while the $(1 - x)$ per cent that sell in the open market get $P > T \geq Q$.

This is a straightforward way of allowing hostile takeovers to discipline executives in a diffuse shareholder situation. The regulator simply increases the toehold limit x to the point at which hostile bids stand a reasonable chance of success. However, the snag is that shareholders are not treated equally. The lucky ones get P (which could be as high as $V - C = £10$ in our example) while the unlucky ones who sell into the market rise only get T (which could be as low as $Q = £7$). Moreover, if insider dealers get wind of the bid, this increases the proportion of the original shareholders who sell at T above the toehold limit of x per cent.

Thus, when assessing the appropriate level at which to require disclosure of shareholdings, a regulator should balance the costs of insider dealers and false markets against those of inefficient and overpaid executives. However, capital market regulators are naturally more concerned about the first type of distortion than the second. Consequently stake disclosure rules tend to be very tight, making it difficult for a bidder to acquire an initial stake on the cheap. In the UK for example $T = 3$ per cent (see Box 7.1 on the UK takeover code).

Unfortunately, disclosure rules can allow insider dealers to take an advantage of a bid situation. These rules prevent the bidder building a significant toehold, but allow groups of insiders to acquire sizeable stakes. These come into play when the bid is made, allowing the bidder to avoid the free-rider problem and succeed. This process is often organized through a dealing ring to facilitate collusion. Indeed the bidder may be in collusion with the dealing ring: a device known as a 'concert party'. The takeover of Guinness by the Distillers Company in 1988 (discussed in Chapter 4) gives one of the more notorious examples of a concert party. However, this means that many of the gains go to inside dealing rings rather than the original investors. Stock exchanges are constantly on the lookout for this kind of conspiracy, but it is extremely difficult to prove.

7.6. Dilution of minority rights

Grossman and Hart (1980) show that the free-rider problem can be removed by allowing the raider to extract value from the reorganized firm in addition to their share entitlement. Again, this is illegal in most countries. For example, the US Andrews Act 1934 and the UK Companies Act 1985 both insist that all shareholders must be treated equally. Grossman and Hart suggest a change in the legal framework to allow companies to relax this and facilitate hostile takeovers.

Grossman and Hart assume that the company's articles of association are amended to allow the new company board to transfer value *ex post* from minority shareholders to a successful bidder. Since this mechanism dilutes minority rights, it is known as the 'dilution factor': F (per share). They rework their earlier analysis, noting that all shareholders will now accept any tender price in excess of the reorganized value less the dilution factor $(V - F)$. Equation (7.2) becomes:

Bid acceptable if: $P > \max(V - F, Q)$. $\qquad$ (7.3)

Combining this with (7.1) gives the conditions:

Bid succeeds if: $F > C$, $\qquad$ (7.4)
$$V > Q + C.$$

It is important to see that because all shareholders should accept an offer described by (7.3), F should never be inflicted upon anyone. This punishment is simply a notional one, devised to facilitate the bid by threatening free riders. That is why (7.1) remains the feasibility condition: the bidder would not expect to be left with a residual minority to exploit.

Nevertheless, the dilution factor does affect the likely bid price, the likelihood of takeover, and hence the behaviour of incumbent management. First, with $V - F > Q$, an increase in F reduces the minimum bid that shareholders are forced to accept (via (7.4)). Moreover, a fall in the potential bid price $V - F$ is likely to depress the market price Q, leaving shareholders prey to an exploitative offer. If shareholders were worried about this then they should set F so that it just satisfies (7.4). This strategy would however give bidders little profit, reducing the threat of takeover and allowing incumbents to shirk their responsibilities. This would also be reflected in a low Q value.

In theory, the dilution factor could be set in a way which traded off these opposing effects. In practice this calculation would depend critically upon the nature of the industry and the competitiveness of the takeover market. If the company's affairs are well understood by outsiders and the market is contestable, then the articles could set F at a high value without fear of an opportunistic offer, since any such bid would be topped by a competitive one. In this case the incumbents must be very careful since they are easily displaced. Otherwise, F should be set to just satisfy (7.4) and prevent extortionate bids.

Realistically, there is little chance of amending company law to permit dilution of minority rights in the way that Grossman and Hart suggest. Nevertheless, there are in practice a variety of ways in which executives transfer value from one group to another, however doubtful they may be legally. For example, the bidder might be able to extract value through transfer pricing—selling the reorganized company's output to a related enterprise at an artificially low price. Similarly, the new management might award itself an artificially high remuneration or perks, as discussed above. Finally, as Chapter 9 demonstrates, value can be extracted through intercompany loan arrangements.

7.7. Asymmetric information

The basic Grossman and Hart (1980) model assumes that all parameters are known (2). They note, however, that in practice a lot of the key factors (notably V) are uncertain. It is in the incumbents' interest to make them as unpredictable as possible to make it harder for the bidder. Moreover, as they note, the incumbents may have a 'White Knight' option. This means that if a hostile bid emerges, the incumbents give their inside information to a friendly bidder or White Knight. In principle this puts the raider in a no-win situation by allowing the White Knight to make a more informed offer.

If the hostile bidder underestimates the value of the firm, the White Knight will win with a higher bid. The hostile bidder loses his costs. Because the new owner is friendly, the incumbent management probably keep their jobs. On the other hand, if the raider overestimates this value he succeeds but pays too much, and again makes a loss. *Ex ante*, the possibility of a White Knight coming to the rescue helps to deter hostile bids and again provides protection for the incumbent management.

More recent theoretical papers have relaxed the Grossman and Hart (1980) assumptions, allowing for large shareholders, private benefits, and asymmetric information. Bagnoli and Lipman (1988) examine the finite shareholder case. Grossman and Hart's subsequent (1981) and (1988) papers analyse the effect of asymmetric information and private benefits accruing to incumbents and rival managements.

Another important extension is provided by Shleifer and Vishny (1986). They assume that

1. there is one large shareholder and a 'fringe' of atomistic shareholders who cannot influence the outcome of the bid individually, and
2. because the large shareholder has an incentive to monitor he is better informed about the *ex post* reorganization value than the fringe.

By relaxing the first of Grossman and Hart's (1980) assumptions, (1) gives the large shareholder a 'toehold' and increases the chances of a successful bid. However, (2) reduces the chances of success by introducing asymmetric information. Because a takeover is informed (like an inside share deal), uninformed shareholders will condition their beliefs upon this, raising their evaluation of the firm and the premium which the bidder must pay to succeed.

Shleifer and Vishny show that an increase in the size of the large holding increases the *ex ante* probability of a bid but reduces the size of the premium paid in a successful bid (their proposition 1). This is essentially because the larger is the bidder's share, the smaller is the increase in the reorganized value which he can afford to accept. On balance, an increase in the large shareholding increases the *ex ante* share price. *Ex post*, a bid reveals positive information and should increase the value attached to the firm by small uninformed shareholders, even if it does not succeed.

The Shleifer and Vishny analysis suggests that once a large holding is accumulated, it is difficult to sell piecemeal in the open market and is likely to be sold as a block. Moreover, when the firm repurchases equity from small shareholders, this increases the relative size of the large holding and increases value. This is the case even if there is no tax advantage to the buyback. The Shleifer and Vishny analysis has many other interesting implications.

These models of the takeover process raise important questions for policy makers. They suggest that the notion of fairness may be misplaced and may simply protect incumbent management from the takeover discipline. They certainly suggest that takeover codes, disclosure rules, and the like should take into account the need to discipline managers, particularly if other methods fail. We take up these questions in the final section. But before judging this, it is important to consider another perspective on the subject of takeovers, which is that they encourage short-termism.

7.8. Takeovers and contractual relations (Shleifer and Summers 1980)

The threat of a takeover can disturb managerial objectives and make these 'short-termist'. Although this just looks like the conventional wisdom, Shleifer and Summers (1980) show that this idea can be underpinned by implicit contract theory. This theory is based on the observation that long-term relationships are important whenever investments are relationship-specific. This means that once investments are undertaken they have a higher economic value when the relationship continues than when it does not. Examples include worker training that is specific to the firm as well as to the worker (Becker 1964). Similarly, suppliers may site their factories next to the buyer's plant, or invest in machines which are specifically geared to producing the component design required by the buyer.

Once made, these investments have the effect of locking the various parties into a long-term relationship, which it is difficult to handle properly through a succession of short-term supply contracts. The problem is that the investment expenditure, once undertaken, becomes a sunk cost. This means that the *ex post* economic rent (or gross cost saving) from the investment is not allocated by the market but by bargaining between the parties to the relationship. Splitting this rent in this way by using short-term supply contracts may cause socially profitable investment opportunities to be overlooked.[2]

In this case, one market solution is for the supplier to enter into a long-term supply agreement that allows it to achieve (at least) a market return on the investment cost. (*Ex ante* Nash bargaining would then allow it to

---

[2] For example suppose that a supplier can reduce net costs by $15,000 a year in perpetuity by spending $100,000 on a machine which is only worth $5,000 a year in its next best use. This investment is socially optimal if the interest rate is less than 10 per cent. However, if the investment cost is met by the supplier and the cost savings are divided equally with the buyer (as would be the case under *ex post* Nash bargaining for example), the investment will only go ahead if the interest rate is below 5 per cent.

divide the *ex ante* surplus or net cost saving with the buyer.) Long-term supply contracts are observed in the mining and energy supply industries, for example, when product is homogeneous, investments are very long term, and transport costs may bind parties together geographically. However, it may be difficult to specify all contingencies or actions that can affect the outcome of a long-term agreement. So a more rudimentary, incomplete, or implicit contract format is often used. This tends to happen in the case of the labour market, where long-term relationship-specific investments are important but hard to specify.

Implicit contracts are informal agreements bound by conversations or understandings which are not enforceable in law. For example, it may be understood that an employer keeps the workforce on in a recession. The *quid pro quo* is that workers are prepared to develop firm-specific skills which are of little value in the outside labour market. One problem with these implicit contracts is that in the event of takeover the new management may break them, laying off workers and white-collar staff, terminating long-standing relationships with banks, suppliers, and other stakeholders. Raiders can expropriate the value of any firm-specific investments made by outsiders. So stakeholders become reluctant to invest in firm-specific skills and products and in that sense become 'short-termist'. They may also demand higher wages and prices to compensate for risk.

This argument is persuasive and begins to articulate many of the worries which commentators have about the short-term horizon of the stock market and the takeover game. Nevertheless, it does leave some questions hanging in the air. First, if short-term contracts split the gross savings, then why not share the investment costs? Second, if implicit contracts are efficient in terms of binding people together in long-term relationships and sharing risk, then why does the new management not continue them? *Per contra*, if they are inefficient, then why doesn't existing management get rid of them? Presumably the raider must have a higher discount rate and value the initial gain more than the incumbent. Yet if that is the case, the bidder's high discount rate is the root cause of short-termism. This suggests that short-termism in the takeover market may be part of a wider capital market problem (Miles 1993).

7.9. A historical perspective

The historical evidence suggests that changes in the competitive nature of the product market, corporate governance, and management discipline do affect corporate, stock market, and macroeconomic performance. Although a formal analysis of the evidence is not possible here, it is worth reviewing the historical trends from the perspective of this chapter on the capital market and managerial discipline. This carries important implications for both competition policy and capital market regulation.

Until the 1950s, hostile bids were quite rare even in the Anglo-Saxon economies.[3] Until then, these countries experienced voluntary amalgamations aimed at eliminating excess capacity rather than inefficient management. The 'merger booms' of the 1890s and 1920s were certainly of this variety. This may have reflected the much greater historical tendency for managers to have large equity stakes in their companies, aligning shareholder interests and making contested takeovers more difficult.

The 1920s boom in the USA and the subsequent recession gave mergers a bad name, resulting in a great deal of antitrust (Smoot–Hartley 1934) and bank (Glass–Steagall 1933) legislation. Stake disclosure rules (which forced large shareholders to declare their holdings) hastened the end of the 'age of the active investor.' This legislation also prevented bank shareholdings. By the 1960s, company boards were largely immune from both competition in the product market and shareholder control. They were dominated by executives rather than non-executives representing shareholders. J. K. Galbraith (1967) and other observers saw them as 'self-perpetuating oligarchies', serving their own interests rather than those of shareholders. Other observers noted the simultaneous increase in trade union power. They argued that this was a consequence of the increase in product market power, which gave the labour force a source of economic rent over which they could bargain with management.

Product market dominance gave these companies strong cashflow. Since US antitrust (and UK monopolies) legislation made vertical integration difficult, this cash was used to secure horizontal integration. Consistent with the views of the managerial school, directors did not maximize shareholder value. Stock markets performed badly, particularly in the USA where the Dow Jones index showed little overall gain during the 1960s and 1970s, despite the high level of inflation. Finance theorists began to argue that it was inappropriate for company management to reinvest dividends and diversify, saying that these important tasks were better performed by shareholders.[4]

---

[3] Contested bids are still very rare in Germany, Japan, and South Korea.

[4] Similar trends were evident in Japan in the 1980s and Korea in the 1990s, where executives overinvested rather than returning money to shareholders.

These adverse governance trends coincided with a general deterioration in the supply side of the economy. By the 1970s, inflation and unemployment had moved up to levels that were very worrying. Although it is hard to unscramble the many factors that were involved in this deterioration, poor industrial management does seem to have been an important contributory factor. However, by the 1980s, takeover bidders had developed ways around the defences of the incumbents and contested bids became commonplace. Consistent with the views of the neoclassical school, there was a marked shift towards value maximization. Raiders found that they could circumvent stake disclosure rules by developing dealing rings that built up large shareholdings and put them 'into play'. By the mid-1980s, these alliances were routinely operating on a transatlantic basis. Raiders were able to finance hostile bids by issuing non-investment-grade 'junk bonds' which were then supported by the cashflows of the victim. The associated interest payments soaked up this cashflow in a particularly tax efficient way. The remaining cashflow was paid out as dividends, boosting the share price, and facilitating further bids.

These techniques allowed huge bids to proceed, making practically every public company in the English-speaking world vulnerable. At the zenith of this takeover boom, hitherto unknown companies were bidding for the titans of industry: Kohlberg Kravis Roberts (KKR) for RJR-Nabisco in the USA and Hoylake for ICI in the UK. Diversification had proceeded to such an extent that these combines were worth considerably less than the sum of their parts, and could be broken up or 'unbundled' at a huge profit. But by the late 1980s, the boom had gone too far and turned to bust. Deal makers put ideas together just to collect fees, without any intrinsic logic. The regulators began to clamp down on corruption, with successful prosecutions being brought against David Levine (see Section 5.6) and Michael Milken (credited with the invention of the junk bond) in the USA; and in the Manpower/Blue Arrow and Distillers cases (see Section 5.6) in the UK.

At the same time, the problems of the Savings and Loan Associations (which had been a big market for high yield bonds) caused a collapse of junk bond values. The failure of Drexel Burnham Lambert in 1989 (the junk bond specialist) spelled the end of the market. Rising interest rates and the recession of the early 1990s also left leveraged companies prone to bankruptcy. Moreover, by that time incumbents had begun to adopt the weapons of their adversaries—a philosophy of high dividends, high leverage, and shareholder value maximization. Efficiency was also boosted by contracting out, demerger (including management buyouts), remerger, and 'downsizing' (a euphemism for redundancies). This all reduced the potential gains to the bidder.

Examples of this response include ICI's demerger of its pharmaceutical arm into Zeneca in its (successful) defence against the Hoylake bid in 1990. Zeneca remerged with the Swedish pharmaceutical company Astra in 1998. A major plank in Northern Electric's defence against the hostile bid from Trafalgar House in 1995 was to return a large sum of money to shareholders financed by a bond issue.[5] More recently, in 1999, NatWest Bank responded to the bids by the Bank of Scotland and the Royal Bank of Scotland by abandoning its own bid for the Legal and General insurance company and divesting itself of Gartmore, a fund manager (see Box 11.3). Despite the promise of similar cost savings and cash handouts to those offered by the Scottish banks, NatWest failed to prevent the bid because it had lost the confidence of investors. Other examples of largely vertical amalgamations, designed to secure cost savings in production and distribution include BP's 1999 takeover of Amoco and Arco in the USA. These voluntary amalgamations have been important in the financial industry, as in the case of Commercial Union and General Accident (British insurance companies which agreed to merge in 1998).

The move to a more contestable market in management over the last two decades has coincided with a major revival in stock market and supply-side performance in the English-speaking world. Again this may be coincidental, but it seems likely that improved managerial performance and the search for shareholder value have played an important role. The correlation between these factors suggests that capital market regulation and competition policy have important macroeconomic implications. The post-war trends suggest that if the regulatory framework allows oligopolistic industries to be run by executives for their own benefit rather than that of stakeholders then this leads to inefficiency on a macroeconomic scale. The Anglo-Saxon market-driven model of capitalism certainly seems to perform badly in this regime, bringing low rates of return for shareholders and general malaise in the economic system. If the committees that regulate corporate governance in these countries fail to make company boards more representative of shareholders it seems

---

[5] This successfully frustrated the Trafalgar bid, but made it apparent to the stock market and more importantly the electricity regulator that financial engineering could be used to secure a large dividend at the expense of the taxpayer. As a result, the regulator realized that the pricing review which had just been completed had been too generous, and this was substantially revised.

imperative that we retain the takeover discipline, despite the risk of capital market corruption and industrial short-termism.

7.10. The empirical evidence

The empirical evidence strongly suggests that takeovers are Pareto-improving in the sense that target shareholders gain significantly, while bidder shareholders do not lose (and may gain). The *ex post* stock market value of the sum is greater than the sum of the *ex ante* values of the parts. This is the central conclusion of two key studies, first a summary of the US evidence by Jensen and Ruback (1983) and second a large sample study of UK takeovers 1955–85 by Franks and Harris (1989). A subsequent analysis by Franks, Harris, and Sheridan (1991) using US and UK data reached similar conclusions. These studies effectively supersede earlier studies which used smaller samples of data and obtained ambiguous results.

Further support for the value maximization school can be found in Shleifer and Vishny (1988, 1989), who find that targets have tended to underperform the market. Their managements are usually replaced following takeover (Martin and McConnel 1991). Nevertheless, Jensen (1993) suggests that disciplinary takeovers were only a minority of those seen in the USA in the 1980s. Franks and Mayer (2000) argue that these disciplinary takeovers are expensive because the costs of changing control are high. Shareholders in the bidder benefit on average from takeovers, but the variance of these gains is high, with about 46 per cent of bidders losing value.

It is important to note that these studies of *ex post* share price gains and losses do allow for the *ex ante* influence which the disciplining effect of takeovers may exert upon managerial behaviour, which is almost impossible to quantify. In principle, these *ex ante* effects should be felt across all public companies and could dwarf any *ex post* announcement gains. This influence might not be entirely beneficial, because as many have argued, the threat of takeover can distract managers and distort their decisions.

Many other issues remain unresolved. In part, this reflects the many different motivations that there are for takeovers. It is not clear, for example, whether share price gains reflect genuine efficiency gains or increases in monopoly power. Historically, as we have argued, market power and the elimination of capacity were the major factors driving

Box 7.1 The UK 'Takeover Code'

In many countries, the takeover process is governed by the courts. However, the UK has a voluntary code of practice, which (apart from the buyout rule) is not enforceable in law. This was originally drawn up by the City Working Party commissioned by the Bank of England in 1959. This established the Takeover Panel to revise, update, and advise on new developments. For example, the panel restricted the use of derivatives following the use of a loophole exploited by Swiss Banking Corporation (SBC) when advising Trafalgar during its bid for Northern Electric in 1995.

The main provisions are:

- Shareholdings of 3 per cent or more must be announced (disclosure rule).
- A holding of 30 per cent makes a public tender offer mandatory. In other words a 30 per cent holding automatically triggers a bid open to all shareholders.
- Tender offers may be 'conditional':
  - 'as to acceptance' level of 50–90 per cent;
  - upon Competition Commission (formerly MMC) inquiry;
  - upon 'no material change' (for example, compensation claims against the company).
- Tender offers must remain open for:
  - 60 days, unless
  - another bidder emerges, in which case the original offer must run for 60 days from that point. For example, BAC originally bid for Vickers Shipbuilding (VSEL) in late 1994, but the bid had to be extended after GEC bid a few weeks later. Similarly the Bank of Scotland's bid for NatWest Bank in November 1999 was extended (until 14 February 2000) by the Royal Bank of Scotland's bid in December.
- Bids cannot be revised after 46 days have elapsed. After that either:
  - the bid lapses and cannot be resurrected for at least three years, or;
  - if a specified level of shareholder acceptances is reached (50–90 per cent, with bidder latitude) the offer goes 'unconditional': either 'wholly unconditional' or subject to 'no material change'.
- The remaining (typically minority) shareholders then have two weeks to accept the final tender price or remain as minority shareholders, unless the 'buyout rule' is activated under section 209 of the 1985 Companies Act. In this case, a majority shareholder with 90 per cent or more of the outstanding share capital can 'buy out' the minority with 10 per cent or less, again at the final tender price.

mergers in the Anglo-Saxon countries and remain so in Japan and Korea. This is another area where regulation becomes important.

7.11. Competition policy and the capital market

The USA has antitrust law in place to prevent the accumulation of market power. These formidable powers are vested in the Federal Trade Commission. In Britain, the government's powers are of a more discretionary nature, being vested in the Secretary of State for Trade and Industry. He or she is advised by departmental advisers as well as the Competition Commission (formerly the Monopoly and Mergers Commission (MMC)). Market power is an important consideration in areas like defence procurement and other areas where there are few major suppliers (GEC and BAe in the UK). However, this market is arguably contestable, since bids from overseas suppliers are able to ensure a fair price. It may not actually matter if there is only one domestic supplier. Similarly, it might be argued that the contestability of their major credit and deposit markets could make the degree of concentration in retail banking tolerable (see Section 11.4).

   This chapter has emphasized the links between the stock price and management behaviour and in particular the need to ensure a contestable market in management through the takeover mechanism. On the evidence of the previous section, the failure of incumbent management to maximize value provides a major motivation for acquisitions. Support for this thesis can be found in recent academic studies, which generally find that despite the premium price paid for the victim, there is little or no tendency for the predator's share price to fall at the time of the bid, or to underperform longer term. This 'stylized fact' suggests that the takeover market is indeed contestable: there is no evidence that bidders underpay; if anything, they overpay. Again, Jensen and Ruback (1983) provide an interesting review of the evidence.

   The analysis of this chapter raises critical questions for both competition policy and capital market regulation. We have looked at these from the perspective of the Anglo-Saxon market-driven model. However, European industrial integration is proceeding at a rapid pace, making it essential to devise a code for cross-border mergers. The problem is that continental financial markets have very different structures and it is hard to think of a one-shoe-fits-all takeover policy. Continental legal and accounting systems have made the capital markets weaker than in the

USA and the UK and have left the banks with a commensurately larger role (La Porta *et al.* 1997, 1998). Shareholdings are much more concentrated. Takeovers usually take the form of voluntary mergers rather than contested bids (Olivetti's bid for Italia Telecom and Vodaphone's play for Mannesmann in 1999 provide the only prominent counterexamples). They are regulated through the courts rather than through a takeover code, making the takeover process much more cumbersome than in the UK.

Although there is no single European model of corporate governance, banks and other stakeholders are generally better represented on company boards on the continent than in the English-speaking world. The takeover mechanism is to this extent less important as a way of regulating executive excess on the continent. Nevertheless, the agglomeration of pan-European companies makes it imperative to devise a competition policy and a takeover code that are appropriate. This is perhaps one of the most challenging tasks that faces the European Commission.

EXERCISES

Question 1. Assume that the ownership of shares in a company is so widespread that it is sensible for individual shareholders to view the probability of a takeover bid being successful as independent of their decision to accept or reject.

(a) What is the best strategy for existing shareholders to follow if a bid is made and they think that the raider can run the firm more efficiently than the incumbent management?

(b) Suppose that if a majority accept the offer the raider will be allowed to buy out the minority at the offer price. Does this change your strategy? Should such a buyout rule exist?

(c) How would you analyse whether a rule that share ownership in excess of 3 per cent should be made public was optimal?

(d) Should it be mandatory that there be sufficient time for competing bids to be made following an initial announcement of a hostile bid? (University of London, Faculty of Economics, B.Sc. (Econ) Financial Economics, Final Examination, 1996)

Question 2. Hostile takeovers are the main source of insider trading. It is in the interests of an efficient allocation of resources that they be banned.' Do you agree?

Question 3. Discuss the pros and cons of encouraging (a) director share dealings and (b) company takeovers as ways of avoiding equity mispricing.

Question 4. In Britain, the financial institutions are 'using the takeover as the corporate governance mechanism of first and last resort' (*Financial Times*, 10 February 2000). Discuss the validity of this opinion.

8. The Theory of Financial Intermediation

The last three chapters have probed the strengths and weaknesses of capital markets. The key observation is that the openness of these media allows them to aggregate information and disseminate it across the community. This is an important function, helping like any price signal to allocate scarce capital, labour, and other resources efficiently. This observation provides an argument for allowing director share transactions, company share buybacks, and the like, even though the presence of such informed agents in the market may reduce liquidity and could cause a false market.

However, as Hirshleifer (1971) shows, its revealing nature can also handicap the capital market. Takeovers offer the best-known example: news often leaks out, allowing the target's share price to reveal a bidder's hand prematurely. News of pharmaceutical discoveries or important product licensing or development deals often leaks out in the same way. Indeed, the equity market may oblige companies to release strategic information about such matters to avoid mispricing and the threat of takeover, or to support new capital issues. Corporate profit warnings, which frequently become necessary to stop overpricing, also give valuable information about trading performance to commercial rivals.

Privately financed companies are not obliged to publish such information. That helps to explain why companies in knowledge-based industries try to remain private as long as they can, despite their need for risk capital. This phenomenon is known as 'information dilution' and is analysed in a recent paper by Bolton and Freixas (1998). Similarly, equity issues reduce the entrepreneur's managerial control, an effect known as 'control dilution'. Venture capital offers an appropriate solution to the problem of information (though not control) dilution, providing finance to the company while making the venture capitalist an insider through managerial involvement. In this case there are no outside shareholders to free ride on the efforts of the investor. There are many well-known examples of large companies (like Richard Branson's Virgin company) which have found the financial reporting and other requirements on a public company too burdensome and have become private companies again.

Table 8.1. Key features of banking and capital markets

	Capital markets	Banking markets
Transparency	Open	Confidential
Typical investors	Small	Large
Contracts	Equity and bond	Loan and deposit

As we have seen, decentralized capital markets have other flaws. Table 8.1 provides a summary. Private investors have an incentive to undertake company research in order to screen investments and seek out capital gain, but have little incentive to monitor company management over the longer term. Moreover, if small shareholders suspect that there is a management problem, the only action for them is to sell their shares or hope that a bidder comes along. Decentralized monitoring is also hard to coordinate. Another problem that we have seen with these markets is that the equity participation contract is not 'incentive efficient'. Finally, the takeover mechanism may not be a very effective discipline for the reasons discussed in the previous chapter.

For capital markets to thrive they need a legal and accounting structure which helps them to overcome these handicaps. If this framework is not in place, intermediaries like banks may have the advantage. As Table 8.1 indicates, banking markets are very different from capital markets in all of these respects and this can give them an edge in some systems.

This chapter looks at ways in which financial intermediaries like banks can use these characteristics to help to resolve the delegation problem. There are currently two main streams of thought in this area. The first approach is based on the observation that, in contrast to capital market relationships which are open, banking relationships are highly confidential. According to this school of thought, banks are given access to inside information, which allows them to finance a company privately, without revealing its trade secrets to the market and—more importantly—its rivals. The second approach is based on the idea that, as large institutions, banks enjoy 'economies of scale and scope'. In particular, there are economies of scale (and scope) in monitoring borrowers and reducing risk through portfolio diversification. Public debt differs from bank debt in all of these respects and is discussed in Section 9.3.

These are of course very old ideas, but this is not just a case of 'old wine in new bottles'. Modern theoretical research deploys these ideas in a novel way, suggesting ways in which intermediation can overcome many of the problems presented by asymmetric information. To quote Bhattacharya and Thakor (1993), two of the exponents of this new approach, 'Intermediation is a response to the inability of market mediated mechanisms to efficiently resolve informational problems.'

8.1. Confidentiality and the banking relationship

This section looks at the first of these ideas. Consider again the problem of security mispricing discussed in Chapter 4. In this case the share price is out of line with the fundamentals (summarized in V^h or V^l) as they are known to the firm's insiders. The insiders could rectify the situation by publishing more information, but will be reluctant to release details of acquisition, development plans, or other information likely to be of strategic importance to commercial rivals. This confidentiality problem was first analysed by Campbell and Krakaw (1980).

A mature business which was generating a lot of cash but undervalued by the market might consider a share buyback. However, this option is not open to small, rapidly growing companies such as are found in new technology-based industries. For similar reasons, it may not be practicable to signal value through high dividend payouts or equity purchases by directors. The alternative is for the firm to enter into a confidential disclosure agreement with a bank. The bank then is a cash-rich company insider that can signal value by letting it be known that it is making a loan to the company. This idea is due originally to Fama (1985) and was pursued by James (1987).

By making the bank privy to its secrets the company drastically reduces the institution's research cost. Over the longer term, the 'customer relationship' can provide the bank with a great deal of valuable information very cheaply. For example, the company's bank account provides an excellent indicator of cashflow and financial viability. Moreover, in this case the research and monitoring cost is centralized, avoiding the problems of decentralization found in the capital market (Chapter 7). The problem of coordinating a response to an *ex post* verification problem like a bankruptcy is also avoided if the bank is the lead investor.

The economic consequences of temporary security mispricing are unlikely to be severe in practice. However, systematic mispricing is likely to have adverse effects on allocation, particularly if product development and investment require new finance. By funding such developments without a public disclosure of commercial information or discounted equity issues, banks may play a particularly useful role.

Recent research on the US system suggests that announcements of such arrangements provide a strong signal to the capital markets of the value to the firm of new projects. That is essentially because the bank lends on fixed (or perhaps floating interest rate) terms, without any upside from equity participation. To do this on a market-related interest margin the bank's experts must perceive little downside risk to the project. The upside gains accrue to shareholders and should be reflected in a higher share price once the deal is announced. Shareholders ought to be prepared to subscribe for new equity issue, helping to finance the project and provide an equity cushion, which helps in turn to protect the bank's investment from downside risk.

This allows the bank and the company to turn the financial free-rider problem to their advantage. In an open capital market, this problem means that it is rarely worthwhile for small shareholders to scrutinize company management. But if the bank is made an insider, the cost is less significant. Shareholders can free ride on bank research, bidding the share price up on a loan announcement in the knowledge that the bank's accountants and experts have scrutinized the application properly. The bank does not mind, because the extra equity provides more of a cushion for its own investment. This underpins the complementarity between bank loans, public bond issues, and equity seen in the financial system. It helps to explain for example why blue chip companies often borrow from banks with poorer credit ratings than they themselves enjoy in the bond market.

8.2. The evidence for the signalling role of bank lending

Clear evidence of these effects can be found in the US financial system. James (1987) analyses the effect of announcements of bank loans to US firms on their share prices. He finds that the average effect in his sample is to increase the share price by 1.5 per cent and that this is statistically significant. This result stands in contrast to studies of public bond issues, which suggest a negative effect on share prices upon announcement.

A subsequent study by Lummer and McConnell (1989) discriminates between loans to new borrowers and changes in the terms relating to loans to existing customers (for example loan maturity and size, covenants, and interest rate mark-ups.) They find that in the case of new customers, the share price effect is insignificant. However, favourable revisions to existing loan arrangements increase share prices by an average of 0.87 per cent, which was significant. Unfavourable revisions have a statistically significant negative effect, reducing the share price by an average of 3.86 per cent. If the revision is precipitated by the action of the borrower the effect is insignificant, but changes undertaken at the lender's initiative reduce the share price by a very significant 7.22 per cent.

Although shareholders are told about bank loan transactions in the UK and Europe, formal announcements are much less common than in the USA. So it is hard to know whether these effects are important in other markets. The US results are nevertheless revealing. They suggest that although banks may not become insiders immediately, an information advantage builds up over time as the 'customer relationship' develops. The complementarity between banking and capital markets helps to explain why even large companies with AAA credit ratings borrow from banks as well as the bond market.

8.3. The Diamond (1984) model

This signalling theory of intermediation makes a good start, but it has its limitations. The statistical tests analyse the one-off announcement of a loan and suggest that intermediation and in particular long-term customer relationships can, as Akerlof (1970) argues, help solve the problem of adverse selection. However, it is not clear that intermediation helps solve the problem of moral hazard and state verification (Table 1.1). A large bank may have some advantage over small investors in monitoring and verification, but the signalling test framework does not throw any light upon this issue. The results suggest that the bank's inside information helps it mitigate the adverse selection problem through initial screening of loan applications, but are largely silent on the moral hazard and verification problems.

Banks may become insiders in an informational sense, but unlike venture capital firms, they do not typically have day-to-day managerial involvement.[1] Nevertheless, because a bank handles the borrower's transactions account it effectively acts as a company's bookkeeper. This puts the bank in an excellent position to monitor its financial behaviour as well as to screen new applications. This is one of the classic 'economies

---

[1] Even in the German system of corporate governance, the presence of *Hausbank* representatives is usually confined to the supervisory board. Japan is, however, exceptional in this respect. Under the keiretsu system, bank appointees invariably sit on the supervisory board and often hold managerial positions.

of scope' or synergies between borrowing and lending business, providing a rationale for the joint provision of these facilities by banks.

In practice, banks need either to monitor managers or set up incentive contracts which ensure that (a) managers' interests are sufficiently aligned with those of the bank to ensure repayment and (b) they represent the outcome truthfully. The second strand of the theory addresses these problems directly, showing how bank loan contracts and scale economies help to solve the agency problem which lies behind these difficulties.

8.4. Economies of scale in monitoring borrowers

The second strand in this literature starts with the paper by Diamond (1984). This article provides a sophisticated version of the standard portfolio diversification argument, which depends upon risk pooling within a bank's loan book. It relies heavily upon the fixed rate/term structure of bank loan and deposit contracts and the observation that centralized monitoring of borrowers is efficient. It does *not* depend upon the signalling role of bank lending since lender–borrower relationships, including loan terms, are assumed to be completely confidential. Indeed, there are no equity investors in this model at all.

It is reasonable to consider debt instruments as 'safe' if the borrower has plenty of collateral. However, in practice borrowers typically do not have much capital, which is why they need to borrow in the first place. This deficiency can expose the lender to downside risk. Diamond crystallizes this issue by assuming that borrowers do not have any collateral. The bank does not have any collateral either, but finances its loan portfolio by fixed-term, fixed-rate deposits which resemble the loan contract. In effect, the depositors just delegate the problem of monitoring the borrower to the bank.

The problem of bank runs, which stems from the instant access facility which retail banks typically offer depositors, is avoided by assuming that bank liabilities are term deposits, as they usually are for an investment bank. The problem of bank runs and systemic risk is the subject of the Diamond and Dybvig (1983) article, discussed in Chapter 10.

Diamond's (1984) analysis starts from the idea that as soon as anyone makes a loan, this sets up an agency problem with moral hazard and verification costs. The borrower then acts as the agent of the lender since the lender's return depends upon the behaviour of the borrower. Even if a bank can efficiently screen customers when deciding loan applications, it will have to either monitor the behaviour of borrowers or devise a contract structure which is incentive-efficient, ensuring efficiency and truthfulness.

Both of these devices have their drawbacks. Because there is no collateral to forfeit, incentive structures involve non-financial penalties like bankruptcy or prison which are socially wasteful. If a lender monitors instead, competitors in the banking industry, like equity investors, will be able to free ride on this effort. If several lenders make loans to the same borrower, they may find it difficult to coordinate. They may all duplicate each other's monitoring efforts. On the other hand, they may all rely upon each other's monitoring effort, so that no one actually supervises the borrower. Banks are little different from other investors in this respect.

In the Diamond model a large bank solves these informational problems at a stroke by taking the firm off-market and becoming the sole provider of capital. This takes the form of a short-term loan promising a fixed return, financed by deposits with a similar structure. This delegated monitoring arrangement appears to resolve the problem of monitoring lenders, but actually puts it at one remove, because the depositors (acting as principal) have to make sure that the bank (now acting as the agent) is being run properly. They have to either set up an appropriate incentive structure or monitor the bank. This agency cost is called the delegation cost. Because they are assumed to be small, all of the problems of supervisory coordination return. Indeed, there is potentially a double layer of agency costs, since the borrower is the agent of the bank which is in turn the agent of the depositors.

Nevertheless, Diamond shows that if appropriate penalty clauses are built into deposit contracts, this arrangement is incentive-efficient: the bank behaves efficiently and honestly. Furthermore, diversification means that the expected value of the penalty costs becomes negligible as the size of bank increases. Since the bank is more efficient at monitoring borrowers than the decentralized depositors and since the delegation cost is negligible, intermediation provides a neat resolution of the informational problem.

8.4.1. Decentralized loan contracts

We now analyse a simplified version of the Diamond (1984) model. He shows that the deposit and loan contracts are optimal, while I take this for granted. The underlying assumptions are:

1. There are n borrowers each with a project requiring capital of $I > 1$.
2. There are N lenders each with wealth $= 1$ to lend (so $N > n$).
3. Lenders are not risk averse.
4. Project returns are identically and independently distributed.
5. $L \geq I =$ loan repayment promised by each firm (not necessarily achieved).
6. Borrowers do not have personal capital which they can invest in project as forfeit.
7. Borrowers have private knowledge of their own effort and returns.
8. Y is the *ex post* yield of project declared by the borrower, so the actual loan repayment is $r = \min(L, Y)$.
9. $\pi = \pi(L)$ is the probability of individual borrower default, provided that
10. Lender monitors/audits each borrower at cost K, or imposes penalty with a monetary equivalent of P for debt default: $(L \geq R)$.

In order to see the implications of this model we compare the efficiency of decentralized lending with that of centralized (bank) lending. First note that $I > 1$, which means that there are more lenders than borrowers ($N > n$). This is a key (but arguably realistic) assumption. Also, (3) lenders are not risk averse and so do not diversify across projects because this increases the number of loans in their portfolio and hence under (10) the monitoring cost. Assumption (4) means that there is no adverse selection in this model, only moral hazard and *ex post* verification cost.

Under assumption (10) there are two alternative ways of ensuring effort and honesty on the part of borrowers in a decentralized system. The first is for each investor to lend to a single borrower and police at cost K. The second is for lenders to collectively inflict the penalty cost P on a borrower if repayment $r < L$.

Assumption (6) means that the punishment is a non-financial penalty.[2] Because this is a net cost to society and not a transfer payment like a fine, this is wasteful. For example, imprisonment involves a loss of freedom and income for the prisoner as a maintenance cost to the rest of society. Moreover, to deal with dishonest borrowers, P has to be at least equivalent to L to ensure that it is optimal for a borrower to be honest when $Y > L$. If $P < L$ then the borrower can make a gain of $L - P$ by falsely declaring $Y = 0$. Similarly, if $P < L$ then the borrower can make a gain of $L - P$ by simply running off with L. The laws of fraud and theft respec-

---

[2] For petty crime, 'community service' may provide an alternative to fines which effectively takes the form of a transfer payment.

tively must be tough enough (and the probability of conviction high enough) to ensure incentive efficiency in these cases.

This still leaves the lender exposed to moral hazard. This could take the form of slacking or shirking by the manager, but in the case of fixed interest contracts excessive risk-taking is potentially more problematic, as the next chapter shows. This is a 'non-contractual wealth transfer' and as such is not illegal. However, the law of contract provides a way of dealing with this by allowing lenders to stipulate what the loan is used for, and by writing in covenants which protect their investment.

I will use a special interpretation of the Diamond model in which the criminal law is sufficient to deter dishonesty and the lender is only concerned about moral hazard. Lenders can avoid this and maximize the probability of repayment by either monitoring at cost K or by imposing a penalty P in bankruptcy. Debtor's prison gives an obvious historical example of such a penalty. For a modern financial system, the stigma of bankruptcy is assumed to be sufficient to ensure efficiency and prevent excessive risk-taking. Loss of earnings owing to the business handicap of bankruptcy might be an added punishment.

Lenders and borrowers agree to the monitoring or 'policing' method if this has the lowest social cost:

$$\text{total decentralized monitoring cost} = NK < nP\pi$$
$$= \text{expected penalty cost.}$$

Otherwise (if $NK > nPp$) they agree to the punishment approach. Because the number of lenders is large relative to the number of borrowers, this loads the dice in favour of the latter in the decentralized system. Either way, these costs are a deadweight cost to society.

8.4.2. Quis custodiet custodes?

Now consider the situation of a single bank in a contestable market. The bank also incurs cost of K for monitoring each borrower. But because $N > n$ it is cheaper for the bank to monitor incur costs of nK by policing n firms than for N lenders to incur NK by monitoring their own loans. The bank avoids lender duplication and solves the monitoring coordination problem efficiently.

It remains possible that the decentralized penalty solution is even more cost-effective than bank monitoring:

$$NK > nK > nP\pi,$$
$$\text{i.e. } IK > K > P\pi, \tag{8.1}$$

Table 8.2. Cost effectiveness in policing or punishing borrowers

Method/level	Decentralized	Centralized
Policing	NK	$> nK$
Punishment	$nP\pi$	$= nP\pi$

in which case lenders and borrowers agree to use the punishment system and that is the end of the story. However, because P is likely to be large relative to K, the policing method is likely to be cost-effective: $K < P\pi$. If this is the case, then banks have a cost advantage at this stage.

8.5. Portfolio diversification

Introducing a layer of intermediation brings its own costs: ultimate lenders must either monitor the bank or inflict a punishment for default. This is the delegation cost. Assume conformably with (6) that:

6'. there is no bank equity stake.

Although nL is the total repayment of loans promised to the bank by ultimate borrowers, the concavity of the relationship describing each repayment as a function of Y, means that the bank is likely to get less than this.[3] Let $X = E[R] = E[\min(L, Y)] < L$ be the expected value of a single repayment. Then, because the expectation of a sum is the sum of the expectations, the bank can expect to get nX in total. Deducting the total monitoring cost nK gives:

5'. $n(X - K) =$ total repayment bank can realistically promise depositors *ex ante*.

Subtracting the net funds available to the bank *ex post* $(\Sigma_i R_i - nK)$ gives the shortfall: $nX - \Sigma_i R_i$. The bank is in default if this is strictly positive. Now assume conformably with (10) that:

10'. $\bar{P} =$ punishment inflicted on bank for default. To maintain the bank's efficiency we need $\bar{P} \geq nP$.

Under these assumptions the probability of bank default is:

9'. $\bar{\pi} = \text{prob}(nX - \Sigma_i R_i > 0) = \text{prob}(X - \Sigma_i R_i/n > 0)$.

---

[3] The effect of concavity and convexity in loan markets is analysed more systematically in the next chapter.

Importantly, X is the probability limit (plim) of $\Sigma_i R_i/n$. In other words as n tends to infinity the average $\Sigma_i R_i/n$ converges on X for sure.[4] The implication is that, provided the depositors threaten the bank with $\bar{P}$ for default to ensure honesty, the bank will never default. This means that we can forget about the delegation cost because we can make its expected value as small as we like by increasing the scale of the bank and reducing the probability of default by diversification. Whether intermediation is effective or not depends simply upon whether the bank's costs (as the most efficient monitor) of nK are less than the expected penalty cost $n\pi P$, which just depends upon the cost of monitoring one borrower being less than the expected penalty cost per borrower: (8.1).

In this representation of the model I have assumed for simplicity that penalty costs take the form of a lump sum. Diamond assumes that the monetary equivalent of any punishment was exactly equal to the scale of the financial shortfall. In the immortal words of Gilbert and Sullivan, he makes the punishment fit the crime. However, if intermediation is cost-effective, punishment simply acts to deter bad bank behaviour and is never deployed. It is akin to the dilution factor of the Grossman and Hart (1980) model used in the previous chapter. The precise nature of the punishment structure is irrelevant provided that it is large enough to prevent moral hazard.

Similarly, this model just identifies the lowest social cost option without saying what the final incidence of these costs will be. It is reasonable to think that because one large borrower negotiates with many small lenders, the lenders will end up footing the bill. So, for example, if the most cost-effective option is for lenders to transact directly with borrowers, using the threat of punishment to ensure good behaviour, they must give the borrowers *ex ante* payments to compensate for the expected value of the punishment. However, the way in which the social costs are divided up does not really matter.

8.6. Extending the basic model

Unless borrowers have capital which they can pledge as collateral, fixed rate instruments are prone to downside risk. The Diamond (1984) paper

---

[4] Technically: $\lim_{n \to 0} \text{prob}(X - \Sigma_i R_i/n > 0) = 0$. That is because $E[\Sigma_i R_i/n] = X$ and the central limit theorem tells us that because this is the average of a sum of independent variables, the variance goes to zero as n tends to infinity.

crystallizes this problem by assuming that neither borrowers nor banks have capital to forfeit. Instead he assumes a punishment structure which makes debt and deposit contracts optimal.[5] Individual loans are subject to downside risk, but diversification within the bank's loan book makes deposits risk-free. Consequently, there is no need for a regulator in the Diamond model.

Diamond's model shows how a large intermediary can provide an efficient centralized solution to the problems posed by asymmetric information in the financial system. It assumes that lending risks are independent and the intermediary can be effectively punished for failure. The extra layer of cost from delegating the monitoring role to the intermediary can be reduced to arbitrarily small proportions by increasing its size. The gains from diversification and delegation are not as powerful if project returns are correlated but they still work in favour of large intermediaries.

This paper has generated an extensive literature on the efficacy of delegated monitoring. Subsequent papers go well beyond the assumptions of the original article. For example, as Bhattacharya and Thakor (1993) show, centralized monitoring can alternatively be explained by investor risk-aversion. This causes investors to diversify across more than one borrower, increasing the decentralized monitoring cost. Even if the penalty cost mechanism is not effective, the scale effect can sustain an equilibrium in which it is efficient for the depositors to monitor the bank and for the bank to monitor the borrowers.[6] The cost-effectiveness of this centralized monitoring method is enhanced if it is easier for investors to monitor the bank (typically a large, well-known Plc) than the borrower (typically a small private firm or individual). As remarked earlier, the bank's inside track may make it better at monitoring and audit than a private investor.

This literature provides a very useful framework for thinking about the theoretical effect of economies of scale in banking. However, to the extent that it relies upon non-financial penalty costs rather than collateral it must be treated with caution. Non-financial penalties like debtor's prison have been important enforcement devices historically, but are not a

---

[5] This part of the model builds upon work by Townsend (1978) which analyses the optimality of debt contracts and is taken further by Gale and Hellwig (1985) and Grossman and Hart (1986).

[6] For example, suppose that risk aversion causes the decentralized investor to lend to two borrowers. Also suppose that $N = 10n$. Then the decentralized monitoring cost is $2KN$, while the total intermediation cost is $(N + n)K = 1.1NK < 2NK$. Intermediation is again cost-effective. Also, the degree of diversification is likely to be much greater in the case of a diversified bank portfolio than the two-asset portfolio held by the decentralized investor.

feature of a modern financial system. Bankruptcy may have a significant non-financial cost and this may help prevent moral hazard (as in my interpretation of the model), but it is unrealistic to think that this stigma is sufficient to deter dishonesty. Ultimately, this deterrent has to be provided by the criminal law. Efficiency and truth-telling have to be encouraged by making sure that banks and other borrowers have their own money at stake. In practice, it may be necessary for there to be a regulator to ensure that banks are adequately capitalized. We examine this idea in Chapter 11.

The next chapter looks at some of the phenomena which can be found in debt markets when there is no collateral and no non-financial penalty. Section 9.4 discusses the different attributes of bank and public debt: loan instruments like bond term corporate bonds that are issued in the capital market. In the case of public debt, the markets are open and investors may be small and uncoordinated. This makes the public bond markets very different from both equity and banking markets.

EXERCISES

The customer relationship

Question 1. Consider the period of time over which you have had your current bank account and the information about your financial affairs that this gives your bank manager. What bearing do you think this would have if you applied for a new personal loan? Now consider the kind of questions you would be asked (and references you would have to provide) if you applied for a loan from a new lender. Do you think someone with (a) a good and (b) a poor relationship with their bank would stand a better chance with the new lender? How is this likely to affect the sample of borrowers attracted by new entrants to the loan market?

Financial intermediation under the binomial distribution

Question 2. Use the Diamond (1970) intermediation model to answer the following problems.

(a) An Internet entrepreneur can invest £3 million in a project. She will get a return of £17 million with a probability of 50 per cent, nothing otherwise. What is her expected rate of return?

> The expected payoff is £17 million $\times$ 0.5 = £8.5 million and the rate of return is $(8.5 - 3)/3$ or 183 1/3 per cent.

(b) This entrepreneur has no collateral and needs to borrow the £3 million cost.

The risk-free interest rate is zero. Venture capital investors are indifferent to risk but each has only £300,000 of capital to invest. They can only ensure that the distribution of returns is as described in (a) either (i) by each incurring a non-financial monitoring cost equivalent to £125,000 or (ii) by jointly inflicting a non-financial penalty worth £4 million upon the entrepreneur if she defaults. Show that method (i) is the most cost-effective way of securing this distribution of returns.

> In this case $n = 1$, $N = 10$. The default probability is 0.5 and the expected penalty cost of £2m exceeds the total monitoring cost of £1.25m $= N \times 125,000$.

(c) Calculate (i) the breakeven interest rate which lenders would have to charge to compensate for this cost and recoup their initial investment and (ii) the breakeven share of the payoff required by an equity investor.

> Each lender needs to recover £850,000 if the project is successful, to generate an expected payback of £425,000 $= 0.5 \times$ £0.85m and offset the investment and monitoring costs. This means building in an interest rate charge of 550/300 or 183 1/3 per cent. An equity contract which gave investors (in total) a 50 per cent share of the payoff would give the same result.

(d) Are there any problems with this monitoring approach?

> The problem is that coordination is difficult—lenders may assume that others are monitoring, making it possible that no one monitors.

(e) Suppose that a bank has enough capital to finance two entrepreneurs, raising deposits from twenty investors. They are as described in (a) and (b), and the payoffs on their two projects are independently distributed. It can monitor each entrepreneur for the equivalent of £125,000, only a tenth of the total monitoring cost under b(i). However, the bank's effective performance has to be ensured by either (i) monitoring at a cost equivalent to £125,000 per depositor or (ii) inflicting a non-financial penalty with a monetary value of £8 million in the event of default. The bank has no collateral and uses standard deposit and loan contracts. Taking into account the monetary value of the bank's monitoring and penalty costs, show that under (ii) the breakeven interest rate charges are 33 1/3 per cent for deposits and 175 per cent for loans.

> If an entrepreneur is successful the bank gets a payoff of £8.25m (275 per cent of £3m or 3 × 11/12m) and nothing otherwise. Half of the time only one will be successful. In this case the bank receives £8.25m, which is just enough to pay the depositors the £8m total promised (133 1/3 per cent of £6m) and compensate the bank for the total monitoring cost equivalent of £125,000 per project. A quarter of the time both will be successful, the bank will receive £16.5m, pay depositors £8m and keep £8.25m, worth £8m after monitoring costs. The rest of the time both will fail, the depositors will get nothing, the bank will experience a non-financial penalty worth £8m and monitoring costs of £250,000. The table shows the pattern of gains and losses in these cases.

Project successes	Prob.	Bank receives	Bank pays	Other costs	Net	Depositors get	Depositors pay	Net
2	1/4	16.50	8.00	0.25	8.25	8	6	2
1	1/2	8.25	8.00	0.25	0.00	8	6	2
0	1/4	0	0	8.25	−8.25	0	6	−6
Expected value					0.00	6	6	0

Overall, the depositors and the bank break even. Entrepreneurs gain £17m less payments of £8.25m if successful, with an expected value of £4,375,000. This is £125,000 more than in the decentralized case, reflecting the lower interest rate charge.

(f) Is this intermediation cost-effective?

Yes. This is indicated by the net gain made by the entrepreneur. We can check by comparing the total expected non-financial cost. In (e) this is £2.25m or £1.125m per entrepreneur. This compares with £1.25m under b(i). Intermediation works because monitoring is centralized and risk pooling with $n = 2$ lowers the bank failure rate to 1/4, from 1/2 for an individual entrepreneur.

(g) What would happen to the breakeven and bank failure rates if the number of depositors and entrepreneurs became very large?

The total payment to the bank has a Bernoulli (or binomial) distribution. If n is the number of entrepreneurs and s the number that are successful, then the expected value of the fraction s/n is 1/2. The variance of s is $p(1 - p)n$ and the variance of the fraction s/n is thus $p(1 - p)/n = 1/(4n)$. This vanishes as n increases. Consequently, the bank can afford to offer entrepreneurs loans at an interest charge 133 1/3 per cent, while the bankruptcy and breakeven deposit rates become negligibly small.

Financial intermediation under the normal distribution

Question 3. An entrepreneur wants to borrow £1 million to invest in a project promising a mean return of £1.3 million with a standard deviation of £0.1 million. These returns are normally distributed.

(a) What is the probability of the return being enough to repay the £1 million principal L plus interest r at 10 per cent?

When variables are normally distributed we set up a Z-variable which shows the number of critical standard deviations σ. Then we look up the probability of this event in a table of the cumulative normal density. In this case we find the number of standard deviations the project return can fall below the mean μ before a shortfall on $L(1 + r)$ occurs:

$$Z_1 = [\mu - L(1 + r)]/\sigma = [1.3 - 1.1]/0.1 = 2.$$

The standard tables show that the probability of this happening is $\pi = 0.0228$, about 1 in 44.

(b) Now consider a bank that has £10 million of deposits and invests £1 million in ten such projects. If the returns on these projects are statistically independent then what is the probability that the bank will be able to meet a repayment of principal and interest to depositors of £11 million?

> It may look as if everything is scaled up by a factor of ten. That is true of loan and mean return values and hence the numerator in the Z-ratio. However, the variance of a sum of independently distributed variables equals the sum of the individual variances. Consequently, the variance of the return to ten independent projects is ten times the variance of a single project and the standard deviation (the square root of variance) is only 3.16 times that for a single project. The denominator thus increases by a factor of 3.16. The new Z-ratio is thus
>
> $$Z_{10} = 10 \times [\mu + L(1 + r)]/3.16 \times \sigma = [13 - 11]/0.316 = 6.33.$$
>
> This value is so high that it is not reported in the standard tables; that is, the probability of a shortfall is negligibly small.

(c) Suppose that borrowers are as described in (a). Lenders are indifferent to risk but each has only £100,000 of capital to lend. They can only ensure that the distribution of returns is as described in (a) either (i) by incurring a monitoring cost of £1,000 per lender or (ii) by jointly inflicting a non-financial penalty worth £100,000 per entrepreneur in the event of failure to repay in full. Assume that the monitoring costs will be passed on to the borrower and that penalties are a deadweight loss. Show that method (ii) is the most cost-effective way of securing this distribution of returns.

> In this case, $n = 1$, $N = 10$, and from (a) $\pi = 0.0228$. So for each borrower:
>
> $$\text{Monitoring cost} = 10 \times 1,000 = 10,000 > 2,280 = 0.0228 \times 100,000$$
> $$= E[\text{penalty}].$$

(d) Now suppose that the bank in (b) can also monitor each entrepreneur for £1,000. That obviously results in savings compared with c(i) and c(ii). But the bank's effective performance has also to be ensured by either a monitoring cost of £1,000 per depositor or a penalty of £1 million in the event of a failure to repay the £1.1 million in full. Is this intermediary cost-effective?

> First establish that the bank monitors the borrowers:
>
> $$\text{Bank monitoring cost} = 1,000 < 2,280 = 0.0228 \times 100,000 = E[\text{penalty}].$$
>
> Then note that if depositors threaten to punish the bank, the likelihood of this happening is effectively zero (result (b)). So the total cost under intermediation is just the bank monitoring cost of £1,000 per borrower, which is less than the minimum cost under decentralized lending of £2,280 (result (c)).

Financial intermediation and capital markets

Question 4. Explain how asymmetric information can adversely affect the operation of the capital market. Can financial intermediaries resolve this problem more efficiently? (University of London, Faculty of Economics, B.Sc. (Econ) Financial Economics, Final Examination, 1999)

Question 5. Why does so much finance get channelled through financial intermediaries rather than the capital markets, even in the USA and the UK?

Question 6. How can the confidential nature of their business help financial intermediaries to win business from large firms? When can a bank loan agreement act as a signal to the capital markets? (University of London, Faculty of Economics, B.Sc. (Econ) Financial Economics, Final Examination, 1999).

9. Convexity, Excessive Risk and Bank Regulation

The previous chapter showed how non-financial penalties could achieve incentive efficiency in a debt-financed system without collateral. However, in practice, the likelihood of detection and prosecution may not be a sufficient deterrent to financial crime. Moreover, non-financial penalties may not be enough to prevent moral hazard. Capital requirements are normally essential to support honesty and effort in financial markets, and banking markets are no exception. Indeed, their deposit liabilities can encourage banks to take excessive risks because borrowers exclusively enjoy the fruits of successful outcomes, while their creditors share the cost of failure. This is essentially due to the 'convexity' of the payoff to borrowers once a loan agreement is signed, and is a form of moral hazard.

This chapter looks at moral hazard in the bank loan and public bond markets and the ways in which investors in these markets can protect themselves from it. We take up a point first made in Chapter 7, which discussed various ways in which shareholders could align company directors' interests with their own. It was noted that if these devices are effective, they align manager interests with those of shareholders and not those of debtholders (or depositors). These mechanisms set up another agency problem, with the shareholder/managers acting as the agent of bondholders and others who have fixed claims on the company.

9.1. The agency cost of debt finance

A simple model can be used to illustrate the potential for moral hazard when managers align themselves with shareholders and there are fixed claims upon the firm. This apparatus shows what happens to the value of fixed claims (like bonds, loans, and deposits) and residual claims (like shares) if there are no default penalties and managers can influence the riskiness of a business or project. Assume that profits (Y) are verifiable. But for simplicity assume that the borrower has no equity, and that the loan principal (I) finances the whole of the project.

Figure 9.1 shows the payoff functions for fixed and residual claimants. The continuous lines show the payout ρ to debtholders. This is equal to L provided that Y is enough to finance this. Otherwise it is equal to Y:

$$\rho = \min(L, Y). \tag{9.1}$$

This is a concave function, because a line drawn between any two points on this structure always lies *below* it. The 'yardstick' shaped schedule lying below this shows the payoff π to shareholders. They get nothing if $Y < L$, but otherwise get the surplus:

$$\pi = \max(0, Y - L). \tag{9.2}$$

This yardstick is the same as that used to describe the terminal value of a call option with an exercise price of L on a security worth Y. This is a similarity which I will draw upon extensively. This sort of structure is convex, because a line drawn between any two points on this function lies everywhere *above* it.

Now consider two investments, both financed by loans promising to repay principal and interest of L. The residual value goes to shareholders.

Project A: This yields $Y = L$ for sure. Therefore debtholders are always repaid L and shareholders never get anything.

Project B: This returns Y_1 and Y_2 each with equal probability, where $Y_1 < I < \bar{Y} < Y_2$ as shown in Figure 9.1. Importantly, the average return is the same as in project A: $(Y_1 + Y_2)/2 = \bar{Y} = L$, where $\theta = (Y_1 - Y_2)$ is

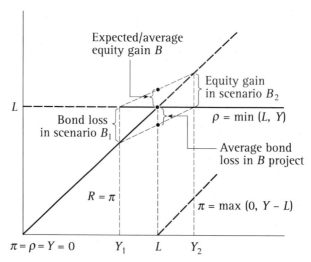

Figure 9.1 Convexity and the returns to equity and debt

known as the 'spread'. In this case, if $Y = Y_1 < L$ then bonds only get Y_1. Equities still get nothing. Otherwise, bonds get paid L in full while shares get the surplus $Y_2 - L > 0$.

It is important to see that with project B, bondholders lose (relative to project A), while equities gain. This illustrates the fundamental principle that risk transfers value from debtholders to equity holders. Moreover, the bigger the spread, the bigger is the transfer of value. Mathematically, this follows from the fact that the expected value of a concave function of a random variable falls as the dispersion or risk increases. This is why expected utility (a concave function of consumption) falls when uncertainty about consumption increases. The opposite happens for a convex function, which is why the value of a call option (a convex function of the underlying security price) increases with the variance of the security price.

In this example, shareholders get a payoff in the 'good' state if project B is selected. Substituting Y_2 into their payoff function (9.2) and multiplying by the probability of $1/2$ gives the expected payoff:

$$E[\pi_B] = \max(0, Y_2 - L)/2 = (Y_2 - L)/2 = \theta/4 > E[S_B] = 0. \qquad (9.3)$$

The transfer of expected value $E[\pi_B]$ is proportional to the spread in this case. Remember that the mean return of the two investments is the same, so the move from project A to B is a 'mean-preserving increase in spread'. This is a particular kind of shift in the probability distribution which makes extreme outcomes more likely, and always has the effect of increasing the value of a security (like an equity or a call option) with a convex payoff structure and reducing the value of one (like a bond or debt instrument) with a concave structure. The financial implications of convexity are very important, particularly in the area of bank regulation.

9.2. Asset substitution (or excessive risk-taking)

Although equity and call option contracts are similar in having a convex payoff structure, there is an important difference between them. In the case of a call option, it is reasonable to assume that the holder cannot influence the riskiness or variance of the underlying security. Yet manager-shareholders *are* in a position to influence the riskiness or variance of the underlying business. They have a clear incentive to increase the degree of risk, because that boosts the theoretical value of the shares by transferring value from bondholders. This phenomenon is known in the corporate finance literature as 'asset substitution', because management has an incentive to substitute high-risk projects for low-risk ones once a debt is incurred. Convexity can encourage manager-owners with debt liabilities to undertake risky projects that have negative social value, because they neglect the negative effect on bondholder value. This is known as 'excessive risk-taking' in the banking literature.

Executive share options, which are valued as convex functions of convex pay-off functions, may amplify this effect. The effect can also be exaggerated by capital loss, which reduces the collateral, reputation, or other investments which the manager may have invested in the project, and hence the weight attached to low outcomes. As this stake is reduced towards zero, the manager has nothing to lose, and is tempted into increasingly risky positions as a way of increasing the chances of recovery. This is the slippery slope which can turn security dealers into 'rogue traders', making it important to monitor their trading positions closely. Nick Leeson, the trader who broke Barings Bank in 1996, is one of many examples.

Company managers can transfer value in more subtle ways. For example, they can neglect the maintenance of company assets and other factors which support the value of the firm in bankruptcy, when ownership passes to fixed claimants. (In the context of our simple model, they would adopt a policy that boosted Y_2 at the expense of Y_1.) Managers have an incentive to declare artificially high earnings and dividends. This has the effect of reducing collateral and increasing the probability of default, at the expense of fixed claimants.

9.3. Moral hazard, bond covenants, and the accounting system

There are various ways in which lenders and other creditors of the firm can protect themselves from moral hazard. For example, a closer alignment of interests can sometimes be achieved by manager/shareholder loan collateral (a device most often used by banks) and the issuance of convertible bonds (bonds with share purchase options). These devices have to be buttressed by efficient monitoring or accounting procedures.

In the case of a public bond issue, the investment bank sponsoring the issue will usually attempt to protect its bond investors from any value transfer by writing covenants into the prospectus that limit the scope for asset substitution and the issuance of new debt. Standard covenants prevent the firm from paying a dividend which is not covered by the company's earnings. Cashflow covenants require the firm to trade at a profit. Net value covenants prevent the firm from trading unless its assets exceed its fixed liabilities. A survey of covenants most frequently found in the USA is provided by Smith and Warner (1979). In the absence of these injunctions, the firm and its shareholders effectively have an option which allows them to trade on in the hope of recovery until the situation is so dire that it is no longer worth putting equity into the company in a reorganization (Mella-Barral and Perraudin 1996).

It is the bond investor's responsibility to ensure that these covenants are adhered to. This requires an element of monitoring which can only be realistically done with an objective set of accounts, describing trading profits, earnings, and net worth on a standardized basis. If the company's accounts can be fudged, the covenants become meaningless. Consequently, although an effective accounting system is not necessary for bond investors to overcome the verification problem, it is necessary to buttress any covenants used to minimize moral hazard.

9.4. Bank loan and public debt instruments

Formal covenants are much less common in the case of bank loans. Instead, banks find other ways to protect their investments from bad borrower behaviour. If it can, a bank will protect a loan by collateral or securing it against specific assets, both of which are difficult to organize to support a bond issue. A bank will typically rely on an informal client agreement or understanding that can be monitored effectively from its position as bookkeeper. It does not need to rely upon standard covenants and accounting conventions as a bondholder does.

The long-term benefits of the customer relationship are such that a borrower is unlikely to prejudice this through bad behaviour. Indeed, as Section 2.6 suggested, the long-term nature of lending relationships means that reputations and repeat purchases (in the form of future loans) play an important dynamic role. This point is particularly relevant in the case of high-growth companies with intangible assets that cannot be pledged as collateral. It is also relevant in the case of sovereign (international government) debt. In this situation, there is no collateral and no punishment other than exclusion from future borrowing. Eaton and Gersovitz (1981) show how these reputational effects can sustain an equilibrium in the sovereign debt market. Diamond (1989) shows how firms establish reputations for being good borrowers.

Bank loans are typically short term, allowing them to be renegotiated or rescheduled more flexibly than public bond issues. Moreover, as noted in the previous chapter, bond investors tend to be smaller than banks. This also makes it easier to renegotiate a bank loan. Shleifer and Vishny (1997) argue that the problem of coordinating small lenders makes public debt a much tighter discipline upon company managers than bank debt. This is the reverse of the situation in the equity market, where, as we saw in Chapter 7, a large investor usually has more control over management than a lot of small shareholders.

The choice between public and bank debt has been modelled by Bolton and Freixas (1998), who set up a theoretical structure in which companies can finance themselves by issuing equity, public debt, or by borrowing from a bank. Equity issues involve information loss and dilute control. In this model, the bank has the inside track and can afford to be more flexible than bondholders when a company gets into trouble, but the cost of intermediation makes bank debt more expensive than bond finance. In equilibrium, small companies which need a sympathetic lender tend to rely upon bank finance despite the cost, while larger companies use the bond market. These observations have important implications for the structure of the financial system, and are discussed in Section 12.2.

9.5. Creditor protection

Company law provides another important safeguard against shareholder exploitation of creditors. The degree of creditor and debtor protection varies internationally. La Porta *et al.* (1997) provide an excellent review. The surveys by Harris and Raviv (1991) and Allen and Winton (1995) discuss the implications for the capital structure of a commercial firm.

The general conclusion of these surveys is that debtor protection in the USA is relatively strong, forcing bondholders to rely upon the covenant mechanism. There is a tradition of debtor protection in the English-speaking countries which can be traced back to the Magna Carta of 1215. In the case of the USA, Chapter 11 of the 1978 Bankruptcy Reform Act affords business debtors who are in default some protection from creditors because it allows managers to apply to the courts for time to restructure the business. (In contrast, Chapter 10 of the previous (1898) Bankruptcy Act provided for trustees to take over the management of a defaulting firm.) Many commentators have argued that this provision can be abused by borrowers, and that creditor protection is too weak. This in turn makes creditors reluctant to lend and increases corporate bond yields. However, public bond issues are a much more important source of finance for companies in the USA than in other countries (see Section 12.2).

British legislation on the other hand is currently inclined if anything in favour of creditors. The 1986 Insolvency Act greatly strengthened the creditor's position by bringing in two basic tests of insolvency: defined as 'a company's ability to pay its debts as they fall due'. Under the first (cash-flow or liquidity) test, 'a company is unable to pay its debts if it cannot pay them as they fall due out of cash or readily realizable assets' (section 123(1)). This criterion is relatively straightforward. Proof by the creditor that his debt has not been paid is *prima facie* evidence that the company is insolvent (Pennington 1995).

Under the alternative test, 'a company is unable to pay its debts if the value of its assets is less than the amount of its liabilities, taking contingent and prospective liabilities into account as well as its debts which are immediately payable' (section 123(2)). Under this criterion, a company is 'unable to pay its debts if it has no reasonable prospect of paying all of them by a ready realization of all its assets, and in applying this test it will be immaterial that the company can pay its accrued debts out of its liquid resources' (Pennington 1995). This rule involves complex accounting and valuation issues, on both the asset and the liability side (see, for example, the discussion of Goode 1997).[1] There is a complementarity between the legal and accounting systems here as elsewhere.

The UK government has set up an HM Treasury–DTI working party to consider the working of the insolvency law and in particular the view that it should be made more like the US one that allows a chance for companies to restructure before creditors move in. (The Company Director Disqualification Act is also being reassessed, with the idea of removing some of the stigma attached to bankruptcy.) The US Congress appears to be moving in the opposite direction and is considering legislation to make it more difficult for borrowers to resist the demands of creditors.

---

[1] The 1986 Act also includes an important safeguard (section 8(1)) against directors and share-holders who (in the style of the Mella-Barral and Perraudin 1996 paper) know that the firm is trading at a loss which is likely to be sustained, but who nevertheless inject capital in the hope of recovery. Creditors can petition the courts for an administration order 'if the company is likely to begin or continue trading at a loss without recovery prospects' (Goode 1997). Moreover, directors who allow an insolvent company to trade without petitioning for insolvency are liable to disqualification and other penalties (Goode 1997). Kim, Ramaswamy, and Sundaresan (1993) analyse the effect of a cashflow covenant, which is akin to the UK legal test of solvency.

9.6. Depositor protection

These remedies may work tolerably well in a commercial firm, since the gearing is not normally very high. But in the case of a bank, the high gearing of deposits relative to shareholders' capital means that such devices are unlikely to prove adequate. Excessive risk-taking must be ruled out by restricting the types of asset that banks can invest in. That is why, as Davis (1993) argues, bank managers are usually restricted to fixed-rate lending, which has no 'upside' to tempt them. It is particularly important to curtail equity investment, which is highly risky and would expose depositors to a 'heads the bank wins, tails the depositors lose' game with potentially disastrous consequences for financial stability and the economy.

Nevertheless, this approach to regulation supposes that banks are able to prevent their borrowers from exploiting the convex nature of the bank loan contract by selecting risky projects. There would be no point in designing a contract which prevented banks from engaging in excessive risk if this simply allowed borrowers to behave in this way, exposing the depositor indirectly to excessive risk-taking. The next section analyses the effect of convexity in the credit market and some of the ways in which banks can contain its effects. This model generates a coherent set of prudential rules for regulating a competitive banking system, discussed in the conclusion to this chapter.

9.7. Bank loan markets and convexity

Credit is rationed when there is unsatisfied demand by borrowers at the existing (or a slightly higher) interest rate. This can happen in many different ways. It can emerge as a result of government policy: for example, in the early post-war years, the UK government rationed mortgage and consumer lending while keeping interest rates relatively low to encourage industrial borrowing and investment (Box 11.2). It can occur because interest rates are slow to adjust to an increase in the demand for credit. But what interests us here is the phenomenon of equilibrium credit rationing. In this case, although there is no government intervention, there is no tendency for the interest rate to change despite an unsatisfied demand by borrowers.

How can this phenomenon be sustained in equilibrium? Why don't banks simply raise their interest rate to choke off the surplus borrowers?

The seminal paper by Stiglitz and Weiss (1981) argues that the twin effects of adverse selection (low-risk borrowers would leave the market) and moral hazard (those left would take up riskier projects) mean that the expected rate of return can fall when interest rate charges rise, making this suboptimal. Their basic assumptions are:

1. All borrowers invest in projects with same mean return, but different degrees of risk: represented by the spread θ.
2. The bank cannot distinguish between borrowers with high- and low-risk projects, so all borrowers pay the same interest rate (pooling equilibrium).

This effect can be illustrated using a simple model in which projects are as described in Section 9.1. There are two types of borrower. Both have the convex payoff function (9.2). Half are of type A and can only invest in project A, and the rest (type B) can invest in project B. Now write:

$$L = I(1 + r_L), \tag{9.4}$$

where r_L is the loan rate. The breakeven loan rate for type A borrowers is found by setting L equal to the known payoff $\bar{Y}$ and solving (9.4) for r_L. This gives the maximum rate which they would be willing to pay:

$$r_L^* = \bar{Y}/I - 1 > 0. \tag{9.5}$$

If the loan rate r_L strictly exceeds this critical value r_L^*, then the type As drop out of the market. Adverse selection occurs, because type Bs remain in the market. Substituting L into (9.3) we see that the Bs' expected payoff is:

$$E[\pi_B] = \frac{1}{2} \max(0, Y_2 - L) = \frac{1}{2}(Y_2 - I(1 + r_L)). \tag{9.6}$$

Setting this to zero gives their breakeven rate:

$$r_L^{**} = Y_2/I - 1 > r_L^*. \tag{9.7}$$

At yet higher interest rates, type Bs also drop out.

Now consider the position of a bank in a competitive market. From this perspective, the deposit rate r_D is exogenous. The bank makes a sure profit of $I(r_L - r_D)$ on loans to type A borrowers. Substituting Y_1 and Y_2 into (9.1), a loan to a type B borrower returns the bank $L = I(1 + r_L)$ in the 'good' state but returns only $Y_1 < L$ in the 'bad' state. The net expected return on type B loans is thus $\frac{1}{2}I(r_L - r_D) + \frac{1}{2}[Y_1 - I(1 + r_D)]$. So, if $r_L < r_L^*$ and both types borrow, the average expected profit is:

$$E[\rho(r, r_D)] = \frac{3}{4} I(r_L - r_D) + \frac{1}{4} [Y_1 - I(1 + r_D)], \tag{9.8}$$

for $0 < r_L < r_L^*$.

This is linear and increasing in r_L. However, at $r_L = r_L^*$ the type As drop out. The first term in the above equation disappears and the bank's average profit falls abruptly to:

$$E[\rho(r, r_D)'] = \frac{1}{2} I(r_L - r_D) + \frac{1}{2} [Y_1 - I(1 + r_D)], \tag{9.9}$$

for $r_L^* < r_L < r_L^{**}$.

This is also increasing in r_L, up to the point $r_L = r_L^{**}$, at which point the Bs also drop out and the bank's profit falls to zero. A monopoly bank would push r_L up to r_L^* or r_L^{**}, whichever yielded the higher profit, possibly rationing in the first case. But what about a bank in a contestable market?

9.8. Competitive pooling equilibrium

In a contestable market, (9.8) or (9.9) defines the equilibrium relationship between r_L and r_D. Setting (9.8) to zero and solving for r gives:

$$r_L = r_D + \frac{1}{3} [1 + r_D - Y_1/I], \tag{9.10}$$

for $r_L \leq r_L^*$, i.e. $r_D \leq r_D^* = \frac{3}{4} \frac{\bar{Y}}{I} + \frac{1}{4} \frac{Y_1}{I} - 1.$

This says that provided r_D is below the critical value r_D^*, the competitive loan rate is a mark-up on the deposit rate, where the mark-up allows for losses against type B loans in the bad state. This mark-up is the product of the prospective default $[1 + r_D - Y_1/I]$ and the relative probability of 1/3. This relationship is represented by the lower of the two schedules in the top right-hand quadrant in Figure 9.2. The highest deposit rate at which the bank can break even lending to As and Bs is r_D^*. This is equal to the bank's expected return when it sets $L = \bar{Y}$ and gets this back 3/4 of the time, with Y_1 being returned otherwise.

If the deposit rate is higher than r_D^* the bank would need to charge a loan rate higher than r_L^*. However, that would mean lending exclusively to the high-risk B types. The breakeven relationship between r_L and r_D for this high-risk lending is (9.9). Setting this to zero gives:

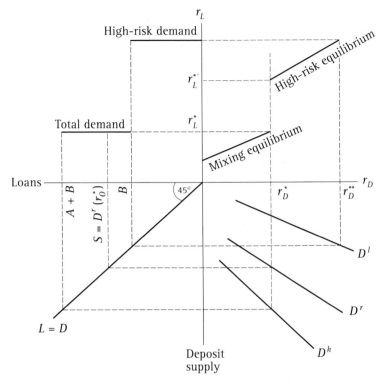

Figure 9.2 Equilibrium credit rationing

$$r'_L = 2r_D + 1 - Y_1/I, \tag{9.11}$$

for $r^{*\prime}_L \leq r'_L \leq r^{**}_L$, i.e. $r^*_D \leq r_D \leq r^{**}_D = \bar{Y}/I - 1.$

This is shown as the higher schedule in the top right-hand quadrant in Figure 9.2. Importantly, if the deposit rate is r^*_D then a bank has two potential breakeven options. The first is to charge r^*_L and consequently lend to a mix of As and Bs. The second is to charge $r^{*\prime}_L$, knowing that it will only be lending to the high-risk types. We solve for this rate by substituting r^*_D from (9.10) into (9.11):

$$r^{*\prime}_L = \frac{\bar{Y}}{I} + \frac{1}{4}\frac{Y_2 - Y_1}{I} - 1.$$

It will never charge a rate between r^*_L and $r^{*\prime}_L$ since that would mean lending to B types at a rate insufficient to cover the cost of deposits.

9.9. Equilibrium credit rationing

The other three quadrants in Figure 9.2 allow the implications of this relationship for market equilibrium to be illustrated. First, we look at two cases in which the market clears, then at the case of equilibrium credit rationing. The top left quadrant shows the demand for loans as a function of r_L. At rates below r_L^* there is demand from both types at point $A + B$ while for rates between r_L^* and $r_L^{*\prime}$ the demand falls back by a half, to point B. The lower right quadrant shows the supply of deposits as a function of r_D. The line in the bottom left of the figure shows the relationship between the supply of deposits and the supply of loans. In this case it is drawn as a 45° line, assuming that all deposits are lent on as loans. (Fractional reserve requirements and other factors reducing the supply of loans could be allowed for by varying the slope of this line.)

The outcome depends critically upon the deposit supply schedule. If there are enough deposits forthcoming at a rate at or below r_D^* to finance all the demands of type A and B borrowers, then a simple competitive pooling equilibrium results in the loan market. This case is illustrated by the schedule D^h. Alternatively, if there are just enough funds forthcoming at a rate between r_D^* and r_D^{**} to accommodate the Bs, then a high-risk market equilibrium results, illustrated by D^l.

However, if the supply of deposits (S) at r_D^* is more than enough to accommodate the Bs but insufficient to accommodate the As and the Bs when the loan rate is r_L^*, then the equilibrium involves rationing. This is illustrated using the deposit schedule D^r in the figure. By construction, there is an excess demand at all loan rates at or below r_L^* and an excess supply at all higher rates. So there is no rate which is consistent with a market-clearing equilibrium.

The only equilibrium is one in which the deposit rate sticks at r_D^*. As we have seen, two breakeven strategies are then open to the bank. One is to charge r_L^* and lend to both As and Bs subject to availability and the other to charge $r_L^{*\prime}$ and lend to the Bs. However, in this model, only the former is used.[2] That is because, faced with this choice, type Bs always find it more profitable to mix with the low-risk types and take their chances of getting funded at r_L^* in the pool rather than getting funds at $r_L^{*\prime}$ for sure.[3]

---

[2] Stiglitz and Weiss (1981) argue that both stategies will be used in equilibrium (Theorem 5). However, that is not the case in this model.

[3] In the first case, if they are successful in getting funds, their expected profit is $E[\pi_B(r_L^*)] = \frac{1}{2}(Y_2 - I(1 + r_L^*)) = \theta/4$; using (9.5). Weighting this by the probability of getting funds: $1/2 < \phi = S/(A + B) < 1$; gives an expected return of $\phi\theta/4$. On the other hand, if they go to a bank offering funds for sure at $r_L^{*\prime}$ their expected return is: $E[\pi_B(r_L^{*\prime})] = \frac{1}{2}(Y_2 - I(1 + r_L^{*\prime})) = \theta/8$, which is less than $\phi\theta/4$.

9.10. The Stiglitz–Weiss analysis

The Stiglitz–Weiss analysis is more general than this illustration. It is based on the behaviour of convex and concave value functions under a 'mean preserving increase in spread'. However their general argument can be understood from the perspective of option pricing theory. In effect, the bank owns the underlying value of the project and the final payoff (Y), but sells a 'call' option to the borrower with a strike price of L and hence the terminal value indicated by (9.2). The put–call parity theorem means this is equivalent to the bank owning a risk-free asset with terminal value L and selling a put option to a borrower with a terminal value $\max(0, L - Y)$. This point is taken up in Chapter 11 when we note that, abstracting from collateral, the bank's position is effectively owned by its depositors, who can protect themselves from the default risk by buying a similar 'put' in the form of deposit insurance.

As illustrated by the simple model, the convexity of the call or surplus function (9.1) means that a mean-preserving increase in spread increases the value of the 'call' and hence the breakeven rate the borrower is willing to offer. Consequently, as the loan rate rises, low-risk types drop out and average risk rises. Again, the net effect on the bank's expected return may or may not turn negative. If such a point is reached then the bank will ration credit rather than increase the interest rate. Moral hazard works in a similar way once the loan contract is signed.

9.11. Implications for the prudential regulation of banks

Although convexity analysis was first used to describe asset substitution and credit rationing phenomena, it has been applied to a wide range of different problems in economics. For example, De Meza and Webb (1987) use this to analyse industrial investment and find that, counterintuitively, asymmetric information can actually lead to overinvestment. In this section we look at the implications for bank prudential regulation.

The Stiglitz–Weiss analysis can be used to design a watertight regulatory regime for banks. It shows that if banks are allowed to invest only in bank loan instruments (and perhaps reserve assets like Treasury bills and bonds) then they achieve an expected rate of return of r_D. This may be a market-clearing rate or a rate such as r_D^* which implies credit rationing. That is not particularly relevant in this context. What is important is that the lack of information about borrowers and the nature of the loan contract ensures that the bank cannot influence this return. Assuming that the loan portfolio is well diversified and there is adequate collateral, the bank will always be able to pay this rate to depositors and will expect a zero (or normal) profit for shareholders.

However, if these twin assumptions are relaxed, regulatory loopholes appear and the model begins to unravel, with adverse consequences for depositors. This shows just how watertight such rules have to be. Suppose for example that the bank has no collateral and the rules permit it to lend to a single large borrower (or equivalently for a set of projects with identical returns). Then its shareholders do best if it puts all of its eggs in this one basket. If it offers this loan at the market rate $r_L \le r_L^*$ determined by (9.8) then 75 per cent of the time it will make a profit for its shareholders of $I(r_L - r_D) > 0$ and be able to pay depositors in full. However, the other 25 per cent of the time it will be unlucky and lend to a type B in a bad state. Then it will make a loss of $[Y_1 - I(1 + r_D)]$ on its loan and will not be able to pay depositors in full. In this case the social return r_D is still optimal, but is split unfairly between shareholders and depositors.

The bank might actually do better by increasing its lending rate, knowing that it can still attract business from risky borrowers, and make the higher margin $I(r_L - r_D)$ for its shareholders 50 per cent of the time. This would be a classic example of excessive risk-taking, with a subnormal social return. Of course, the bank is in an even better position if it is allowed to invest in equity. The implication of this is that the bank must be monitored to make sure that it restricts itself to well-diversified lending at a market-related rate and has appropriate collateral. Otherwise it is another case of heads the bank wins, tails the depositors lose.

If these prudential controls are watertight, then as the Stiglitz–Weiss system shows, the bank should not be able to afford a supernormal *deposit* rate. However, if there are no prudential controls or banks can somehow circumvent these, the deposit rate becomes an important instrument of regulation. In this case, the Stiglitz–Weiss analysis can be applied to the deposit market. Banks with high-risk profiles will be able to offer higher deposit rates than other banks (as appears to have happened in the case of BCCI, Box 2.2). Uninsured depositors should know this and be wary of putting their funds in such banks. High-risk banks (like the type B borrowers in our simple loan model) will generally do better to pool with low-risk banks and attract whatever funds they can at the going rate. Consequently, there would be a danger in a poorly regulated system that adverse selection and moral hazard could cause the riskiness of deposits to increase with the level of the deposit rate. This might be used to justify a deposit rate ceiling (such as 'regulation Q' introduced in the USA under the Glass–Steagall Act of 1933). However, such a restriction would clearly be an anticompetitive second-best solution, an admission that prudential controls had failed.

EXERCISES

Question 1. (a) Banks can invest in 'loans' or 'investments' and shareholders enjoy limited liability. The returns on these assets are measured after deducting the banks' costs. Loans yield a 10 per cent return with a probability of 0.9 and just repay the principal otherwise. Investments appreciate by 20 per cent with a probability of 0.5 and depreciate by 10 per cent otherwise. Banks promise depositors 9 per cent interest. Banks initially put up £1 of collateral (capital and reserves) for every £8 of deposits and are indifferent to risk.

(i) What is the best initial investment strategy for the banks' shareholders?

> They invest exclusively in loans because these have the highest expected rate of return. If the bank puts its cash into the investment, for every original pound of collateral it gets a gross payoff of £10.8 = 9 × 1.2 in the good state. Deducting the £8.72 paid to depositors reduces this to £2.08. In the bad scenario it gets £8.1 = 9 × 0.9 gross, which is not enough to pay depositors in full, so it gets nothing net. The expected payoff is thus £1.04 = 0.5 × 2.08, which means the rate of return would be 4 per cent. For loans a similar calculation gives a return of 9 per cent: £1.09 = (0.9 × 9 × 1.1 + 0.1 × 9) − 8.72. The banks are still solvent in the bad state.

(ii) What is the expected rate of return on deposits?

> There are no bankruptcies under this strategy so the depositors get the 9 per cent promised.

(iii) Is the industry in equilibrium (assuming that it is contestable)?

> Banks make the same rate of return on their collateral as depositors, so there is no tendency to enter or leave the industry.

(b) Now suppose that a bank experiences a bad outcome and gets no interest back on any of its loans. It pays depositors interest out of collateral. Shareholders do not put up any more capital and are paid a 9 per cent dividend out of collateral. The public is not aware of this and the bank can still raise the same amount of deposits as before by promising them 9 per cent interest.

(i) Describe this bank's liability structure;

> The bank pays out dividends and interest of £0.81 = 9 × 0.09 out of each pound of collateral and now has just 19p of capital and reserves for every £8 of deposits.

(ii) What is the bank's best investment strategy now?

For every 19p of collateral it gets a net payoff of £1.108 = (8.19 × 1.2 − 8.72) from the investment in the good state. In the bad state there is a gross investment payoff of only £7.371 = 8.19 × 0.9, which again is not enough to pay depositors. The bank is insolvent and the shareholders get nothing. The expected payoff is, however, £0.554 = 0.5 × 1.108, which represents a rate of return of 192 per cent on the residual 19p of collateral. In the loan market this calculation gives £0.2601 = 0.9 × (8.19 × 1.1 − 8.72), i.e. a rate of 37 per cent. So the bank engages in asset substitution by switching out of loans into investments.

(iii) What is the expected rate of return on deposits? Comment on your result.

The bank engages in asset substitution by switching out of loans into investments, which now have a higher rate of return for the bank. Depositors get £8.72 in full in the good state but are left with the gross figure of £7.371 otherwise. Their average return is £8.0455 = 0.5(8.72 + 7.371), which is a percentage gain of just over 0.5 per cent. The average total payoff is 0.5(1.2 + 0.9) = £1.05, so the social rate of return is 5 per cent and virtually all of these returns go to the bank. This situation is socially suboptimal because 5 per cent is less than the social return of 9 per cent on loans, and the investment route is only taken because the low capitalization distorts bank incentives. This illustrates the idea that losses which reduce collateral encourage banks to pay uncovered dividends and engage in asset substitution. A solution is for a bank inspector to scrutinize the books regularly and ensure an adequate level of collateral.

Question 2. Consider the implications of the 1996 Barings Bank collapse for (a) trader remuneration structures, (b) risk management, (c) the compartmentalization of multi-role finance houses, (d) systemic risk, and (e) international regulatory cooperation.

Question 3. Why is there no role for a regulator in the Diamond (1984) model of bank financial intermediation? Is there a case for regulating banks in Britain in the year 2000? (University of London, Faculty of Economics, B.Sc.(Econ) Financial Economics, Final Examination, 1999).

Question 4. Carefully explain how asymmetric information can affect the market for bank credit.

10. Bank Runs, Systemic Risk, and Deposit Insurance

One of the simplifying features of the Diamond (1984) model is the assumption that bank liabilities are fixed-term loans. Investors make these loans to the bank rather than to ultimate borrowers in order to delegate the monitoring role. But in practice, retail bank liabilities largely consist of deposits that can be withdrawn without notice. Depositors' liquidity requirements are uncertain and one of the functions of the monetary and banking system is to finance these needs.

This seriously complicates the problem of bank management and regulation, because banks cannot lend their deposit funds in this way (except to each other through the interbank market). Bank borrowers would find an instant recall option too disruptive. However, banks have a scale advantage in managing their deposits, similar to the one which they have in monitoring their loans. They typically have a large number of depositors whose demands for cash are unlikely to be perfectly correlated or coordinated. For the banking system as a whole, these demands are normally inversely correlated, since one person's debit is another's credit. This scale effect means that a bank is in a much better position to offer an instant recall facility than a single borrower financed by just a handful of investors. This allows a bank to raise instant access deposits and invest some of the funds in term loans or long-term securities at higher interest rates. The bank can learn to judge the natural ebb and flow of funds and arrange its balance sheet accordingly. Once interbank financing arrangements develop, further economies in holdings of cash can be made at the level of the banking system.

The snag is that if for some reason people panic and demand their money back without having a genuine cash requirement, a bank will not be able to repay everyone. Interbank financing arrangements may help, but not if this loss of confidence is contagious and spills over from one bank to another. This effect puts the entire banking system at risk. Liquidation costs for longer-term investments mean that although those first in the queue get paid in full, those at the end get nothing. Recall that in Chapter 8 it was argued that banks made loans on the basis of confidential information and long-term customer relationships. This information is not available to those who bid for bank assets in a distress situation, resulting in a 'fire sale'.

Asymmetric information plays a key role here because the bank does not know whether an individual's need for cash is genuine. If it did, then it could delay payment until a depositor really needed cash, by which time its long-term assets could be liquidated at a reasonable price. Dybvig and Diamond (1983) analyse three mechanisms for ensuring that people tell the truth about their liquidity needs and do not withdraw their funds until they actually need them. The first mechanism is the suspension of convertibility used historically by banks to conserve their assets. The others are techniques based upon government or central bank intervention: deposit insurance and the lender of last resort facility. Dybvig and Diamond show that in the absence of risk, these devices run-proof the system at no cost. But in practice the moral hazard associated with these two devices implies a need for government or central bank regulation.

10.1. The Dybvig and Diamond (1983) model

The Dybvig and Diamond model captures these features in a relatively simple way. The model resembles the two-state model used in Chapter 3, except that in this case, preferences rather than production outcomes are state dependent: people need early or late consumption depending upon which state materializes. Dybvig and Diamond used this feature to motivate the demand for liquidity. There is no aggregate uncertainty in this model, so mutual insurance schemes like those analysed in Chapter 3 increase welfare. However, the problem is that private information makes this insurance difficult to organize.

Dybvig and Diamond assume that:

1. There are 3 periods: numbered 0, 1, and 2.
2. Primary investments cost 1 in period 0, and yield 1 if cashed in period 1, $R > 1$ if cashed in period 2.
3. Individuals are identical and have wealth of 1 unit in period 0. However, in period 1 they learn that they are either of type 1 or type 2. Type 1s die and consume C_1 in period 1 with utility level $U(C_1)$ while type 2s die and consume C_1 in period 2 with utility $U(C_1 + C_2)$. This is private information. Because $R > 1$, the type 2s optimally set $C_1 = 0$.
4. Individuals know that there will be p per cent type 1s and $(1 - p)$ per cent type 2s. Taking the probability-weighted average, their expected utility in period 0 (before anyone knows what type they are) is
$$EU = pU(C_1) + (1 - p)U(C_2).$$

5. The utility function $U(C)$ is defined over consumption (C) with $U' = \partial U/\partial C > 0, \partial^2 U/\partial^2 C < 0$. It satisfies the Inada conditions: $U'(0) = \infty, U'(\infty) = 0$.
6. Current consumption is a normal good in the sense that it falls in response to an increase in its relative cost (R). Technically this means a relatively high degree of intertemporal substitution: $-(\partial^2 U/\partial^2 C)/C(\partial U/d\partial C) > 1$.

10.2. Autarchy

In this model, 'early death' and consumption drive the need for liquidity. Suppose first that there are no financial markets. Those who die in period 1 are unlucky because they have to liquidate the primary investment early and with $C_1 = 1$ have a lower utility $U(1)$ than those who survive into period 2 and enjoy $U(R)$. This is the cost of early death in this model. Taking the probability-weighted average, expected utility in period 0 (before anyone knows what type they are) is $EU = pU(1) + (1-p)U(R)$.

Since the utility function is concave (assumption 5) investors are risk averse and this 'autarchic' solution is inefficient. Risk-sharing agreements (like life assurance) spread the costs of 'early death' and provide a better outcome. Suppose for example that there are only two individuals, one of whom will die early and the other late. In this case $p = 1/2$. Life expectancy is verifiable (known to both players) at time 1 since they both know what type they are and therefore what type the other is. If there is some mechanism for enforcing this contract *ex post*, they can set up a 'social insurance contract' whereby the one that is going to live longest pays the other a fixed sum.

10.3. Optimal social insurance

We can find the appropriate scale of this transfer using the approach set out in Chapter 3. This two-person situation is in fact identical to the textbook case in which one person allocates their own consumption over two periods. Suppose that the players agree beforehand that the type 2 will pay the type 1 a (nominal) amount π in period 1. The type 1 can then consume the early liquidation value of their own wealth plus the transfer π. This leaves the type 2 with $(1 - \pi)$ invested at the end of period 1, which returns $R(1 - \pi)$ in period 2. Our problem is to choose this to maximize the individual's *ex ante* expected utility

$$EU = U(C_1) + U(C_2) \tag{10.1}$$

(for convenience this is rescaled by multiplying by 2) subject to $C_1 = 1 + \pi$, $C_2 = R(1 - \pi)$. Solving for π as $C_1 - 1$ and substituting into C_2 gives the two period budget constraint $C_2 = R(2 - C_1)$.

This is identical to the standard two-period budget constraint faced by a single individual with initial wealth of 2 in period 1, consumption of C_1 in period 1 and $C_2 = R(2 - C_1)$ in period 2. R is effectively 1 plus the one-period rate of interest (r). If this individual has an additive utility function like (10.1), then the two optimization problems are identical. An easy way to solve this is to substitute $C_2 = R(2 - C_1)$ into (10.1) which gives

$$\max_{\{C_1\}} U(C_1) + U(R(2 - C_1)).$$

Differentiating this with respect to C_1 gives the standard result:

$$U'(C_1)/U'(C_2) = R = (1 + r),$$

which says that the marginal rate of substitution of C_1 and C_2 in consumption must equal their marginal rate of transformation. Together with the budget constraint, this defines the optimal values C_1^* and C_2^* and hence the transfer π^*.

Figure 10.1 uses a standard two-period indifference curve diagram to show the welfare gain. The negatively sloped line is the budget line, indicating that 'society' can consume 2 units in period 1 or $2R$ units in period 2 or any convex combination of these. The curves are indifference curves joining points of equal expected utility or social welfare. Point a has coordinates $(1,R)$ and shows the autarchic consumption point. Under assumption (6) the indifference curve passing through a cuts the budget line from above,[1] as shown in the figure. This means that a higher level of social welfare can be obtained by moving down the budget line to a point of tangency such as b. This means a transfer from the type 2 to the type 1, to give the socially optimal values $1 < C_1^* < C_2^* < R$.

---

[1] This point is a point of tangency between the budget line and an indifference curve in the case of logarithmic utility $(-(\partial^2 U/\partial^2 C)/C(\partial U/d\partial C) = 1)$, but this is ruled out by A(5). If the rate of intertemporal substitution is greater than implied by the logarithmic utility function $(0 < -(\partial^2 U/\partial^2 C)/C(\partial U/d\partial C) < 1)$ then the indifference curve cuts from below and welfare is improved by a transfer from the type 1 to the type 2. This allocation could be assimilated by a deposit contract which paid out *less* than the primary asset in period 1. In other words, this contract is always incentive compatible because there is never any incentive for a type 2 to declare themselves to be type 1. This system would be run-proof.

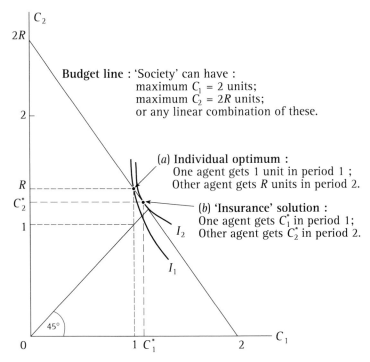

Figure 10.1 How 'insurance' improves allocation

10.4. The deposit contract

The problem with this social insurance contract is that life expectancy and cash needs are not verifiable if there are more than two players. However Dybvig and Diamond show that the same allocation can be achieved by a non-tradable deposit contract that pays out $C_1^* > 1$ (for a unit deposit) in period 1 and $C_2^* > C_1^*$ if held until period 2. Moreover since $C_2^* > C_1^*$ it pays type 2 individuals to keep their money in the bank in period 1, *unless they fear a bank run*.

There is no fundamental basis for such fears in this model since the budget constraint ensures that if C_1^* is paid out only to ($p = 50$ per cent) type 1 individuals in the first period, then there will always be enough cash left to pay C_2^* out to type 2s in the last period. However, there is no leeway in the bank's budget calculation for error. Consequently, if just one type 2 individual panics and withdraws cash, another depositor will get less than promised. Indeed if there is a general panic and all type 2s

Table 10.1. Expected utility

Regime/utility	Type 1	Type 2	Expected utility
1 Autarchy	$U(1)$	$U(R)$	$\dfrac{U(1) + U(R)}{2}$
2(a) Bank deposits (no run)	$U(C_1^*)$	$U(C_2^*)$	$\dfrac{U(C_1^*) + U(C_1^*)}{2}$
2(b) Bank run (no insurance)			$\dfrac{U(C_1^*) - \pi U(0)}{C_1^*}$
2(c) Bank run (with insurance)	$U(1)$	$U(1)$	$U(1)$

attempt to withdraw funds in period 1, the bank will run out of cash and some depositors will get nothing.

In this case there is a 'bank run' and all assets are liquidated in period 1. If there are N depositors, bank liquidation of assets gives total proceeds of N that are available for distribution, while total deposit claims are $NC_1^* > N$. Only a fraction $f = 1/C_1^*$ of depositors can withdraw the amount C_1^*. This means that $1 - f = \pi/C_1^*$ (the last in the queue) get nothing. These proceeds are shared out very badly. Table 10.1 shows that social welfare (or *ex ante* expected utility) is $[U(C_1^*) - \pi U(0)]/C_1^*$.

This welfare index is below that in the autarchic level. There are two reasons for this: the distribution effect and the premature liquidation effect. If the tax system is used to reverse the first effect, so that all depositors consume 1 with utility 1, then this maximizes welfare subject to the available resources. However expected utility is then $U(1)$ which is less than the autarchy value $[U(1) + U(R)]/2$ because of the liquidation effect.

The Dybvig and Diamond deposit model thus has two Nash equilibria (defined as situations in which agents behave autonomously and disregard the aggregate effect of their actions). The first 2(a) is a good equilibrium in which nobody panics and the bank deposit resembles optimal social insurance in the two-person case (i.e. with state verification). Expected utility is higher than in the baseline 1(a). But the second is a bad equilibrium in which people panic, pushing expected utility well below the baseline.

10.5. Suspension of convertibility

This model shows that bank deposit contracts can improve economic allocation and explains why historically banks which were prone to runs could nevertheless attract deposits. The twin-equilibrium solution neatly characterizes a situation in which periods of confidence can be punctuated by episodes of panic. Diamond and Dybvig discuss various ways in which the situation can be improved, by reducing or in some cases eliminating the possibility of a bank run. One way to reduce this risk is to ease the competitive pressure on the banking system. This allows banks to set the first-period payout below C_1^*. However, as long as this exceeds unity (the liquidation value) it is still possible for its assets to be depleted by a panic, so this modification does not eliminate the problem.

Diamond and Dybvig show that (in their non-stochastic model) there are three ways in which the bad Nash equilibrium can be eliminated. The first is the historical device of 'suspension of convertibility': the bank shuts its doors once it is clear that a panic is developing, allowing it time to liquidate assets in an orderly way, in the hope of repaying depositors in full at a later date. In the Diamond and Dybvig model, the bank announces that it will close its doors in period 1 as soon as it pays out a fraction $p = 1/2$ of depositors. If some type 2s withdrew their funds early, then this would leave some type 1s very badly off: with a utility index of $U(0)$. However, the suspension facility ensures that no matter what happens, the bank will always have enough to pay the type 2s $C_2^* > 1$ in the next period. This device gives the type 2s a clear incentive to keep their money in the bank until they need it. It therefore eliminates the bad Nash equilibrium 2(b) and makes the good equilibrium 2(a) unique.

In this model, suspension never occurs. That is because the asset returns and the aggregate liquidity need ($p = 1/2$) are known. However, Diamond and Dybvig show that if the aggregate liquidity requirement is uncertain, no uninsured bank deposit mechanism can replicate the optimal allocation provided by a social planner. This is the case even with suspension of convertibility. As we might expect, they show that suspension of convertibility helps to improve upon the result obtained by the uninsured deposit mechanism by preventing bank runs. However, suspension is sometimes necessary in equilibrium, leaving any type 1s who are unable to get funds very badly off.

10.6. Deposit insurance

Dybvig and Diamond show that government-backed deposit insurance offers another way of eliminating bank runs. They note that the tax system can be used to claw back funds after they have been paid to depositors. Dybvig and Diamond argue that because banks have not got this recall ability, this makes government intervention effective. Suppose for example that the insurance guarantees the original deposit, not the interest. If people panic, then those who are lucky and manage to withdraw C_1^* pay a tax of π. This is sufficient to pay a subsidy of 1 to those who do not, leaving everyone with $U(1)$ as indicated in the bottom right cell in the table.

We have seen that this outcome reverses the distribution but not the liquidation effect and still leaves type 2 individuals worse of than in the autarchic case. However, as in the case of the suspension facility, these type 2 individuals have nothing to gain by withdrawing their deposits prematurely even if they are worried about the possibility of a bank run. If the worst comes to the worst and there is a bank run, they still consume 1. Consumption is at least as high as it would be if they took their money out early. Since there is always some chance that there will not be a panic (and that they will get paid $C_2^* > 1$) they leave their money in the bank until they need it. In other words, the good Nash equilibrium is again unique.

The insurance mechanism (like convertibility) effectively removes the information asymmetry and ensures that individuals never lie about their type. The government only needs to ensure that all individuals receive the same after tax in period 1 to get this result. In this case it just insures the original deposit. This is important because that is all the government can guarantee in this simple economy if there actually is a bank run. The resource constraint means that unless it has other resources at its disposal, it can no more guarantee to pay everyone C_1^* than the bank can.

In practice, the tax system may be distortionary or costly to run, in which case the government guarantee would have to be partial. However, provided everyone gets the same consumption in period 1, tax-based deposit insurance L still avoids runs and secures the optimal outcome. The tax system is never used in equilibrium, and so it does not matter whether taxes have distortionary effects or not. However, if aggregate liquidity requirements are uncertain, this does matter. In this case, the bank has to guess what p is in order to be able to calculate C_1^*. If p turns out to be higher, a shortfall will occur, reducing the resources available for the type 2s. In this case, the government has to use the tax system to reduce the consumption of the type 1s appropriately. Diamond and Dybvig note that if the tax system were very perverse, social welfare could be higher (in a stochastic system) without it.

10.7. The lender of last resort

Finally, Diamond and Dybvig consider the way in which a lender of last resort facility at the central bank can support the deposit contract. They note that deposit contracts are monetary instruments with repayment structures specified in nominal terms. This means that if there is a bank run, the government can always print enough money to allow the bank to liquidate assets and meet the demands of depositors. In the Diamond and Dybvig model, if there is a run the government can print money and buy the primary assets from the bank at the inflated price C_1^*. This allows the bank to meet all of its depositors' nominal demands even if there is a run. However, in this case, the resource constraint means that the price level rises and the nominal repayment of C_1^* is only worth 1 in real terms. In other words, there is an inflation tax of π per depositor. But as in the suspension and insurance models, this makes it optimal for the type 2s to leave their money in the bank in the hope of getting a real repayment of $C_2^* > 1$ if a run is avoided. So again, the bad Nash equilibrium is eliminated costlessly.

10.8. Mutual fund banking

The Diamond and Dybvig (1983) model focuses a great deal of theoretical light upon the nature of a bank run. However, in order to keep the model relatively simple, it incorporates some extremely simple assumptions. In particular, individuals express extreme preferences for early or late consumption, consuming everything in a single period. It is more reasonable to assume smooth preferences, making it optimal for individuals to spread consumption across several periods. Subsequent research has relaxed these assumptions and provided a better understanding, albeit at the cost of more complexity.

An important paper by Jacklin (1987) shows what happens when financial instruments can be traded. Jacklin first notes that there is nothing special about bank deposits in the basic Diamond and Dybvig structure, since the same risk-sharing outcome can be produced by an equity or mutual fund arrangement, avoiding the bank run problem altogether. For example, a fund can issue equities or capital units worth 1 in period 0 and invest in the primary asset. Each unit promises a dividend of pC_1^* in period 1 and a liquidating or residual dividend of $R(1 - pC_1^*)$ in period 2. If everyone buys these units then a competitive market in the ex dividend rights in period 1 secures the optimum.

With $p = 1/2$, each type 1 exchanges her ex dividend rights for a dividend received by a type 2. She therefore has two dividends each worth $C_1^*/2$ for consumption in period 1, thus achieving the optimum. The type 2 on the other hand is willing to enter into this trade because $R(1 - C_1^*/2) > C_1^*/2$. In total, he gets two ex dividend rights units that each give a liquidating dividend of $R(1 - C_1^*/2)$ for consumption in period 2, thus attaining the optimum of $C_2^* = R(2 - C_1^*)$.

Jacklin then shows that the Diamond and Dybvig deposit arrangement unravels if deposits are tradable, like certificates of deposit (CDs). Suppose that a 'deviant' institution offers a tradable CD that pays r in period 2 and nothing in period 1. Provided that relative prices are not affected, a 'deviant' investor is better off buying this security in period 0 no matter which state occurs. If he becomes a type 2 then obviously he gets $R > C_2^*$. If he becomes a type 1 then he can sell this claim in the ex dividend share market. Since it pays r in period 2 and an ex dividend unit only pays $R(1 - C_1^*/2)$, in period 1 it is worth $1/(1 - C_1^*/2)$ times the ex dividend price of $C_1^*/2$. So the deviant depositor gets $C_1^*/2(1 - C_1^*/2) > C_1^*$.

In a more positive vein, Jacklin shows that if preferences are 'smoother' and both types of individual spread consumption across periods 1 and 2, deposits can allow the economy to attain outcomes which are better than equity markets or mutual funds. Bank runs can again present a problem. However, these arrangements also unravel if deposits can be traded in a secondary market. A subsequent paper by Jacklin and Bhattacharya (1988) develops these ideas and allows the return on the primary asset to be risky. This is important because it allows bank runs to be triggered by poor information about 'fundamentals.' Information-based financial crises are also considered in an important paper by Morris and Shin (1998).

10.9. Systemic risk

In view of these problems, we should be cautious about using theoretical models of bank and depositor behaviour to directly inform analysis of the regulatory process. We need to be particularly careful when considering systemic risk and moral hazard, which are absent from these theoretical models.

The role of the discount window is to protect the banking industry from systemic risk and not to rescue individual banks from liquidity problems. Central banks normally act as the lender of last resort, offering the discount facility to banks that they regard as solvent. In some countries this facility is only used when the system as a whole is under pressure owing to the contagious effects of bank failures. In this situation, the failure of one bank reduces public confidence in other banks, and can produce a domino or contagion effect. These negative externalities mean that even the most solvent banks can collapse unless they are able to liquidate their assets quickly without depressing prices. To prevent this, the lender of last resort buys or lends money against bank assets and provides the system with the liquidity necessary to meet depositor demands without unduly depressing capital values.

Commercial banking systems are particularly prone to asymmetric information-based panic because their deposits are fixed-value callable claims upon an unobservable-value loan portfolio. This form of contagion is less likely in the case of investment banks, since their deposits are small compared to their broking and other business activities and are usually time rather than sight deposits. Their assets are normally marketable, with observable values. However, counterparty risk is still a problem in such systems. Although margin requirements and other collateral devices can in principle contain these risks, counterparty contagion effects can threaten the financial system, as was demonstrated by the Long Term Capital Management hedge fund rescued by Alan Greenspan in 1998 (see Box 11.1).

The liabilities of US mutual funds and UK unit trusts are callable but valued in terms of the underlying asset portfolio and not fixed in terms of currency. This makes such institutions much less prone to asset substitution, insolvency, and contagion than banks. That is why regulators can allow these funds to offer chequing and other payment facilities to their clients without subjecting them to prudential regulation.

10.10. Moral hazard

The basic Diamond and Dybvig model assumes that the investment technology is riskless. However, they note that if the technology is risky and the government insures deposits, moral hazard reasserts itself. This is a serious problem in practice. Depositors have little or no incentive to monitor the bank if they are going to be bailed out by the government. Depositors do best to put their funds in the bank offering the highest deposit rate, even though (as in the case of BCCI (Box 2.2)) this is a sign of a risky asset portfolio. The taxpayer then pays for moral hazard and bankruptcy. If the deposit insurance scheme is financed by the industry, cautious bankers (and depositors) subsidize risky banks (and their depositors). The implication is that because bank managers are no longer kept on their toes by depositors or shareholders with money at stake, the government or central bank regulator should monitor them instead.

The connections between government deposit insurance, the lender of last resort facility, and regulation can be seen by extending the option theory developed in the previous chapter. First, if bank shareholders have unlimited or multiple liability, they have the incentive to monitor borrowers, just as the bank manager does in the Diamond (1984) model with non-financial penalties.

Under limited liability this incentive is seriously weakened. As pointed out in the last chapter, bank equity effectively becomes a call option on the loan portfolio. The put–call parity theorem says that this is equivalent to ownership of the loan portfolio plus a 'put' option bought from depositors. The put option allows the bank's shareholders to hand everything over to the depositors in a bankruptcy state and walk away without liability. Consequently, depositors either need to monitor limited liability banks or impose penalties for default as in Diamond (1984). As we have established, neither of these alternatives is easy to organize on a decentralized basis.

The alternative is deposit insurance. Merton (1977) views the deposit insurance contract as a 'put' option bought by depositors from the deposit insurer. If this happens, the deposit insurer and not the depositors bears the downside risk and must monitor or penalize banks. As Davis (1992) argues, this delegated bank monitoring solution should be efficient in the same way that delegated monitoring of ultimate borrowers is efficient (Chapter 8). The bank regulator may have the advantage of a confidential relationship with the bank. Indeed, in many traditional systems (such as the one which prevailed in Britain until the establishment of the FSA), the central bank acts both as the regulator and the 'banker's bank'. A centralized regulator also enjoys economies of scale and scope, avoiding the problems of coordinating decentralized monitoring and punishment

Central bank support for a bank in distress may also play a signalling or coordinating role in banking markets, similar to the role of a bank loan in the James (1987) model. In this case, lending through the discount window or government bailout indicates that the central bank's experts are satisfied that the underlying position of the bank is sound. Seeing this, the depositors and other commercial banks are normally prepared to resume a normal business relationship with the troubled bank, allowing it to recover. This free rider effect works in the central bank's favour, limiting the scale of the funds which it has to commit.[2]

EXERCISES

Nash equilibrium strategies

Question 1. Explain what a Nash equilibrium strategy is. Which of the following are Nash equilibrium strategies: (a) standing up to see better at a football match; (b) driving on the left-hand side of the road in London; (c) driving on the left-hand side of the road in Paris; (d) tax evasion; (e) 'holding out' by not accepting a takeover bid; (f) withdrawing money from your bank account in response to a bad press comment?

The Dybvig and Diamond model

Question 2. Illustrate the model of Section 10.1 using the utility specification

$$U(C) = 1 - 1/C.$$

(a) Derive algebraically the utility levels of the type 1 and type 2 individuals under autarchy.

$$U(C_1) = 1 - 1/1 = 0; \quad U(C_2) = 1 - 1/R.$$

(b) Design an optimal mutual insurance contract for this pair.

> Our problem is to choose R to maximize the individual's average or expected utility:
>
> $$EU = U(C_1) + U(C_2).$$
>
> The easy way to solve this is to substitute $C_2 = R(2 - C_1)$. With $U(C)$ defined above this gives
>
> $$\max_{\{C_1\}}[- 1/C_1 - 1/R(2 - C_1)].$$
>
> Differentiating this with respect to C_1 and setting this to zero yields the first-order condition
>
> $$C_1^2 = R(2 - C_1)^2,$$
>
> which we can rearrange as $C_1 = \sqrt{R}\,(2 - C_1)$ to get
>
> $$C_1^* = 2\sqrt{R}\,/(1 + \sqrt{R}).$$
>
> Substituting this into $C_2 = R(2 - C_1)$ we get

---

[2] It can be argued that the International Monetary Fund can transmit a similar lender of last resort signal on the international stage. Typically what happens (for example in Mexico in 1996 and South Korea in 1998) is that a country runs into economic problems like overconsumption or overinvestment. These are reflected in a balance of payments crisis and eventually capital flight, which leads to a loss of exchange reserves or currency depreciation. IMF lending to such countries is normally made conditional upon reforms designed to rectify the fundamentals. It signals to the markets that things are back in order. Once international investors see this the capital flight usually begins to reverse, allowing the IMF loan to be repaid.

$$C_2^* = 2R/(1 + \sqrt{R}).$$

Note that these formulae satisfy $1 < C_1^* < C_2^* < R$.

(c) Assume $R = 1.21$ (the two-period rate of interest is 21 per cent). Calculate the arithmetic value of C_1^* and C_2^* and check that $1 < C_1^* < C_2^* < R$. Calculate the arithmetic levels of utility in situations (a) and (b) for the type 1, the type 2, and their average.

Note that $\sqrt{R} = 1.1$. So $C_1^* = 2\sqrt{R}/(1 + \sqrt{R}) = 1.04762$.

$C_2^* = 2R/(1 + \sqrt{R}) = 1.15238$. Check $1 < C_1^* = 1.04762 < C_2^* = 1.15238 < R = 1.21$.

Substituting $C_1 = 1$, $C_2 = R$ into the utility specification above gives the levels of utility under autarchy, as shown in the first row of the table:

	Type 1	Type 2	Expected utility
(a) Autarchy	$U(1) = 0$	$U(R) = 1 - 1/1.21$ $= 0.1735$	$\dfrac{U(1) + U(R)}{2} = 0.08677$
(b) Mutual insurance	$U(C_1^*) = 1 - 1/C_1^*$ $= 0.04545$	$U(C_2^*) = 1 - 1/C_2^*$ $= 0.1321$	$\dfrac{U(C_1^*) + U(C_1^*)}{2} = 0.08877$

Substituting C_1^* as derived at (b) gives the second row, which implies a higher level of expected utility. Individuals expect to gain more in state 1 than they lose in state 2.

(d) Now assume that there are many individuals, but that the two types are evenly matched. In period 0 they all invest their capital in bank deposits designed to replicate the insurance contract at (b). Discuss the utility levels which emerge with and without a run on the bank.

These deposits pay C_1^* in period 1 and C_2^* in period 2. If there is no bank run, they replicate the utility levels of the mutual insurance contract that are as shown in the lower row of the table. However, if there is a run, only $1/C_1^*$ or 95.45 per cent of individuals get paid. They have a utility value of zero. The remaining 4.55 per cent get nothing. Their utility level is minus infinity. The average level of utility is also minus infinity, making this the worst outcome considered.

(e) Can deposit insurance improve welfare in this situation?

It removes the bad Nash equilibrium and improves welfare. Moreover since the type 2s never panic, there is never any need for the government to pay compensation. There is no moral hazard in the Diamond–Dybvig model, but this assumption is unrealistic. In practice deposit insurance is expensive for the government.

Prudential regulation

Question 3. A bank can invest in two types of asset. The first is a loan with an expected rate of return of 25 per cent and the second a safe asset with an expected return of 5 per cent. Loan returns are normally distributed and have a standard deviation of 40 per cent.

(a) Assume that a bank raises £1 million of deposits upon which it pays 10 per cent for the period. It has equity capital of £150,000. Suppose that it uses all of these funds to acquire 1 loan. What is the probability of default?

Default occurs when the proceeds from the loan portfolio are not sufficient to repay depositors $D(1 + r)$ in full. To find the probability of this we set up a Z-variable which shows the number of critical standard deviations σ (as in Question 3 of Chapter 8) that these proceeds can fall below the mean μ. Then we look up the probability.

In this case $D(1 + r) = 1.1$ and the expected return μ from the loan of 1.15 is $1.15 \times 1.25 = 1.4375$. The standard deviation is $1.15 \times 0.4 = 0.46$. Putting this together gives

$$Z_a = [\mu - D(1 + r)]/\sigma = [1.4375 - 1.1]/0.46 = 0.734.$$

Looking this up in standard tables gives a probability of bankruptcy of 23.1 per cent.

(b) Now the bank invests 15 per cent of its assets in the safe asset and the rest in loans. What are the chances of bankruptcy?

In this case $\mu = 1.25 + 0.15 \times 1.05 = 1.4075$ and $\sigma = 0.4$. This gives

$$Z_b = [1.4075 - 1.1]/0.4 = 0.768.$$

This reduces the probability of bankruptcy to 22.1 per cent.

(c) A regulator wants to reduce the probability of bankruptcy to 10 per cent. She assumes that the bank will use all funds to acquire loans. How high does she have to set the equity capital requirement for a bank raising £1 million from deposits?

We set $L = (1 + E)$, where E is the requirement (in £m). Then $\mu = 1.25(1 + E)$ and $\sigma = 0.4(1 + E)$. The tables show that the value of Z associated with a tail probability of 10 per cent is 1.28. Substituting these values into Z_a gives

$$1.28 = Z = [\mu - D(1 + r)]/\sigma = [1.25(1 + E) - 1.1]/0.4(1 + E),$$

which we can solve to get $E = 0.49$.

Question 4. Suppose that banks can hold N types of asset, which we label A_1, A_2, ..., A_n. The expected returns on these assets are R_1, R_2, ..., R_n and the standard deviation of these returns s_1, s_2, ..., s_n. A regulator decides to introduce a capital adequacy scheme to control insolvency risks. The minimum amount of capital for every £1 of asset of type i will be denoted by £c_i.

(a) Consider the pros and cons of each of the following capital adequacy rules:

Rule 1: $c_i = ks_i$ where $k > 0$.
Rule 2: $c_i = cR_i$ where $c > 0$.
Rule 3: $c_i = d(R_i - \bar{R})$ where $d > 0$ and $\bar{R}$ is the average return on the N assets.
Rule 4: $c_i = bs_i/R_i$ where $b > 0$.

(b) What extra information would be useful in designing capital weights? (University of London, Faculty of Economics, B.Sc. (Econ) Financial Economics, Final Examination, 1997).

11. Bank Regulation in Practice

Because of their special nature, banks are more heavily regulated than other financial institutions. Banks are vital social institutions because they operate the payments transmission system. They benefit from economies of scale and scope, and so tend to be relatively large. Their deposits are fixed claims, and high deposit to capital ratios encourage excessive risk-taking. Bank loan values are subjective and most bank deposits are callable at short notice, making the system prone to asymmetric-information-induced panics.

Monetary history offers examples of a range of regulatory regimes, varying from laissez-faire to prohibitive systems which severely restrict bank portfolio selection. However, in most countries, the present banking regime is based on limited liability for shareholders and the public provision of insurance for depositors. In the USA, for example, insurance provides complete cover for all deposits up to $100,000. These devices are designed to maintain confidence and ensure that the banking system is run-proof. But they also remove the incentive for stakeholders to monitor the bank.

Supervision in the current regime is undertaken instead by government agencies like the central bank, with the potential loss from the deposit guarantee providing an incentive for effective monitoring. Prudential controls vary internationally, but there has been a degree of convergence in recent years as capital mobility has increased and regulators have tried to reduce regulatory arbitrage. Although some countries still have a prohibitive approach which restricts competition and asset choice, most rely upon capital adequacy requirements which are believed to cause fewer distortions. Excessive risk-taking is also curtailed by restricting bank investment in equities. The sanctions open to the regulator also vary from country to country, but the threat of bank closure always provides the ultimate sanction.

This regime is coherent and has theoretical appeal. It capitalizes upon the government's ability to maintain confidence through its power to redistribute and print money. Diamond and Dybvig establish that the deposit insurance and lender of last resort mechanisms are unequivocally beneficial in a non-stochastic world, run-proofing the system at zero cost. In practice, however, outcomes are uncertain and moral hazard is a serious problem, forcing the government agencies to monitor banks much more closely than non-banks. Although the government has a theoretical advantage as a delegated monitor, its track record has been very poor.

Most commentators agree that in recent years there have been too many failures for comfort. The last decade has seen mass failures of Savings and Loan institutions in the USA. More recently, the Japanese and South Korean banking systems have also seen massive bailouts. As Calomiris (1990) remarks, these losses dwarf those in the USA in the 1930s. Although the losses have not been on the same scale, faith in the UK system has been eroded by a succession of failures: Johnson Matthey, BCCI, and Barings Bank. Losses at LTCM (Box 11.1) and banks (Box 11.3) in 1998 raise further questions about risk management systems in banking and other highly leveraged institutions.

This chapter reviews these problems and looks at proposals for root and branch reform. After looking at the radical changes made in New Zealand, we look at some of the piecemeal changes being made elsewhere. The emphasis here is upon prudential regulation. However, we conclude the chapter with a look at some of the important competition issues which arise when the banking system is dominated by a few large institutions, as it is in Britain. The argument for combining the prudential regulation of banking and insurance with the supervision of other financial institutions is addressed in the next chapter.

11.1. Problems with the present regulatory regime

The critics of the present system argue that these failures reflect a fundamental problem, which is that the balance between market discipline, insurance, and liquidity assistance is awry. The emphasis upon deposit insurance leads to moral hazard, which in turn causes bank failures and bailouts.

This regime involves multiple layers of agency: the borrower is the agent of the bank manager, who is the agent of the central bank, which ultimately acts for the taxpayer. It effectively absolves shareholders and depositors from responsibility and thus places a heavy burden upon the regulator, raising unrealistic expectations among the general public about the efficacy of prudential controls and the safety of their investments in the banking system. This is especially true in sophisticated banking systems with a high level of deposit insurance cover like the US system. But even in countries without formal deposit insurance schemes like New Zealand there is arguably a de facto obligation upon the central bank to bail banks out when they get into difficulties.

In my view, this incentive problem is compounded by the increasingly complicated and derivative nature of banking transactions. The complexity of this business makes it extremely difficult for any outsider, whether it be a central bank, rating agency, depositor, or shareholder, to assess the risk profile of a bank's balance sheet and the effectiveness of its risk controls. The problem is that although reforms may give outsiders every *incentive* to monitor a bank's activities, they may increasingly lack the *ability* to do this.

Critics of the present system also argue that regulators always leave it too late before taking action, for fear of precipitating a crisis. This was allegedly the case in the Bank of England's closure of BCCI and in the case of many US Savings and Loan institutions. The public inevitably blames the regulator when things go wrong, even if internal management is largely culpable. These observations have led to a critical re-evaluation of the regulatory system.

Many different proposals have been made for reforming the current regime. Yet there is little consensus about the way in which the system should be reformed. Economists like Dowd (1989) and Glasner (1989) follow Hayek (1978) in arguing for an unregulated banking system. They play down the uniqueness of banks and government deposit guarantees. Others like Friedman (1959), Laidler (1992), Benston and Kaufman (1996), and Calomiris (1998), while generally critical of government intervention, believe that the banking and monetary system is one area where it is inevitable. On this view, we need to devise better rules for monetary management and prudential regulation.

11.2. Radical reform proposals

These reforms seek to make managers, shareholders, and depositors more responsible by giving them more of an incentive to monitor. However, it is arguably of equal importance to see that these agents have the ability to monitor effectively. Outsiders may be given every incentive to monitor, but do they have the ability to understand, monitor, and control what is going on inside a complex modern bank operating in a fast-moving market?

11.2.1. The case for free banking

Free bankers like Glasner (1989) and Dowd (1989) argue that there is nothing special about the banking firm. They are deeply suspicious of any deposit guarantee based upon the government's power of redistribution. They are also critical of the government's monopoly of the printing press, which they say has been grossly abused, causing depression in the 1930s and inflation post-1945. They claim that their theoretical arguments are supported by the historical evidence that the monetary system functions well in the absence of government regulation.

Many countries have experienced this kind of laissez-faire system, notably the USA 1837–1913, Canada 1817–1914, Sweden 1831–1902, and Scotland 1716–1844. These systems all exhibited a remarkably low failure rate: in particular, there were no bank failures at all in Sweden between 1831 and 1902. These systems were innovative and competitive; the Scottish banks, for example, pioneering the payment of interest on demand deposits and the overdraft system. The US banks were able to pay interest on demand deposits until this was prohibited by the Glass-Steagall Banking Act of 1933. The level of government regulation was minimal in these historical episodes. It was usually confined to the prohibition of small-denomination banknotes, designed to protect small unsophisticated individuals. In the USA, some states, following the lead of the New York 'safety fund' in 1829, set up compulsory deposit insurance schemes, but these quickly became insolvent.

These laissez-faire monetary systems provided both currency and deposits, which were usually convertible upon demand into gold or silver. This limited the money supply and kept the rate of inflation more stable than in the modern fiat money system. Banks accepted each other's notes and cheques and settled these through a clearing house. The 'law of reflux' meant that excessive expansion by a bank led to a deficit on clearing which had to be financed by asset sales, curtailing further expansion.

Membership of the clearing house was vital to an institution in a free banking regime. It gave its peers information about the bank's business, while the threat of exclusion gave them a sanction for misbehaviour. The clearing house also allowed members to economize on reserves of base currency (Laidler 1992). In some systems (such as the National Banking System which operated in the USA between 1865 and 1913) the clearing house could act as a lender of last resort, helping banks which were deemed to be solvent but had a liquidity problem.

The members of the clearing house thus had an incentive and a comparative advantage in monitoring each other's performance, placing them in a position similar to that filled by the central bank in the current system. However, unlike the present system, in which stakeholders have little incentive to monitor, this was reinforced by effective shareholder and depositor scrutiny. Laidler (1992) notes that deposit banking during the free banking era was confined to the business community, 'which could be relied upon to understand banks and monitor their behaviour'. He argues that the prohibition of small denomination notes and ultimately the move to government monopoly of the note issue was justified by the need to protect small unsophisticated users.

Historically, the liability of shareholders for the bank's losses gave them a strong incentive to scrutinize the bank. For example, in the USA, double shareholder liability was the norm until the reforms of the 1930s. This meant that if a bank failed, shareholders not only stood to lose their equity stake but could also have an additional and equal sum confiscated. In Scotland, only the three big Edinburgh-based banks had a charter granting limited liability. West coast banks (like the Glasgow Bank, which had 130 branches throughout Scotland at the time of its collapse) had unlimited liability.

Proponents of the laissez-faire system argue that the failure of a bank is little different from that of a commercial firm. However, it is not difficult to find examples which suggest that bank failure is a much more serious affair. For example, in Scotland the sudden failure of the Glasgow Bank in 1878 bankrupted large sections of the city's entrepreneurial class. Of its 1,819 shareholders, only 250 remained solvent after the collapse. This precipitated the bankruptcy of many industrial firms, with long-lasting repercussions for the region's trade and industry.

Nevertheless, unlimited liability did work well in the small, often family-owned banks seen during the eighteenth and nineteenth centuries. The managers of these banks typically had a strong financial incentive to ensure that prudent policies were being followed. This gave outside shareholders the reassurance they needed to invest on an unlimited or multiple liability basis. In turn, shareholder liability reassured depositors, providing a cushion, in addition to that provided by the bank's own capital reserve. Even so, the level of bank capital was much greater in these systems than under the present system. Kaufman (1992) tells us that in the USA, bank capital ratios were over 40 per cent before the civil war, 20 per cent around the turn of the century, and around 15 per cent when the Federal deposit insurance was introduced in 1933–4.

Nowadays, the concentration of equity and the level of shareholder activity are much lower than they were historically. This change is partly explained by equity disclosure rules that were introduced in the USA in the 1930s and have been adopted by several other countries since. These rules have been retained and reinforced (Box 7.1) to make it difficult for takeover bidders to acquire stock cheaply in the market before revealing their hand. However, they have the side-effect of discouraging large holdings and thus reducing the incentive for shareholder activism and monitoring (Section 7.1).

11.2.2. How would laissez-faire work in a modern banking system?

With these safeguards in place, free banks succeeded as part of a close-knit financial community. The historical experience of laissez-faire shows that it is important for stakeholders to become actively involved in bank management. However, it is not clear that laissez-faire would work in a modern financial community based on anonymity and limited liability. Although it would place more responsibility upon shareholders and depositors, it is hard to see how they could be made insiders to the extent necessary to effectively scrutinize a modern bank.

Admittedly, large professional investors might be able to look after their deposits, but this would leave a mass of small depositors with little knowledge or understanding of the situation, free riding on the activity of others. Small depositors would thus be prone to rumour and herding behaviour and liable to cause a run on the bank. If this happened, then liquidation costs could mean that even a bank with 20 per cent capital reserves could be pushed into insolvency. This in turn would surely make even the most sophisticated depositors prone to panic. Monetary history is mute on this point, since legislators excluded the uninformed from participation.

Clearing house members should also have an advantage in scrutinizing bank management, and might even be willing to bail out a competitor that was facing liquidity problems, providing that members knew this competitor to be solvent. However, there is no reason to think that this informational advantage would be any better than that enjoyed by a central bank under the present system.

A modern free banking system might therefore be just a privatized version of the present one—but without government deposit guarantees. It is possible that private institutions could provide this insurance instead, and historical examples are provided by Calomiris (1990) and Calomiris and Kahn (1996). However, Calomiris (1998) argues that de facto government insurance would make this difficult now. Free banking theorists suggest that confidence could be maintained instead by the publication of high capital reserves. Yet historically, even with the cushion of shareholder assets, these had to be much higher than in the present scheme of regulation.

The argument for a self-regulating payments system will become influential if the growth of m-commerce forces the development of new digital money systems. So far, e-commerce has relied upon the credit and debit card payment systems for transactions settlement. Yet as the scale and scope of the Internet grow, the shortcomings of this plastic money system are likely to become apparent–notably the inefficiency of using these devices for making micropayments and their inability to settle peer-to-peer transactions. New sophisticated electronic systems (like PayPal, Visacash, and Mondex) are available for use on the Internet and elsewhere but have yet to reach critical mass. Alan Greenspan and the Federal Reserve want to allow these new systems to develop outside the framework of prudential regulation and deposit insurance. So, if these systems do catch on they will furnish a modern example of a self-regulating monetary system and provide an interesting test bed for free banking theory.

11.2.3. The Calomiris blueprints for a new global financial architecture

Charles Calomiris is a professor at Columbia Business School whose reputation in this area is based largely on his highly respected historical studies of American free banking systems. His 'blueprints' emphasize the basic principles laid down for the lender of last resort by Bagehot (1873), who stressed the need for a central bank to lend freely, but at penal rates and only on collateral to solvent banks. However, this proposal sets the reform of the banking system in an international context, following the international financial crisis of 1998 which led to massive bailouts of East Asian countries by the IMF.

Calomiris argues that market discipline and liquidity assistance can be combined to give a system which is much more robust than the present one in the face of bank runs and other speculative attacks, while avoiding moral hazard. Like Friedman (1959) he proposes a rule-based system that leaves the authorities with very little discretion.

His first blueprint shows how to reconstruct the domestic financial architecture. Credible rules are established at the national level that deliberately expose bank shareholders and bondholders to loss in the event of failure and confine the support that the taxpayer provides to insured deposits. Particular emphasis is placed on a minimum (2 per cent) subordinated debt requirement. This basic idea was originally due to Wall (1989). These junior debts are last in the queue of creditors in the event of a bankruptcy. They are not covered by the deposit guarantee. Their values are not swollen by the asset substitution problem affecting equity values. Governments can credibly pre-commit not to bail out these bond-holders, who are largely sophisticated investors, in a way which is not possible in the case of small depositors. In fact, bondholders as well as shareholders lost their money in the Barings Bank failure, despite a strong lobby in their favour.

The Calomiris version of the subordinated debt requirement is designed to reduce the degree of moral hazard, to furnish an indicator of market risk, and ultimately to provide an automatic market mechanism for contracting excessively risky bank balance sheets. He proposes that these should be short-term (two-year maturity) instruments and that banks should not be permitted to issue these bonds if their yield spreads exceed 5 per cent. Debt redemptions would then shrink the capital base and hence the bank's business until the market risk rating improved. This discipline is buttressed by subordinated debt cross-holding rules that encourage banks to monitor each other. This market assessment of risk would be reflected in the cost of capital, encouraging good behaviour, and helping to offset any perverse incentives set up by deposit insurance and regulation.

Calomiris proposes free entry into banking to increase transparency and international diversification of ownership. He wants to bring back asset-side restrictions in the form of a 20 per cent liquid asset requirement and a novel 20 per cent 'global securities' requirement, aimed at reducing risks through international diversification. As noted earlier, Calomiris reluctantly accepts the need for deposit insurance to combat the problem of asymmetric-information-induced contagion.

The second blueprint is designed to reform the international monetary architecture. Reflecting Bagehot, Calomiris argues that international support from the IMF and other agencies would be automatic but at penal rates and restricted to countries that adopted the banking reform. He argues that the established IMF method of lending in staggered amounts or tranches conditional upon macroeconomic policy criteria is inappropriate when large amounts of liquidity are needed quickly to staunch speculative outflows and restore confidence. Penal rates give an incentive for policies designed to bring early repayment. IMF lending programmes have involved tranches of finance at above-market rates, although these are not as high as Calomiris would like.

Calomiris accepts that these international arrangements would be exclusive and that many countries would not be able to meet such conditions. He argues that governmental aid and other institutions are the appropriate means of support in this case, subject to democratic approval. He concludes by saying that if vested interest prevented its reform, then he would side with Schwarz (1998) in arguing for the abolition of the IMF.

11.2.4. The Narrow Banking scheme

The problem of the small uninformed depositor is explicitly addressed by the Narrow Banking proposal. This scheme was originally proposed by Litan (1987). *The Economist* (1996) has strongly supported this proposal: that lender of last resort and deposit insurance facilities should be restricted to a narrow range of retail banking institutions catering for small depositors with instant access. As a *quid pro quo*, the narrow banks would be required to invest exclusively in safe government debt and would be closely monitored by government. Again, a historical precedent can be found in the USA in the nineteenth century, where some states required their banks to invest exclusively in municipal or federal securities. Britain's Trustee Savings Banks (now deregulated and part of the Lloyds TSB group) offer additional historical examples of institutions catering for small unsophisticated depositors and facing prohibitive regulation structures.

This would leave a free banking regime for 'wide' banks catering for sophisticated corporate and professional investors. These banking institutions would offer term deposit facilities at market-related interest rates under a regime of *caveat emptor*. The theory is that depositors would monitor these banks, while fixed maturity deposits would help protect against runs. The narrow banking idea may thus be seen as a variation on the free banking idea, which by trying to cater for the small unsophisticated depositor provides a solution to one of the main problems with the free banking mechanism. In a similar vein, Merton and Bodie (1993) argue that the regulation of banks enjoying a government deposit guarantee should be a prohibitive one, with restrictions on bank portfolio choice.

These proposals attempt to get the best of both worlds by drawing upon the strengths of both regulated and unregulated models. However, the danger with all such proposals is that they may precipitate the worst of both worlds. The regulated sector might be free of moral hazard, but it would be little more than a government bank and would offer a very low rate of return. In good times, unsophisticated depositors would surely be tempted into the high rates offered by the unregulated sector, making this prone to capital flight in times of crisis. The use of time deposits cleverly anticipates this problem, but might not prove adequate in the event. It also removes an important discipline on management. Moreover, this proposal still does not deal with the monitoring problem: uninsured outside depositors may have a strong incentive to monitor the wide banks, but how can they find out what is really going on?

11.3. Recent reforms of bank regulatory regimes

Although these various reform proposals involve different degrees of government involvement in banking markets, all suggest that there should be less government discretion and more market discipline. Recent changes in the rules have moved bank regulatory regimes in broadly the same direction. New Zealand has taken a radical step towards a free banking system. Other regulators have been much more cautious.

11.3.1. The 'Brash' approach

Don Brash became Governor of the Reserve Bank of New Zealand in 1988. Like many bank regulators, he felt that the central bank's de facto responsibility for bank failure had led to an unrealistic attitude on the part of the public. Under the New Zealand reforms, instituted in 1996, the Reserve Bank continues to monitor banks, but only on the basis of publicly available information and without culpability. With the exception of the Basel Capital Adequacy ratios, all prudential rules are eliminated. This is designed to place more of the burden of monitoring banks upon stakeholders.

This switch from government to stakeholder responsibility is buttressed by an attempt to make managers more accountable and ultimately culpable for failure. Banks are required to publish more loan risk and other information on a more timely, quarterly basis. More frequent external audits are also required. Moreover, bank directors are required to attest to the accuracy of this information and the adequacy of internal controls. In principle, they can be sued by depositors, shareholders, and liquidators if these risk control arrangements fail. This is perhaps the most revolutionary aspect of the new arrangements, since it effectively reintroduces the principle of unlimited liability for bank management. Like any market-based mechanism it reduces the costs of compliance for both the regulator and the regulated and gives management a strong incentive to acquire a good credit rating and bring down the cost of capital.

It remains to be seen how well these arrangements will work in practice. Its critics say this reform is only practicable because New Zealand banks are subsidiaries of foreign banks (like Standard Chartered, based in the UK) and are ultimately supervised by overseas regulators (like the Bank of England). Ninety per cent of New Zealand deposits are held with branches of foreign banks. This observation is important but it should not be given too much weight. No one would suggest that local supervision is redundant under the Basle Concordat or that the Reserve Bank did nothing under the *ancien régime*. Surely no one would suggest in the wake of the Leeson affair that the Bank of England can effectively supervise offices in far-flung outposts like Singapore and Canterbury without local cooperation? Does anyone really think that British taxpayers provide de facto deposit insurance in the antipodes? The success of these reforms will provide a recipe for radical changes in governance rules designed to increase market discipline, combined with arm's-length regulation and the abolition of deposit insurance.

Another criticism is that the risk of being sued for negligence could deter good managers with personal capital and attract poor managers with nothing to lose. However, in a flexible labour market like New Zealand and other Anglo-Saxon countries we would expect the rise in risk levels to be compensated by a rise in remuneration rather than an exodus of good managers. Moreover, the fact that well-heeled bankers are prepared to put their personal capital at risk should signal a low-risk prospect as in the Leland and Pyle (1977) model. This is arguably a more telling indicator of confidence and viability than the high capital reserves of the free banking school, the credit ratings of the latest Basel proposal (Box 11.2), and even some of the clever bond-based indicators proposed by Wall (1989) and Calomiris (1998).

I have reservations about these proposals, but for a different reason. It may be the case that the operational risks inherent in the modern banking industry are so opaque and so difficult to manage that managers may not be able to get on top of them. In this case, no reasonable level of remuneration could compensate for the risk. If so, this reform will fail. But if managers cannot effectively control what is going on then no one can. If this reform does fail, then this will indicate that the risks in the present system are essentially uncontrollable, suggesting a move back to a prohibitive system of regulation.

The new New Zealand regime represents the most interesting of the recent banking reforms. Its emphasis upon corporate governance is surely the correct one, an attempt to get to the heart of the principal–agent problem. Elsewhere, more orthodox proposals are being implemented. Like monetary rules or inflation targets in the macroeconomic area, these reforms accept the need for central bank intervention in money and banking, but try to make the present system function better. In the meantime, in Britain, Japan, and some other countries, banking supervision is being merged with other types of regulation. However, this reform is of a more general nature and is discussed in the final section of the next chapter.

13.3.2. Structural Early Intervention and Resolution (SEIR)

This is the name given to the reform suggested by Benston and Kaufman (1988, 1996). Their proposal strongly reflects contemporary US attitudes towards financial regulation. They are very doubtful about the regulator's ability to control risk in bank portfolios by restricting asset choice. Similarly, like Kroszner and Rajan (1994) and others, they regard the dichotomy between investment and commercial banking enshrined in the Glass–Steagall Act (1933) as anachronistic.

Benston and Kaufman reluctantly accept the need for deposit insurance and government regulation of banking. However, they suggest two ways of improving the regime. First, like many US commentators, they argue that deposit insurance should be restricted to small deposits and that premia should be related to the riskiness of the bank's portfolio. Second, they propose a gradualist approach to regulation, with much less reliance upon bank closure. They suggest that the regulator should monitor the situation on a more timely basis and impose a sliding scale of penalties as a bank gets into trouble rather than wait until it is close to bankruptcy. This scheme is based on a higher level of capitalization, which is maintained through capital injections as the bank makes losses. Fines are also incurred if losses are made. The ultimate sanction of closure is held in reserve to make sure that these equity injections are made, either by the original shareholders or other interested parties.

Merton's (1977) analogy between banking and option markets offers an insight into this line of reasoning. As his paper points out, the value of a bank's equity can be seen as a call option on the loan portfolio. Remember, a call option contract carries the right but not the obligation to buy the underlying asset or loan portfolio at a price fixed in advance. This is a worry in the case of a bank loan portfolio, because if the value of the portfolio drops, then gearing and the temptation for excessive risk-taking increases.

In contrast, a futures contract carries both the right and the obligation to buy. The obligation is enforced by continuous margin requirements operated by the futures exchange. In particular, if the price of the under-lying asset falls, the holder of a futures contract has to make up the dif-ference immediately. The Benston and Kaufman (1988) proposals effectively emulate this system, with the bank's capital base playing the role of the margin. The switch from an option to a futures risk model removes the effect of convexity. That is because the bank's shareholders now have to treat losses and gains in the loan portfolio symmetrically, accounting and compensating for any deficiency on a timely basis by new equity injections (resembling margin calls).

The idea of imposing fines for large losses as well as recapitalization has been criticized because these fines could push a bank over the brink into bankruptcy. This would happen if the losses occurred suddenly because of an abrupt or 'jump' change in value, an effect which options and futures trading mechanisms find difficult to handle. Also, with a sys-tem of fines in place shareholders should give more weight to losses than gains. In contrast to the usual case of excessive risk-taking, this could make shareholders and managers excessively cautious. With these reser-vations, the Benston and Kaufman proposal seems sensible. It was clearly reflected in the FDIC Improvement Act (1991). The Act's Prompt Correc-tive Action Provisions are very similar to the SEIR proposal and should help to ensure that the US regulators act in a more timely and automatic fashion.

This automatic mechanism seems particularly appropriate in the case of investment banks that have portfolios of traded securities that are rou-tinely 'marked to market' at the end of every trading day. The analogy with the futures margin mechanism is close in this case, since, in line with the standard theory, the underlying securities trade at prices which are continuously observable. However, commercial bank loan portfolios are not priced in the market. Their value to the bank depends upon confi-dential 'credit' (or default) risk information that may not be available to outsiders like the regulator. The valuation of the bank's loan portfolio (and a fortiori its effective capital reserve) may be difficult in practice. The risk characteristics of a loan portfolio may also be difficult to assess.

11.3.3. Basel 1999: towards a new capital adequacy framework

A simple way of classifying credit risk has been developed by the Basel Committee on Bank Supervision (1995a) and enshrined in the 1988 Basel Accord between bank regulators of the G10 countries (Box 2.3). They agreed that banks operating within their jurisdictions should have enough capital to cover at least 8 per cent of 'weighted' assets. The asset risk weights vary from one type of loan to another, with government debt for example attracting a zero risk weight, residential mortgage debt a 50 per cent weight, and commercial and consumer lending a 100 per cent weight. Reflecting criticisms of the 1988 Accord (Box 2.3), the Committee published a consultative paper on a new capital adequacy framework in June 1999 (Basel Committee, 1995a). This consists of three proposals, known as the 'three pillars'.

The first pillar represents a development of the 1988 capital requirement. The four risk bands of the existing system are preserved, and the 50 per cent weighting for residential mortgages remains in place. However, the paper proposes the use of external agency risk ratings to grade assets within each of the other groups. For example in the case of sovereign debt, AAA to AA− rated debt still has a zero weight; A+ to A− is weighted at 20 per cent; BBB+ to BBB− at 50 per cent; BB+ to B− at 100 per cent. Unrated sovereign debt has a risk weighting of 100 per cent, but all government (or other) paper rated at B− has a risk weight of 150 per cent. Several different risk assessment systems are proposed for banks, including two systems based on agency credit ratings. The paper discusses the use of credit risk systems based on banks' own private assessment, and, more radically, the use of internal credit risk modelling techniques.

The second pillar proposes a framework for supervisory review. This would oblige signatories to check the overall institutional risk profile and impose discretionary increases in capital where this was thought to be appropriate. This is already common practice in most large countries and is designed to discourage any perverse incentives produced by loopholes in the risk weighting system and to allow for special features such as weaknesses in bank management or risk control systems which the weighting system does not reflect. The third proposal is to introduce more transparency and market discipline. Reflecting the Brash reform, banks would be required to publish more comprehensive and timely accounts, as well as information on risk exposure and risk management systems. This would allow the markets to provide a better assessment of risk. This assessment would be reflected in the cost of capital, helping to offset any perverse incentives set up by anomalies in the risk weighting system.

Although they pay lip service to the use of risk modelling techniques, the Committee's basic proposals remain very simple, especially compared with the techniques currently employed by the banking industry. They look at assets in isolation, without allowing for correlations (possibly negative) between different assets which critically influence the overall risk profile. The risk weights only reflect 'credit' risk and do not address 'market' risk stemming from variations in macroeconomic variables like interest rates. These factors can influence the price of long-term government debt, even if this has no credit risk and enjoys a zero risk weight. The use of agency ratings is also questionable, since these ratings are only roughly correlated with historical risk and usually lag behind market perception. The use of subordinated debt spreads as proposed by Wall (1988) and Calomiris (1998) would appear to offer a better way to harness market discipline.

However, when assessing these proposals it is important to remember that the use of relatively simple and objective criteria facilitates international agreement in this important area. It also reduces the scope for differential interpretation at the national level and hence regulatory drift. As the 1998 crisis revealed, the use of rapidly moving market or risk-model-based risk assessments can be destabilizing, placing banks in double jeopardy by prescribing an increase in the target capital base when losses are actually contracting the base. Finally, these are minimum rules which the national authorities can extend using more sophisticated methods. The 1999 proposals would surely bring an improvement in the international regulatory environment, if only by blocking some of the more obvious loopholes in the present system.

11.3.4. The European dimension

The Basel arrangements offer an example of international coordination designed to minimize regulatory arbitrage – the migration of large 'footloose' banks to centres with the most lax supervisory standards. As Chapter 2 argued, this risk rises as technology increases capital mobility and as international barriers are dismantled, and is a particular worry in Europe. Investment and wholesale banking is much more footloose than retail business and the European Commission's (1993) Capital Adequacy Directive (CAD) explicitly recognizes this fact. This directive imposed uniform capital requirements for the traded assets of all securities houses and banks in the European Union and was effective from 1 January 1996.

The European Commission's Second Banking Directive (1992) makes the central bank of a bank's 'home country' formally responsible for its supervision and that of its subsidiaries, wherever these are located. However, as the BCCI (Box 2.2) and LTCM (Box 11.1) crises proved, financial stability is an international issue and requires close cooperation between supervisors at different levels in different financial centres. This was recognized in the Maastricht Treaty, which handed the operation of Euro-zone monetary policy over to the ECB. The Treaty left the national central banks responsible for supervising their own banking systems.[1] The ECB must nevertheless be consulted on legislation concerning bank regulation. Moreover, the Maastricht Treaty contained a clause which left it open for supervisory powers to be given to the ECB in the future. Recent statements by Wim Duisenburg, the President of the ECB, have argued that cross-border consolidation in the European banking industry may now require supervision by the ECB.

11.4. Competition issues in bank regulation

One of the ways in which banks differ from other institutions is that they tend to be large, taking advantage of economies of scale and scope. With the notable exception of the USA, most developed countries have banking systems that are dominated by a handful of large institutions. Besides the prudential aspects, this makes competition issues important in the regulation of this industry. These aspects are normally handled by separate prudential and competition authorities, but are interconnected.

In concluding this chapter we return to the competition issues raised in Chapter 7 and explore the connection between industrial concentration, competition, and solvency in banking. It is important to stress here that industrial concentration does not necessarily mean a lack of competition. If markets are contestable (Baumol 1970), then potential entrants can keep profit margins at low levels even if there is a single supplier. Indeed, that is the simplifying assumption used in many of the mathematical models deployed in this book. Some examples of contestable banking markets were discussed in Section 2.7. Bank of England (1991: table A) provides a useful summary of contestable features of various bank product markets. Nevertheless it remains clear that banks have market power in many areas. For example, in Britain the market for small business services has been an abiding concern of the competition authorities. An interesting survey of the US empirical literature on structural concentration and market performance is provided by Gilbert (1984).

The basic regulatory issue in this area concerns the agency problem and the tension that this induces between competition, incentives, and failure

---

[1] These central banks intervene in the money market on behalf of the ECB, and could in principle act as lender of last resort to the Euro-system. However, it remains unclear how the lender of last resort facility will be operated (if at all) in the event of a crisis.

Box 11.1. The Crisis at Long-Term Capital Management (LTCM)

LTCM was a hedge fund set up in 1994 by John Meriwether, Robert Merton, and Myron Scholes. These founders were all famous in their own way. Myron Scholes is the 'Scholes' in the Black–Scholes option pricing model and a Nobel prize winner in Economics. Robert Merton is the pioneer of continuous time finance, another well-published academic and Nobel laureate—my bibliography is testimony to his contribution. John Meriwether, known as the King of Wall Street, made his name as a bond trader at Salomon Brothers.

Like all hedge funds, LTCM operated on the principle that asset price anomalies could be exploited by setting up an appropriate hedge position. For example suppose that we think that a corporate bond is underpriced relative to a government bond. In other words, the yield 'spread' is too large, compared to the normal (or perhaps the theoretical) value. In this case we buy the corporate bond and hedge out the interest rate risk by short-selling the appropriate amount of the government bond (or bond future). The size of the short position is calculated from the hedge ratio, which depends upon the relative sensitivity of the two bonds to interest rates. There are two 'legs' to this position, which cancel out interest risk, leaving the exposure to the spread. (This is why the gross positions of a hedge fund are very large compared to the net exposure.) Once this position is set up, it will increase in value if the market perception of the firm's risk improves and the spread falls. But, of course, the opposite can happen.

Securities like government bonds are short-sold by borrowing them from institutional holders (usually through a sale and repurchase agreement or 'repo' arranged through an intermediary) and then selling them in the market. This exposes the institution (or intermediary) to the risk of a collapse of the hedge fund. This counterparty risk is often managed by a system of margin calls (Chapter 9). When futures are used, margin calls are designed to insulate the futures exchange and its clients. (However, see Section 1.6.)

LTCM was initially very successful. With their reputations, the founders did not find it difficult to attract equity investors and institutions willing to trade in the repo market. With an equity capital base of just over $3 billion (and borrowing thought by the market to be about $100 billion) it made a return of 21 per cent (after fees and expenses) for its investors in 1994, its first year of operation. A return of 43 per cent was made in 1995 and 41 per cent followed in 1996. These returns put LTCM at the top of the hedge fund league. However, things began to go wrong in the summer of 1997. A financial crisis that began in Thailand quickly spread to other East Asian countries. Although LTCM was not directly involved in this area, a 'flight to quality' began: western investors sold corporate and other high yield bonds to buy government bonds like US Treasuries that LTCM had sold short. The spreads that LTCM had bet would narrow began to widen. During the summer of 1998, LTCM increased its hedge positions in high-yield bonds, believing that a return to normal

(*continued*)

would generate huge profits. This involved even more borrowing, straining the equity base.

Then, on 14 August 1998, the Russian government unexpectedly defaulted on its rouble debt payments. Spreads widened dramatically and LTCM began to make much bigger losses. Four days later, it lost half a billion dollars in a single day, effectively wiping out its remaining equity. At this stage the problems at LTCM became apparent to its creditors, who began to worry about counterparty risk. They had not realized until then how much LTCM had borrowed in total. Their problem was that if they asked for their money to be returned, this would have forced LTCM to liquidate its positions, resulting in even wider spreads and larger losses. This would almost certainly have precipitated bankruptcies at other hedge fund managers. Counterparty exposure had the potential to cause failures at banks and other financial institutions that were not directly involved in spread trades.

Thus it became apparent to the Federal Reserve that LTCM had the potential to cause immense damage to the western financial system, even though it was not a bank. It was highly geared and had relationships with practically every major firm on Wall Street, as well as banks in London and elsewhere (see Box 7.1). Alan Greenspan, the Fed chairman, chose to avert the risk of systemic damage by organizing a bailout. The Fed persuaded LTCM's major creditors to take over the fund and subscribe another $3.5 billion of equity funding. LTCM's original investors were left with nothing, but a serious collapse was avoided. Regulators are now taking the threat of counterparty contagion very seriously. The Brockmeijer Report (Basel Committee, 1999b) provides a useful insight into the latest official thinking on this subject.

rates in the financial industry. This tension is particularly acute in the banking system. The problem (Section 7.2) is that a financial structure that motivates bank operators to behave in the public interest requires a 'reasonable' rate of return, which may not be forthcoming if banking markets are open and competitive. Allowing entry to all comers, for example, might increase competition but could put depositors' funds and ultimately the payments system itself at risk.

Largely for this reason, most post-war banking systems were cartelized in the hope that restricted entry and secure profits would promote safety and soundness and offer the government a tool for interventionist policies. (see Box 11.2). The link between size and efficiency meant that large banks can exploit economies of scale and scope, offering the government a useful source of tax (including inflation tax) revenue. Don Cruikshank, a former telecommunications utility regulator appointed to conduct a review of competition issues in UK banking, rightly remarked that the payments system has many of the features of a natural monopoly. Natural

Box 11.2. A prohibitive regulatory regime: British banking 1945–71

Until the reform of 1971, the UK banking system was organized along highly pro-hibitive lines. The big clearing banks (members of the London Clearing house) oper-ated as a cartel. This was organized by the Bank of England. The cartel restricted competition and boosted the value of equity in banking. Solvency and confidence were maintained by a 'hidden' capital reserve known only to the Bank of England's regulators. Prudential rules were supported by a reserve asset requirement which said that 28 per cent of the assets had to be invested in liquid assets. Credit was allocated at a low interest rate in line with government guidelines that favoured industrial borrowers. There were strict lines of demarcation between banks and other financial institutions.

Following a critical report by the Labour government's Prices and Incomes Board, the Bank Rate cartel was abolished in 1971. This opened the way to a more com-petitive system. Banks set deposit interest rates to attract funds. The interbank market provided individual banks with (so-called liability-side) liquidity, and reflect-ing this the reserve asset ratio was reduced to 12.5 per cent (and was then abolished in 1981). Credit was allocated by the market, not government rules. Other markets, like those for mortgages and credit cards, based on new information technology, arguably became contestable. Hidden reserves were abolished as part of a gradual move to an explicit system of capital adequacy, culminating in the adoption of the Basle 8 per cent ratio in 1988. The operation of competitive forces in this system is reviewed by Wilson (1978) and the Bank of England (1991).

monopolies have historically been heavily regulated. Cruikshank also highlighted the delicate trade-off between competition and prudential considerations in banking (see Section 11.5).

This philosophy did not affect the USA, which historically has exhib-ited a distrust of large banks. Some commentators have traced this back to the dislike which the merchant adventurers of London had for big banks and in particular their worry about a Bank of England monopoly. These concerns were clearly reflected in the debate over the chartering of the second Bank of the United States early in the nineteenth century. The failure to recharter this national bank left bank regulation to individual states. Interstate banking laws then prevented the development of large nationwide banks.

In the twentieth century, the Glass–Steagall Act (1933) and the appli-cation of antitrust laws to the banking sector during the 1950s and 1960s reinforced this bias towards decentralization. Despite the liberalization of the interstate banking laws in the 1980s, the US banking system remains highly decentralized, with about 9,000 separate banking firms running 12,000 banks with 46,000 branches. The size distribution is highly skewed, however, with the top 3 per cent of banks holding three-quarters of the system's total assets.

11.5 Current UK competition issues

In contrast to the USA, the post-war industry was dominated in England and Wales by the 'big five': Barclays, Midland[2], Lloyds, Westminster, and National Provincial. This became the 'big four' in 1970 following the merger of the last two banks into NatWest. In Scotland, the Royal Bank of Scotland, the Bank of Scotland, and the Clydesdale dominated the landscape. Besides the large British banks, there are a large number of building societies and there were the Trustee Savings Banks. The former are mutual institutions that provide mortgage and banking services to personal customers. From the perspective of monetary theory, they are non-bank financial institutions because they are not members of the London clearing house. They settle day-to-day cash imbalances by holding accounts with the clearing banks rather than the Bank of England.

In 1971 the prohibitive post-war UK regime was reformed. The Competition and Credit Control reforms of that year opened the way to competition between banks, building societies, and overseas competitors. Reflecting this, the Bank of England (1991) indicates that between 1970 and 1990 the clearing banks experienced substantial erosion of market share and profit margins in their traditional markets.

Nevertheless, the British competition authorities remain concerned about banking competition. There is the perennial doubt about competition in the provision of medium finance to small companies. Provision of comparative product information is another area of current concern, as is the monopoly of the payments system by the large banks. Cross-subsidization is an issue here as in the case of natural monopolies. This potentially allows firms to use products where they enjoy market power (like local telephone monopolies and bank current accounts) to cut prices and deter competitors in complementary markets (like long-distance calls or, in the case of banks, insurance) where they do not.

In the meantime, City investors and analysts have become increasingly concerned about the poor management of some of the larger clearers,

---

[2] Now absorbed by the Hong Kong and Shanghai Banking Corporation (HSBC), (see Box 11.3).

Box 11.3: Developments in UK banking post-1978

This box highlights some of the important landmarks in the development of the present UK banking system.

1978: The Wilson Committee Report. This committee was established to look at competition in the provision of banking facilities to small business customers, and in particular the availability of medium-term credit. This is a worry that goes back to the medium-term funding gap identified by the Macmillan Committee of 1936. Wilson (1978) concluded that the system was working tolerably well, without any serious funding gap. Nevertheless, small business finance remains an important competition issue.

1984: The Building Societies Act. This allowed the societies to provide a wider range of financial services to their personal customers, including unsecured loan facilities. It also paved the way for building societies to become banks, a route which was followed by Abbey National in 1989 and by the Halifax, Woolwich, Alliance and Leicester, and others during the mid-1990s. The Cheltenham and Gloucester was taken over by Lloyds Bank in 1991. As part of this transition, these new banks began to develop corporate banking facilities. The Trustee Savings Banks (which had been owned by the government) were privatized and became the TSB in 1985. The TSB's corporate banking facilities were boosted by the acquisition of the merchant bank Hill Samuel after Big Bang.

1986: Britain's Big Bang reforms allowed the clearing banks to diversify into market making. They had already developed in-house investment banking divisions to service their larger industrial customers. Small business facilities were well developed, with Barclays, NatWest, and the Midland dominating this market.

1987: The October equity market crash. This brought large losses to many of the clearing banks' investment banking divisions, notably the TSB's Hill Samuel and NatWest's County Bank. In contrast, many of the investment banks (like Warburgs, one of the two largest equity market makers) had deftly managed to escape large losses by hedging in the futures markets. Hill Samuel's major units were sold almost immediately. The Midland also closed its equity market division. County Bank remained under threat of closure for some years, but was eventually consolidated within NatWest. In 1989, the Midland Bank, which had been crippled by large commercial losses on the west coast of America, was taken over by HSBC.

1987-90: The clearing banks had to make large provisions for earlier losses on LDC debt. Then in the recession of 1990-2 large losses were made in domestic lending. Foreclosure of business loans by some of the clearers and repossessions by mortgage lenders made these institutions very unpopular.

1993: NatWest acquired the Gartmore group of fund managers. Their move was part of a general move by banks into bank assurance, culminating in the Lloyds TSB acquisition of Scottish Widows and the NatWest bid for Legal and General in 1999. Many City analysts doubted the wisdom of these moves, saying that the

(*continued*)

diversification gains were questionable and that the prices being paid were excessive. The latter move triggered the bid by the Bank of Scotland for NatWest.

1995: Lloyds Bank merged with the TSB. Its earlier losses at Hill Samuel left the TSB vulnerable to takeover and in October 1995 it agreed to a merger with Lloyds. This proved to be extremely successful, resulting in large cost savings. Consequently, there was much speculation in the City about further consolidation, reflected in a strong performance of bank share prices. However, it was generally understood that their dominance of the small business market ruled out a NatWest–Barclays merger on competition grounds. Overseas bidders apart, it was hard to see anyone with the financial clout to mount a bid for these companies given their size. This stalemate was broken by the bid by the Bank of Scotland for NatWest in 1999.

2000: The Royal Bank of Scotland acquired NatWest after a hostile takeover battle. The Royal Bank counterbid in response to the initial offer by its rival, the Bank of Scotland. Competition issues did not arise in the case of the first bid because the geographical and business overlap between the two banks was small. The overlap was significant in the case of the Royal Bank, but the Secretary of State also allowed this offer to proceed. Although the race to secure investor support was initially very close, the Royal Bank gained the edge over its Scottish rival and prevailed. Despite the promise of similar cost savings and cash handouts to those offered by the Royal Bank, the NatWest board failed to prevent the bid because, with its long history of mismanagement, it had lost the confidence of investors.

reflected in large provisions for bad debts and wasteful diversification into areas like investment banking and fund management. There are several important landmarks in the development of the present UK banking system, which serve to illustrate these worries. These are listed in Box 11.3.

Reflecting these concerns, in November 1998 the new Labour government appointed Don Cruikshank to scrutinize the level of competition, innovation, and efficiency in banking, to see if it met the needs of business and other consumers. His interim report in July 1999 caused a stir by recommending that the new FSA should take on competition as one of its primary objectives, rather than just 'having regard' to it as the FSM Bill had indicated. It is unlikely that the government will give the new financial regulator yet another formal responsibility, but it does seem that the FSA will have to pay greater attention to competition issues than the draft Bill envisaged.

EXERCISES

Question 1. Consider the implications of the 1998 LTCM crisis for (a) the capitalization of leveraged non-banking firms, (b) the compartmentalization of multi-role finance houses, (c) systemic risk, and (d) international regulatory cooperation.

Question 2. Critically evaluate the Calomiris blueprint for reforming (a) national bank regulation and (b) the international financial architecture.

Question 3. Consider the likely effect on the British banking system of introducing this reform package:

- the deposit insurance scheme is to be abolished;
- the FSA is to monitor banks on the basis of publicly available information;
- banks are required to publish more loan-risk and other information on a quarterly basis;
- directors are required to attest to the accuracy of this information and the adequacy of internal controls;
- more frequent external audits are required;
- with the exception of the Basle Capital Adequacy ratios, all prudential rules are eliminated.

Question 4. Suppose that in the none too distant future digital money is provided for use in e-commerce by unregulated Internet banks. Assess the possible implications for financial stability assuming that these banks are obliged to convert e-money into national currency at a rate which (a) is fixed (like main street banks), (b) reflects the value of the banks's assets (like an open-ended trust).

12. Financial Structure and Regulation

Financial contracts allow investors to delegate the management of their assets to others. Fund management represents a straightforward example of such delegation, in which the investor retains full legal title to the assets. Equity, bond, and bank-mediated instruments investors surrender their assets in return for control rights that constrain directors and motivate them to pay dividend and coupon payments. These contracts precipitate difficult principal–agent problems and the financial markets have to find ways of solving these effectively given the legal, accounting, and regulatory systems in place. This chapter brings together our analysis of these problems and of the market and regulatory response. It concludes with a discussion of the case for a single financial regulator.

12.1. Legal systems and financial architecture

We have seen that the structure of the financial system is strongly influenced by the relative effectiveness with which the capital and banking markets can resolve these principal–agent problems. The evidence suggests that the Anglo-Saxon tradition of common law, common accounting standards, and open markets results in a bias towards capital-market-mediated finance, while the financial communities of the European continent are inclined towards banking relationships. La Porta *et al.* (1997, 1998) argue that the tendency towards ownership concentration, debt, and bank-mediated finance in continental countries is largely a market response to the lower level of investor protection afforded by their legal, accounting, and regulatory control systems.

Shleifer and Vishny (1997) argue that the rights of small creditors and large shareholders can be based on simple legal interventions that are likely to be upheld even if courts are poorly informed and motivated. The rights of creditors are clear and are defined for the *individual* investor. Violations of these rights – the suspension of interest or debt repayments, for example – are easy for the courts to verify. Any creditor, no matter how small, can sue the company in these circumstances. In contrast, shareholders receive dividends at the discretion of the directors. They do have voting rights, but as Shleifer and Vishny argue, these may be ineffective unless there is an informed legal system to support them. Small shareholders have little incentive to keep informed about the company or to exercise these rights, especially in the absence of a proxy voting system. Shareholder concentration may be necessary to surmount these problems: large shareholders can threaten management with a majority vote, which is easy for the courts to verify. In the absence of such mechanisms, shareholders may find it impossible to secure a proper return on their assets. As Shleifer and Vishny (1997) put it, 'they may never get back anything at all'.

The very mixed experiences of the countries of the former Soviet bloc since the fall of the Berlin Wall have provided a strong reminder that the legal and accounting system is of vital importance to the functioning of a modern market-based economy. Economists no longer just think of financial structure as a reflection of a business culture or as an accident of history.

Importantly, the Anglo-Saxon system provides a relatively high level of protection for *all* investors: shareholders, bondholders, as well as other creditors (La Porta *et al.* 1998). The legal system plays a crucial role in protecting minority shareholders from exploitation by management or majority shareholders as well as allowing lender repossession in default. Indeed, Hicks (1969, 1989) argued that the historical development of the banking system was largely due to the difficulty which small lenders had in enforcing repayments under loan contracts.

Some of these effects are very subtle. La Porta *et al.* (1998) explain the diffusion of shareholdings in the Anglo-Saxon systems by the rights which small shareholders have been able to win over the centuries through precedent and case history. Proxy voting rights, which are surprisingly absent from many continental systems of company law, play a key role in allowing small shareholders to delegate responsibility to directors. The rights of shareholders and in particular minority shareholders have now been enshrined in statute in the USA and the UK (Chapter 7). Less subtle perhaps, but also of importance, is the fact that prudential arguments prevent commercial banks in the English-speaking world from acquiring equity stakes in corporations (Section 9.7).

Effective accounting rules are important in supporting covenants written into public bond issues to protect their holders from asset substitution. They also help shareholders overcome the verification problem (Section 9.2). In the absence of appropriate accounting standards, bank loan contracts, secured against specific assets and supported by collateral (as well as the confidential information provided by the bank's bookkeeping function), are likely to offer a more effective medium. La Porta *et al.* (1998) argue that legal systems based in the German tradition of civil law provide a high level of protection to secured creditors, helping to explain the prominent role of banks in that system.

Current developments in continental Europe provide an interesting test bed for these theories of financial structure. The move to a single market and a single currency is pushing European industrial integration forward at a rapid pace. It is also a factor in the international diversification of continental equity portfolios, although this is a global and not just a European phenomenon. Portfolio diversification is gradually dispersing shareholdings in continental companies and was an important factor in the success of the hostile takeovers of Telecom Italia and Mannesmann. This suggests that the corporate structure and governance of a country is not rigidly dictated by its legal and regulatory structure, but that market size and other economic factors exert a separate and important influence. It is possible that the diffuse shareholdings of American and British companies owe as much to their size and global outlook as they do to the legal backdrop.

These developments are spurring the European Competition Commissioner on in his efforts to forge a code for cross-border takeovers. The German government too has set up a panel to revise its takeover code. It is also planning to abolish capital gains tax on corporate shareholdings. This is designed to allow German companies to unwind their extensive cross-holdings and facilitate industrial restructuring and foreign investment. Indeed, the moves towards the Anglo-Saxon market-based model are nowhere more apparent on the continent than in Germany. Deutschland AG is under great pressure to deliver shareholder value. Mutual fund and individual share ownership is increasing, too, as Germans think about ways of reducing their dependence upon the state in retirement.

12.2. Transparency in financial systems

While Germany and its neighbours may be taking a few hesitant steps towards the Anglo-Saxon model it is important to remember that bank finance remains important even in market-based systems like that of the USA. Small companies are particularly dependent upon banks, as are individuals. Venture capital and banking relationships provide a better way of handling strategic financial issues and information than do transparent capital markets. As Fama (1985) argued and James (1987) and others have shown, capital markets and bank intermediation are highly complementary even when the framework is conducive to the more transparent market-based approach (Section 8.2).

We have seen that the USA and the UK are similar in terms of their diffuse shareholder registers. Besides the legal system, the emphasis upon transparency in these countries also helps explain this (Section 7.5). Nevertheless, the UK remains less open and market-oriented than the USA, where it seems that the tradition of open government and deep-seated distrust of bankers may have been additional factors. In particular, US companies tend to use the corporate bond market as a source of fixed- and floating-rate finance, while UK corporations rely much more heavily upon banks.

The difference between the two systems was highlighted by the very different ways in which they responded to the inflation and interest rate volatility of the 1970s. This change produced a variety of innovations, notably the invention of deposit substitutes like money market mutual funds and the payment of interest on bank deposits. Financial engineers produced a variety of derivative products to allow companies and individuals to hedge themselves against the volatility of interest rates, exchange rates, and other asset prices. These innovations were also a response to regulation: capital requirements encouraged banks to move business off-balance sheet.

Uncertainty about inflation naturally leads both lenders and borrowers to become short-termist, insuring themselves from the capital variation produced by unexpected changes in inflation and interest rates by borrowing and lending short. This effect severely hit the market in debentures (long-term corporate bonds) in the UK in the 1970s and 1980s, practically driving it out of existence. UK Plc largely substituted short-term bank borrowing for long-term bonds. However the US response to inflation was altogether different. Borrowers and lenders stayed with the public debt market. Investors used diversification to counter the specific company risk that high interest rates and inflation brought, either directly or, in the case of small investors, indirectly through mutual funds. Borrowers and lenders also shifted from fixed to commercial paper (CP)[1] and

---

[1] Commercial paper is a short-term unsecured debt instrument (a 1–3 month maturity) issued by an industrial borrower. It is typically held by another corporate, making this an intercompany market.

floating rate notes (FRNs), an innovation that was pioneered in the dollar bond markets.[2]

This switch may have been due to the tight lending criteria applied by US banks as inflation and interest rates increased. However, this affords only a partial explanation, because many large US companies that were still able to borrow freely from their bankers used the new debt facilities to reduce their reliance upon the banks. The high yield (junk bond) market caused further disintermediation, particularly during the 1980s, although the growth of this market was associated with the takeover market (Section 7.9). Whatever the reason for this, the public debt markets increased their role in the US financial system. Bond holdings rose from very small proportions to over 10 per cent of household wealth by 1998.

The FRN market was frequently tapped by UK financial institutions but rarely used by UK industrial companies. Instead, these companies preferred to rely upon a system of revolving short-term loans, negotiated confidentially. The UK overdraft system conveniently lent itself to this form of borrowing. However, these facilities can be withdrawn at short notice and company treasurers have to trust that their bankers will not foreclose when they get into trouble (Section 9.4). FRNs remove the risk of foreclosure and minimize the transactions costs involved in rollover borrowing. Despite the institutional differences, it remains unclear why these CPs, FRNs, and high-yield bonds appealed to corporate borrowers in the USA but not the UK.[3]

National attitudes to openness in financial relationships are also reflected in the transparency and accountability of monetary policy. Alesina and Summers (1993) provide various indices of central bank independence which indicate that in the post-war world the central banks of Germany, Switzerland, and the USA have been the most independent.

[2] FRNs are medium- or long-term public bond issues offering an interest coupon which is not fixed but varies with a short-term market rate like the 3-month US Treasury Bill rate. Like any public issue, an FRN prospectus normally contains covenants designed to minimize moral hazard. A variety of modifications can be used to cap or put a floor under interest payments, or to allow the borrower or the lender the option of converting the FRN into a standard fixed coupon bond. The FRN market developed alongside the interest rate swap market, which allowed companies to raise fixed- or floating-rate finance and then swap it into the alternative form, or another currency.

[3] FRNs also failed to appeal to UK investors. In 1976 HM Treasury issued two floating rate gilts with interest rates linked to the sterling Treasury Bill rate, but these proved to be unpopular. These issues traded at a large discount to par (fair) value and were not repeated. In contrast, HM Treasury successfully raised dollar FRN finance in 1984 (and subsequent dates) through Credit Suisse First Boston, an investment bank which was born and bred in the Eurodollar markets.

These countries all have a federal political structure in which political power is naturally diffuse, making an autonomous central bank a natural development. However, within this group of independent central banks, attitudes towards transparency and accountability could not be more different. The Bundesbank and the Swiss National Bank are highly secretive. The Bundesbank Council, for example, did not publish its minutes and usually surprised the markets with its interest rate decisions. The same is true of the European Central Bank (ECB), which now dictates European monetary policy. The Federal Reserve's Open Market Policy Committee (FOMC), on the other hand, is open and accountable. It publishes detailed minutes and its chairman provides detailed accounts of policy to Congress. It actively uses these devices to keep the markets abreast of its thinking on the economy and interest rates.

The UK and France are centralized states with unitary political structures. Reflecting this, their central banks have been subservient for most of the post-war period to their respective treasuries. Traditionally, they have been very secretive. However, both these central banks have gained their independence in recent years. Consistent with the transparent market approach, the Bank of England's Monetary Policy Committee is remarkably open, more so even than the FOMC, while the Banque de France like the ECB remains secretive.

12.3. Overview: the financial architecture

Table 12.1 attempts to summarize and contrast the detailed structural analysis of earlier chapters. The Introduction argued that retail financial services were the epitome of a credence good, which to be successful requires the consumer's faith in the provider. These activities are shown in the first three columns of the table. The scope for research is limited. These industries are plagued by adverse selection and other informational problems (row 5). The market response to these problems usually leads to the adoption of self-regulatory devices like mutual monitoring and insurance (row 6). Regulators of portfolio managers and advisers mimic the market response, imposing minimum standards through entry requirements and fit and proper conduct tests, backed up by disciplinary procedures (final row).

For the first two activities shown in the table the provider has a unilateral information advantage. The commission structure is either fixed or takes the form of an equity participation or risk-sharing contract. A fund

Table 12.1. The structure and regulation of financial markets

Activity	Basic financial services			Market making	Equities		Public bonds	Bank lending	Retail bank deposits
	Financial advisers	Portfolio managers	General insurers		Large Plc	Smaller company			
Information asymmetry	Unilateral	Unilateral	Bilateral	Multilateral	Multilateral	Unilateral	Unilateral	Unilateral	Unilateral
Market transparency	Confidential	Confidential	Confidential	Open	Open	Open?	Open	Confidential	Confidential
Principal's information and research activity	Exogenous information	Exogenous information	Exogenous information	Search activity	Security research	Exogenous information?	Security research	Screening, scrutiny, audit	Exogenous information, search activity
Agent's payoff	Fixed fee	Equity participation	Convex	Fixed spread	Equity participation	Equity participation	Convex	Convex	Convex
Main flaws	Adverse selection	Adverse selection, verification	Adverse selection, moral hazard, verification	Adverse selection (esp. smaller companies)	Moral hazard, verification	Moral hazard, verification	Asset substitution	Adverse selection, moral hazard, rationing	Excessive risk, verification
Market response	Mutual monitoring and insurance, minimum standards and disciplinary procedures	Performance measures and audit, minimum standards and disciplinary procedures	Mutual monitoring and insurance, minimum standards and disciplinary procedures	Order limits, two-tier pricing	Disclosure rules, audit	Director's dealings, audit	Covenants and audit, default process	Screening, customer relationship, collateral	Collateral, mutual monitoring
Regulatory response	Public monitoring and insurance, minimum standards and disciplinary procedures	Public monitoring and insurance, minimum standards and disciplinary procedures	Capital requirements, public monitoring, ombudsman	Disclosure rules, minimum standards and disciplinary procedures	Disclosure rules, minimum standards and disciplinary procedures, investor protection law	Disclosure of director's dealings, investor protection law	Creditor protection law	Capital requirements	Capital requirements, deposit insurance

manager's fees are related to the size of the portfolio under management for example. Although market making, summarized in the fourth column, is essentially a search good, the price spread also represents a linear reward structure. In all of these cases, the title of ownership remains with the principal and the agent's payment is essentially linear rather than convex (Section 2.1). This means that the regulator need not be too concerned about excessive risk-taking. Nevertheless, capital requirements are needed to cover counterparty, negligence, execution, and other minor risks. An equity participation contract also helps to reduce shirking and other forms of moral hazard. However, as Table 1.1 reminds us, verification remains a problem with equity-based contracts, making auditing important in these industries.

In the case of insurance the information asymmetry is bilateral: the provider knows more about the product while clients probably know more about their own risk characteristics. Since the free assets of an insurance company belong to the shareholder and not the policyholder the reward structure is convex. This makes a framework of prudential regulation backed by law, appropriate. This framework can be prohibitive, but in the Anglo-Saxon system is usually based on capital requirements and stringent reporting procedures.

At the other end of the spectrum, on the right-hand side of the table, we find the public debt and banking markets. These trade fixed- or floating-rate debt contracts which also make the agent's reward structure convex, requiring a prudential approach, backed by law. Banks are similar to insurance companies in this respect, but differ from providers of fund management and other retail services. This type of contract encourages truth telling, and limits the need for auditing to the bankruptcy state (Section 1.10). But it encourages excessive risk-taking or asset substitution. Public bond markets mitigate this effect using the covenant system backed up by audit, while banks rely more upon secured loans, collateral, and their bookkeeping position (Sections 9.3 and 9.4).

The state verification problem emerges in the bank deposit market because, as the Diamond and Dybvig (1973) analysis reveals, it makes it difficult for bankers to respond to a bank run (Chapter 10). Collateral as well as mutual monitoring and support are important market responses to these problems in a free banking system (Section 9.2). Similarly, capital requirements are very important elements in prudential control of the banking system, particularly when deposits are insured by a public body (Chapter 11). In the case of the banking industry, the nature of the regulatory response is qualitatively different from the market response and does not simply mimic the market mechanism. In the absence of moral hazard, deposit insurance and the lender of last resort yield a first-best solution, which the private sector simply cannot replicate. However, once moral hazard is allowed for, this solution is second-best. Since market participants no longer monitor the bank manager, this job falls to government.

Equities represent a borderline case. These contracts delegate the management of a company to its directors, who are remunerated through fixed salary, bonus, and share option schemes. These schemes build in equity participation, and are designed to align managers' interests with those of shareholders. For this system to function effectively, it is important that the legal system supports the rights of small shareholders and that the rules ensure a high level of disclosure and accountability.

12.4. The case for a single financial services regulator

We are now in a position to review the argument for a single financial services regulator. This unified approach was first adopted by the Nordic countries and more recently by the UK, Japan, and South Korea. In this section I will focus upon the model provided by the UK's new FSM legislation. The new system brings the supervisors of bank and non-bank financial institutions together under one roof, at the Financial Services Authority in London's docklands. The primary argument for a single regulator is that convergence between banks, building societies, and insurance and other financial firms has led to 'bank assurance' institutions that sell similar products and should be supervised by a coordinated authority (HM Treasury 1998).

The previous system was fragmented, employing nine separate regulators for different types of business. It involved the industry in a great deal of cross-reporting and duplication (Section 2.9). It also ran the risk that some financial firms could 'slip through the cracks', as BCCI had done on the international stage in 1991 (Section 2.11). The crisis at Long-Term Capital Management in 1998 (Box 11.1) provides another argument for a system-wide approach, suggesting that systemic risks are no longer confined to banks but can result from high levels of gearing in other financial industries. In this case the failure of a well-connected hedge fund threatened the banking system and had to be rescued by the Federal Reserve. A subsidiary argument is that a single authority on single site allows economies of scale and scope, for example in the provision of common services like accommodation and staff training. Discussion of common methodological problems like risk measurement are also facilitated.

Cross-provision of financial products is increasingly taking place in the UK high street. At one end of the financial spectrum we now see banks and building societies selling insurance, unit trusts, and other long-term investment products, while at the other we see insurance and fund management companies offering bank deposit facilities and mortgages. Supermarkets, airlines, and other non-financial firms are also moving into retail financial services. The functional differences between banks, non-bank financial institutions, and other firms is becoming less distinct, at least at the retail level. This phenomenon is not so widespread in the USA, where the Glass–Steagall law inhibits cross-provision within the banking sector. However, this has not stopped non-banks from providing banking and other financial services (Section 2.6).

Economies of scope are important in banking services (Section 6.3), but it is not clear that they will bring enduring benefits across the wider financial spectrum. The move by the Scottish banks to take over NatWest suggests that the latter made a serious mistake in attempting to take over fund management companies (Box 7.1). Firms (like the building societies) that have focused on their core business of selling insurance, mortgage, or banking services – often new entrants using new marketing technologies (like Direct Line insurance) – have made inroads into the retail market at the expense of the financial supermarkets. Moreover, although banking laws may have impeded the development of commercial banks in the USA, it is not clear that they have held back the US investment banks. These dominate the world's capital markets despite (or perhaps because of) the Glass–Steagall Act. In the meantime, attempts by European banks to combine commercial and investment banking have been hampered by the cultural divide between the two different types of business. Certainly, attempts by British banks to stride this divide have been expensive failures (Box 7.1).

Coordination between banking supervisors and other regulators has nevertheless become increasingly important both nationally and internationally, as the failure of BCCI in 1991 (Box 2.2) and the crisis at Long-Term Capital Management in 1998 (Box 11.1) demonstrate. Moreover, complaints from the industry about duplication and the need for multiple reporting are also well founded. One way to deal with these problems is to reduce the number of regulators, just as Australia and Canada have done recently. It might be efficient to eliminate cross reporting by organizing a single gateway to the regulator for each firm. However, the issue then concerns what lies behind this interface (a) within the firm and (b) within the regulator. It is crucially important that regulators carefully preserve the distinctions between different types of financial activity as well as between different financial institutions. Otherwise, the single gateway will further blur functional differences between institutions and in doing so will fail to preserve the important distinction between deposit taking, insurance, and other types of financial activity (Table 2.1).

In this environment of one-stop regulation, it will be especially important to separate banking from non-banking divisions within each firm. These business units must be carefully compartmentalized and have their own rules, accounts, and reporting systems even if they do not have separate reporting lines into the regulator. They should be assessed as separate entities by sector specialists and must have their own dedicated capital. It would be a serious mistake to think that the risks inherent in deposit-taking activity can in any sense be compared with those in say capital market activity or that they could somehow be traded-off against each other. There should of course be some overall risk assessment at the level of the firm, but this should be regarded as a secondary and not a primary bulwark against collapse.

The rules and reporting systems of these units should take account of the risk characteristics of different types of business (as highlighted in the discussion of Table 12.1). Capital requirements play a crucial role in the prudential regulation of insurance and banking firms with their geared capital structures. Yet they are of much less relevance in the case of other markets, where reliance upon disciplinary procedures remains important (Franks and Mayer 1989). A one-size-fits-all approach based on common capital requirements would severely handicap the financial system.

One of the risks in harmonizing the rule book is that the legal system (which is used to provide a framework for the banking and insurance sectors in most countries) could be confused with the disciplinary framework (which forms the basis of regulation and the conduct of business in capital markets and other financial services). This is an argument for having one regulator for banks and insurance companies and another for capital markets and other financial services. This is the 'twin peaks' approach taken by the new Australian and Canadian regulatory regimes. There is a risk of confusion in systems like the new UK one, which combines the disciplinary and criminal approaches to market abuse (Section 4.8).

Besides the important distinction between laws and disciplinary rules, there are many other dimensions of financial business which should be carefully preserved in a regulatory system, unified or not. One is the distinction between unsophisticated retail and sophisticated professional investors. The emerging international regulatory regime also distinguishes between prudential regulation (which is based on parent country supervision) and conduct-of-business rules (which are supervised by the host country). These arguments led Goodhart *et al.* (1998) to suggest separate regulators to cover the industry according to activities and the objectives of policy, but this might not be necessary provided that these activities and responsibilities are rigorously separated behind the common gateway.

As the first chapter noted, the arguments for regulating financial institutions differ from those for regulating public utilities. The regulation of utilities is simpler, being based upon competition and environmental considerations and not informational asymmetry. However, the arguments for a single regulator actually fit the case of public utilities rather better than they do the case of financial firms. Competition and cross-provision between utilities is as extensive as that between financial firms. In the UK, the big utility companies are marketing gas, electricity, financial, and telephone services and in some cases also provide water and sewage services. One-stop shopping for utilities is a fact of life for many families. The arguments for economies of scale and scope are also more persuasive for natural monopolies than they are for financial firms. Similarly there are in principle economies of scale and scope to be made in regulation, for example in adopting a common methodology for handling cost of capital and other issues consistently across different industries, regulating the flow of work across different reviews, and reducing the apparent arbitrariness of regulatory decisions. This is not so much an argument for merging the various environmental and competition authorities which control the public utilities as an argument for caution in merging financial regulators and designing new organisational structures.

The new UK system of financial regulation follows the US model in separating the job of prudential control (which has gone to the FSA) from the responsibility for financial stability and the lender of last resort facility (which remains with the Bank of England). This division of responsibility is a feature of other financial systems, including the German one. It has nevertheless been criticized on the grounds that systemic stability and prudential control are indivisible (see e.g. Gowland 1997). On the one hand, prudential control is essential for stability, while on the other systemic support can be undertaken only by lending to solvent banks, which can be identified only by the prudential regulator.

These arguments underline the need for close coordination between the various agencies involved. In the USA, the Federal Reserve, the FDIC, the Comptroller of the Currency, and the state banking regulators work very closely and effectively together. In the UK, HM Treasury arranges a monthly meeting between the regulators from the FSA and those responsible for financial stability at the Bank of England. Provided that the inevitable institutional rivalry can be contained, there is no reason to think that the new system should be less stable than the previous one. Ultimately, financial stability is an international concern and requires close cooperation between supervisors in different financial centres as well as within them.

EXERCISES

Question 1. Consider the implications for corporate governance in Germany of the:

(a)   increasing international diffusion of the German shareholder base;

(b)   prospective abolition of capital gains tax on company cross-holdings;

(c)   introduction of a new British-style takeover code;

(d)   likely merger of Frankfurt, London and other European stock exchanges.

Question 2. Consider the relative importance, given current technologies, of (a) the regulatory regime and (b) markets, infrastructure, and other factors for the geographical location of (i) investment banks, (ii) retail share brokers, (iii) providers of life assurance and pension products, and (iv) providers of retail banking services.

References

Akerlof, G. (1970), 'Market for Lemons: Quantitative Uncertainty and the Market Mechanism', *Quarterly Journal of Economics*, 222: 488–500.

Alesina, A., and Summers, L. (1993), 'Central Bank Independence and Macroeconomic Performance: Some Comparative Evidence', *Journal of Money, Credit and Banking*, 25: 110–21.

Allen, B. (1986), 'General Equilibrium with Rational Expectations', in A. Mas-Colell and W. Hildenbrand (eds.), *Contributions to Mathematical Economics: Essays in Honor of Gerard Debreu*, Amsterdam: North-Holland.

Allen, F., and Winton, A. (1995), 'Corporate Financial Structure, Incentives and Optimal Contracting', in R. Jarrow, V. Masimovic, and W. T. Ziemba (eds.), *Handbooks in Operations Research and Management Science*, Vol. 9, Elsevier.

Arrow, K. J. (1953), 'Le Rôle des valeurs boursiers pour la répartition des risques', *Econometrica*, 11: 41–7.

— (1965), *Aspects of the Theory of Riskbearing*, Helsinki: Yrjo Jahnssonis.

— and Debreu, G. (1954), 'Existence of Equilibrium for a Competitive Economy' *Econometrica*, 22: 265–90.

Bagehot, W. (1873), *Lombard Street*, London: Henry S. King.

— (1971), 'The Only Game in Town', *Financial Analyst's Journal*, 27:12–14.

Bagnoli, M., and Lipman, B. L. (1988), 'Successful Takeovers without Exclusion', *Review of Financial Studies*, 1: 89–110.

Baimbridge, M., and Whyman, P. (1997), 'Institutional Macroeconomic Forecasting Performance of the UK Economy', *Applied Economics Letters*, 4(6): 373–6.

Bank of England (1991), 'The Performance of the Major British Banks 1970–90', *Quarterly Bulletin*, November: 508–15.

Batchelor, R., and Dua, P. (1990), 'Forecaster Ideology, Forecasting Technique, and the Accuracy of Economic Forecasts', *International Journal of Forecasting*, 6(1): 3–10.

— — (1991), 'Blue Chip Rationality Tests', *Journal of Money, Credit, and Banking*, 23(4): 692–705.

Basel Committee on Banking Supervision (1995a), 'Planned Supplement to the Capital Accord to Incorporate Market Risk', Basel.

— (1995b), 'An Internal Model-Based Approach to Market Risk Capital Requirements', Basel.

— (1999a), 'A New Capital Adequacy Framework' (June), Basel.

— (1999b), 'Banks' Interactions with Highly Leveraged Institutions' (October), Basel.

Baumol, W. J. (1971), 'Contestable Markets: An Uprising in the Theory of Industrial Structure', *American Economic Review*, 72: 1–15.

Bayoumi, T. A., and McDonald, R. (1994), 'On the Optimality of Consumption across Canadian Provinces', Centre for Economic Policy Research, Discussion Paper 1030.

Bayoumi, T. A., and McDonald, R. (1995), 'Consumption, Income, and International Capital Market Integration', International Monetary Fund Staff Papers, 42(3): 552–76.

Becker, G. (1964), *Human Capital*, New York: Columbia University Press.

Benston, G. J., and Kaufman, G. G. (1988), 'Risk and Solvency Regulation of Depository Institutions', NYU Monograph Series in Finance and Economics.

— — (1996), 'The Appropriate Role of Bank Regulation', *Economic Journal*, 106: 688–97.

Bernanke, B. (1983), 'Non-monetary Effects of the Financial Crisis in the Propagation of the Great Depression', *American Economic Review*, 73: 257–76.

Bernhardt, D., and LeBlanc, G. (1994), 'Direct Revelation of Information vs Signalling in Financial Markets', *Canadian Journal of Economics*, 858–85.

— Hollifield, B., and Hughson, E. (1995), 'Investment and Insider Trading', *Review of Financial Studies*, 8: 501–43.

Bhattacharya, S. (1979), 'Imperfect Information, Dividend Policy, and "the Bird in the Hand" Fallacy', *Bell Journal of Economics*, 10(1): 259–70.

— (1980), 'Nondissipative Signaling Structures and Dividend Policy', *Quarterly Journal of Economics*, 95(1): 1–24.

— and Ritter, J. R. (1983), 'Innovation and Communication: Signalling with Partial Disclosure', *Review of Economic Studies*, 50(2): 331–46.

— and Thakor, A. V. (1990), 'Contemporary Banking Theory', *Journal of Financial Intermediation*, 3: 2–50.

Bidwell, C. M., (1977), 'How Good Is Institutional Brokerage Research?', *Journal of Portfolio Management*, 3(2): 26–31.

Bjerring, J. H., Lakonishok, J., and Vermaelen, T. (1983), 'Stock Prices and Financial Analysts' Recommendations', *Journal of Finance*, 38(1): 187–204.

Bolton, P., and Freixas, X. (1998), 'A Dilution Cost Approach to Financial Intermediation and Securities Markets', Working Paper, Universitat Pompeu Fabra.

Brealey, R. A., and Hodges, S. D. (1972), 'Portfolio Selection in a Dynamic and Uncertain World', *Financial Analysts Journal*, 28: 58–69.

Breeden, D. T. (1979), 'An Intertemporal Asset Pricing Model with Stochastic Consumption and Investment Opportunities', *Journal of Financial Economics*, 7(2): 265–96.

— (1984), 'Futures Markets and Commodity Options: Hedging and Optimality in Incomplete Markets', *Journal of Economic Theory*, 32: 275–300.

Bresnahan, T., Milgrom, P., and Paul, J. (1992), 'The Real Output of the Stock Exchange', in Z. Griliches (ed.), *Output Measurement in the Service Sectors*, Chicago, IL: University of Chicago Press, 195–216.

Brown, P., Foster, G., and Noreen, F. (1985), *Security Analyst Earnings Forecasts and the Capital Market*, Sarasota, FL: American Accounting Association.

Bulkley, G., and Harris, R. (1995), 'Irrational Analysts' Expectations as a Cause of

Excess Volatility in Stock Prices', University of Exeter, Department of Economics Discussion Paper 96/08, July.

Calomiris, C. W. (1990), 'Is Deposit Insurance Necessary? A Historical Perspective', *Journal of Economic History*, 50: 283–95.

—— (1998), 'Blueprints for a New Financial Architecture', mimeo, American Enterprise Institute for Public Policy Research.

—— and Kahn, C. M. (1996), 'The Efficiency of Self-regulating Payments Systems: Evidence from the Suffolk System', *Journal of Money, Credit and Banking*, 34: 766–97.

Campbell, T., and Kracaw, W. (1980), 'Information Production, Market Signalling and the Theory of Intermediation', *Journal of Finance*, 863–82.

Carhart, M. M. (1997), 'On the Persistency in Mutual Fund Performance', *Journal of Finance*, 52: 345–76.

Carlton, D., Fischel, W., and Fischel, D. (1983), 'The Regulation of Insider Trading', *Stanford Law Review*, 35: 79–120.

Coffe, J. C. (1995), 'Competition versus Consolidation: The Significance of Organisational Structure in Financial Services Regulation', *The Business Lawyer*, 50: 45–77.

Copeland, T., and Galai, D. (1983), 'Information Effects and the Bid–Ask Spread', *Journal of Financial Economics*, 38: 1457–69.

Crystal, G. S. (1992), *In Search of Excess: The Overcompensation of American Executives*, New York: Norton.

Davis, E. P. (1993,) 'Theories of Intermediation, Financial Innovation and Regulation', *National Westminster Bank Review*, May: 41.

De Bondt, W. F. M., and Thaler, R. H. (1985), 'Does the Stock Market Overreact?', *Journal of Finance*, 40: 793–805.

—— —— (1990), 'Do Security Analysts Overreact?', *American Economic Review*, 80(2): 52–7.

Debreu, G. (1959), *Theory of Value*, New York: Wiley.

De Meza, D., and Webb, D. (1987), 'Too Much Investment: A Problem of Asymmetric Information', *Quarterly Journal of Economics*, 102: 281–408.

Dewatripont, D., and Tirole, J. (1994), *The Prudential Regulation of Banks*, Cambridge, MA: MIT Press.

Diamond, D. W. (1984), 'Financial Intermediation and Delegated Monitoring', *Review of Economic Studies*, 59: 393.

—— and Dybvig, P. (1983), 'Bank Runs, Deposit Insurance and Liquidity', *Journal of Political Economy*, 91: 401.

Dimson, E., and Fraletti, P. (1986), 'Brokers' Recommendations: The Value of a Telephone Tip', *Economic Journal*, 96(381): 139–59.

—— and Marsh, P. R. (1984), 'An Analysis of Brokers' and Analysts' Unpublished Forecasts of UK Stock Returns', *Journal of Finance*, 39(5): 1257–92.

Dow, J., and Rahi, R. (1996), 'Informed Trading, Investment and Welfare', Discussion Paper 55, Institute for Financial Research, Birkbeck College.

Dowd, K. (1989), *The State and the Monetary System*, Oxford: Philip Allen.

—— (1996), 'The Case for Financial Laissez-Faire', *Economic Journal*, 106: 679–87.

Duffie, D., and Huang, C.-F. (1985), 'Implementing Arrow-Debreu Equilibrium by Continuous Trading of a Few Long-Lived Securities', *Econometrica*, 53: 1337–56.

Dye, R. (1984), 'Insider Trading and Incentives', *Journal of Business*, 57: 295–313.

Easley, D., and O'Hara, M. (1992), 'Adverse Selection and Large Trade Volume: The Implications for Market Efficiency', *Journal of Financial and Quantitative Analysis*, 27: 185–208.

Eaton, J. and Gersovitz, M. (1981), 'Debt with Potential Repudiation: Theoretical and Empirical Analysis', *Review of Economic Studies*, 48: 289–309.

The Economist (1996), 'International Banking', 27 April, 1–41.

Eichberger, J., and Harper, I. R. (1997), *Financial Economics*, Oxford: Oxford University Press.

Elton, E. J., Gruber, M. J., and Koo, S. M. (1986), 'Effect of Quarterly Earnings Announcements on Analysts' Forecasts', in A. H. Chen (ed.), *Research in Finance*, vol. 6, Greenwich, CT and London: JAI Press, 247–59.

Fama, E. F. (1980), 'Banking in a Theory of Finance', *Journal of Monetary Economics*, 6: 39–57.

—— (1985), 'What's Different about Banks?', *Journal of Monetary Economics*, 15: 29–39.

Fischer, P. (1992), 'Optimal Contracting and Insider Trading Regulations', *Journal of Finance*, 47: 673–94.

Fishman, M., and Hagerty, K. (1992), 'Insider Trading and the Efficiency of Stock Prices', *Rand Journal of Economics*, 23: 106–22.

Fletcher, J. (1999), 'The Evaluation of the Performance of UK American Unit Trusts', *International Review of Economics and Finance*, 4: 34–72.

Franks, J. R., and Harris, R. (1989), 'Shareholder Wealth Effects of Corporate Takeovers: The UK Experience 1955–1985', *Journal of Financial Economics*, 23: 225–49.

—— and Mayer, C. (1989), 'Risk, Regulation and Investor Protection: The Case of Investment Management', Oxford: Oxford University Press.

—— —— (1990), 'Capital Markets and Corporated Control: A Study of France, Germany and the UK', *Economic Policy*, 10: 191–231.

—— —— (2000), 'Takeovers and Market Discipline', *Company Law Review*, forthcoming.

—— Harris, R. S., and Sheridan, T. (1991), 'The Postmerger Share-Price Performance of Acquiring Firms', *Journal of Financial Economics*, 29: 81–96.

—— Schaeffer, S. M., and Staunton, M. D. (1998), 'The Direct and Compliance Costs of Financial Regulation', *Journal of Banking and Finance*, 21: 899–913.

Fried, D., and Givoly, D. (1982), 'Financial Analysts' Forecasts of Earnings: A Better Surrogate for Market Expectations', *Journal of Accounting and Economics*, 4(2): 85–107.

Friedman, M. (1959), *A Program for Monetary Stability*, New York: Fordham University Press.

Galbraith, G. K. (1967), *The New Industrial State*, London: Hamish Hamilton.

Gemmill, G. (1993), 'The Price Impact of Large Trades under Different Publication Rules: Evidence from the London Stock Exchange', Working Paper, City University Business School, London.

Gertner, R., Gibbons, R., and Scharfstein, D. (1988), 'Simultaneous Signalling to the Capital and Product Markets', *Rand Journal of Economics*, 173–90.

Gilbert, R. A. (1984), 'Bank Market Structure and Competition: A Survey', *Journal of Money, Credit and Banking*, 16: 617–45.

Givoly, D., and Lakonishok, J. (1979), 'The Information Content of Financial Analysts' Forecasts of Earnings: Some Evidence on Semi-Strong Inefficiency', *Journal of Accounting and Economics*, 1(3): 165–85.

Glasner, D. (1989), 'Free Banking and Monetary Reform', Cambridge: Cambridge University Press.

Glosten, L. (1989), 'Insider Trading, Liquidity and the Role of the Monopolist Specialist', *Journal of Business*, 62: 211–35.

— and Milgrom, P. (1985), 'Bid, Ask, and Transaction Prices in a Specialist Market with Heterogeneously Informed Traders', *Journal of Financial Economics*, 13: 71–100.

Goode, R. M. (1993), 'Pension Law Reform: The Report of the Pensions Law Review Committee', CM2342 I and II, HMSO, London.

— (1997), *Principles of Corporate Insolvency Law*, 2nd edn., London: Sweet and Maxwell.

Goodhart, C. A. E. (1988), 'Financial Regulation or Over-regulation', Institute for Economic Affairs.

Gowland, D. (1997), *Banking on Change: Independence, Regulation and the Bank of England*, London: Politea.

Gregory, A., Matatko, O., and Tonks, I. (1994), 'UK Directors' Trading: The Impact of Dealings in Smaller Firms', *Economic Journal*, 104(4): 37–53.

Grossman, S. J., and Hart, O. D. (1980), 'Takeover Bids, the Free Rider Problem and the Theory of the Corporation', *Bell Journal of Economics and Management*, 11: 253–70.

— — (1981), 'The Allocational Role of Takeover Bids in Situations of Asymmetric Information', *Journal of Finance*, 36: 253–70.

— — (1988), 'One Share–One Vote and the Mechanism for Corporate Control' *Journal of Financial Economics*, 20: 175–202.

— and Miller, M. (1988), 'Liquidity and Market Structure', *Journal of Finance*, 617–33.

— and Stiglitz, J. E. (1980), 'On the Impossibility of Informationally Efficient Markets', *American Economic Review*, 70(3): 393–408.

Grossman, S. J. (1981), 'An Introduction to the Theory of Rational Expectations under Asymmetric Information', *Review of Economic Studies*, 48: 541–59.

Groth, J. C. *et al.* (1978), 'Security Analysts: Some Are More Equal', *Journal of Portfolio Management*, 4(3): 43–8.

Harris, M., and Raviv, A. (1991), 'The Theory of Capital Structure', *The Journal of Finance*, 46(1): 297–355.

Hayek, F. A. (1978), *Denationalising Money: The Argument Refined*, London: Institute for Economic Affairs.

Heffernan, S. (1996), *Modern Banking in Theory and Practice*, New York: Wiley.

Hicks, J. R. (1969), *A Theory of Economic History*, Oxford: Clarendon Press.

—— (1989), *A Market Theory of Money*, Oxford: Clarendon Press.

Higson, C., and Elliot, J. (1998), 'Post Take-Over Returns: The UK Evidence', *Journal of Empirical Finance*, 27–46.

Hirshleifer, J. (1971), 'The Private and Social Value of Information and the Reward to Inventive Activity', *American Economic Review*, 61: 561–74.

Ho, T., and Stoll, H. (1981), 'Optimal Dealer Pricing under Transactions and Return Uncertainty', *Journal of Financial Economics*, 9: 47–73.

—— —— (1983), 'The Dynamics of Dealer Markets', *Journal of Finance*, 38: 1053–74.

Holmstrom, B., and Tirole, J. (1993), 'Market Liquidity and Performance Monitoring', *Journal of Political Economy*, 101(4): 678–709.

Hurwicz, L. (1972), 'On Informationally Decentralised Systems', in R. Radner and C. B. McGuire (eds.), *Decision and Organisation*, Amsterdam: North-Holland.

Jacklin, C. J. (1987), 'Demand Deposits. Trading Restrictions, and Risk Sharing', in E. Prescott and N. Wallace (eds.), *Contractual Arrangements for Intertemporal Trade*, Minneapolis: University of Minnesota Press.

Jackson, P., Maude, D. J., and Perraudin, W. (1995), 'Capital Requirements and Value at Risk', IFR Working Paper no. 1, Birkbeck College, London.

James, C. (1987), 'Some Evidence on the Uniqueness of Bank Loans', *Journal of Financial Economics*, 19: 217–35.

Jenkinson, T., and Ljungqvist, A. (1996), *Going Public: The Theory and Evidence on How Companies Raise Equity Finance*, Oxford: Oxford University Press.

Jensen, M. C. (1968), 'The Performance of Mutual Funds in the Period 1945-64', *Journal of Finance*, 23: 389–416.

—— and Meckling, W. H. (1976), 'Theory of the Firm: Managerial Behaviour, Agency Costs and Ownership Structure', *Journal of Financial Economics*, 3: 305–60.

—— and Ruback, R. (1983), 'The Market for Corporate Control: The Scientific Evidence', *Journal of Financial Economics*, 11: 5–50.

King, M., and Roell, A. (1988), 'The Regulation of Takeovers', *National Westminster Bank Review*, February: 2–14.

—— —— (1990) 'Insider Trading', *Economic Policy*, 162.

Kroszner, R. S., and Rajan, R. G. (1994), 'Is the Glass–Steagall Act Justified? A Study of the US Experience with Universal Banking before 1933', *American Economic Review*, 95: 810–32.

Kyle, A. S. (1985), 'Continuous Auctions and Insider Trading', *Econometrica*, 53: 1315–36.

— (1989), 'Informed Speculation with Imperfect Competition', *Review of Economic Studies*, 56: 317–55.

Laidler, D. (1992), 'Free Banking: Theory', in P. Newman, M. Milgate, and J. Eatwell (eds.), *The New Palgrave: Dictionary of Money and Finance*, Macmillan.

La Porta, R., Lopez de Silanes, F., Shleifer, A., and Vishny, R. W. (1997), 'Legal Determinants of External Finance', *Journal of Finance*, 52(2): 1131–50.

— — — — (1998), 'Law and Finance', *Journal of Political Economy*, 106(6): 1113–37.

Leland, H. E. (1979), 'Quacks, Lemons and Licensing', *Journal of Political Economy*, 87: 59–97.

— (1985), 'Insider Trading: Should it Be Banned?', *Journal of Political Economy*, 100: 859–997.

— and Pyle, D. H. (1977), 'Information Asymmetries, Financial Structure and Financial Intermediation', *Journal of Finance*, 32: 371–87.

Levis, M. (1993), 'The Long-Run Performance of IPOs', *Financial Management*, 11: 28–41.

Litan, R. (1987), 'What Should Banks Do?', Working Paper, Brookings Institute.

Liu, P., Smith, S. D., and Syed, A. A. (1990), 'Stock Price Reactions to *The Wall Street Journal*'s Securities Recommendations', *Journal of Financial and Quantitative Analysis*, 25(3): 399–410.

Lloyd-Davies, P., and Canes, M. (1978), 'Stock Prices and the Publication of Second-Hand Information', *Journal of Business*, 51(1): 43–56.

Loughran, T., and Ritter, J. R. (1995), 'The New Issues Puzzle', *Journal of Finance*, 50(1): 23–51.

Lummer, B. C., and McConnell, S. L. (1992), 'Bank Credit and Information in Capital Markets', in P. Newman, M. Milgate, and J. Eatwell (eds.), *The New Palgrave: Dictionary of Money and Finance*, Macmillan.

Mace, B. J. (1991), 'Full Insurance in the Presence of Aggregate Uncertainty', *Journal of Political Economy*, 99(5): 928–56.

Madhavan, A. (1992), 'Trading Mechanisms in Securities Markets', *Journal of Finance*, 47: 607–42.

Manne, H. (1965), 'Mergers and the Market for Corporate Control', *Journal of Political Economy*, 73: 110–20.

— (1966), *Insider Trading and the Stock Market*, New York: Free Press.

Manove, M. (1989), 'The Harm from Insider Trading and Informed Speculation', *Quarterly Journal of Economics*, 104: 823–46.

Martin, K., and McConnell, J. (1991), 'Corporate Performance, Corporate Takeovers, and Management Turnover', *Journal of Finance*, 46: 671–88.

Melitz, J. (1999), 'Interregional and International Risk Sharing and Lessons for EMU', Working Paper, ENSA.

Mella-Barral, P., and Perraudin, W. (1997), 'Strategic Debt Service', *Journal of Finance*, 52(2): 531–56.

Merton, R. C. (1977), 'An Analytical Derivation of the Cost of Deposit Insurance Loan Guarantees', *Journal of Banking and Finance,* (1): 3–11.

— and Bodie, Z. (1993), 'Deposit Insurance–A Functional Approach', Carnegie-Rochester Conference Series on Public Policy, 38: 1–34.

Miles, D. (1993), 'Testing for Short-Termism in the UK Stock Market', *The Economic Journal*, 103(4): 1379–96.

Milgrom, P., and Stokey, N. (1982), 'Information, Trade and Common Knowledge', *Journal of Economic Theory*, 26: 17–27.

Mishkin, F. S. (1995), *The Economics of Money, Banking and Financial Markets*, New York: Harper Collins, ch. 9.

Morris, S., and Shin, H. S. (1998), 'Unique Equilibrium in a Model of Self-fulfilling Currency Attacks', *American Economic Review*, 88(3): 587–97.

Mueller, D. (1969), 'A Theory of Conglomerate Mergers', *Quarterly Journal of Economics*, 83: 643–59.

Myers, S. C., and Majluf, N. S. (1977), 'Corporate Financing and Investment Decisions When Firms Have Information Investors Do Not', *Journal of Financial Economics*, 5(2): 506–71.

Obstfeld, M. (1994), 'International Capital Mobility in the 1990s', Discussion Paper no. 904, Centre for Economic Policy Research, London.

O'Hara, M. (1995), *Market Microstructure*, Cambridge, MA: MIT Press.

Padoa-Schioppa, T. (1999), 'EMU and Banking Supervision', LSE Financial Markets Group (March).

Pagano, M., and Roell, A. (1992a), 'Failure of Financial Market', in P. Newman, M. Milgate, and J. Eatwell (eds.), *The New Palgrave: Dictionary of Money and Finance*, Macmillan.

— — (1992b), 'Front Running and Stock Market Liquidity', in V. Conti and R. Hamui (eds.), *Financial Market Liberalization and the Role of Banks*, Cambridge: Cambridge University Press.

— — (1993), 'Transparency and Liquidity: A Comparison of Auction and Dealer Markets with Informed Trading', Discussion Paper 150, LSE Financial Markets Group.

Peacock, A., and Bannock, G. (1995), 'The Rationale of Financial Services Regulation: Is the Current Structure Cost-effective and Working?', Graham Banock and Partners Ltd (June).

Pennington, R. (1995), *Company Law*, 7th edn., London: Butterworth.

Radner, R. (1968), 'Competitive Equilibrium under Uncertainty', *Econometrica*, 36: 31–58.

— (1979), 'Rational Expectations Equilibrium: Generic Existence and the Information Revealed by Prices', *Econometrica*, 47: 655–78.

Ritter, J. R. (1991), 'The Long-Run Performance of Initial Public Offerings', *Journal of Finance*, 46(1): 34–57.

Ross, S. (1973), 'The Economic Theory of Agency: The Principal's Problem', *American Economic Review*, 63(2): 134–49.

— (1976), 'Options and Efficiency', *Quarterly Journal of Economics*, 90: 75–89.

— (1977), 'The Determinants of Financial Structure: The Incentive Signalling Approach', *Bell Journal of Economics*, 8: 23–41.

Rothschild, M., and Stiglitz, J. E. (1976), 'Equilibrium in Competitive Insurance Markets: An Essay on the Economics of Imperfect Information', *Quarterly Journal of Economics*, 90: 629–49.

Schwartz, A. J. (1998), 'Time to Terminate the ESF and the IMF', Foreign Policy Briefing No. 48, Cato Institute, August.

Sharpe, W. F. (1964), 'Capital Asset Prices: A Theory of Market Equilibrium under Conditions of Risk', *Journal of Finance*, 19: 425–42.

Shiller, R. J. (1993), *Macromarkets: Creating Institutions to Manage Society's Largest Economic Risks*, Clarendon Lectures in Economics, Oxford: Oxford Univesity Press.

Shleifer, A., and Summers, L. H. (1988), 'Breach of Trust in Hostile Takeovers', in A. J. Auerbach (ed.), *Corporate Takeovers: Causes and Consequences*, NBER Project Report Series, Chicago, IL: University of Chicago Press.

— and Vishny, R. W. (1986), 'Large Shareholders and Corporate Control', *Journal of Political Economy*, 95(2); reprinted in M. J. Brennan, (ed.), *The Theory of Corporate Finance*, Cheltenham: Elgar, vol. 1: 145–72.

— — (1997), 'A Survey of Corporate Governance', *Journal of Finance*, 52: 737–79.

Silber, W. (1983), 'The Process of Financial Innovation', *American Economic Review*, Papers and Proceedings, 89.

Simpson, D. (1996), *Regulating Pensions*, Institute for Economic Affairs.

Smith, C., and Warner, J. (1979), 'On Financial Contracting', *Journal of Monetary Economics*, 7: 117–61.

Steil, B. (1996), *The European Equity Markets*, Royal Institute of International Affairs.

Stickel, S. E. (1992), 'Reputation and Performance among Security Analysts', *Journal of Finance*, 47(5): 1811–36.

— (1993), 'Accuracy Improvements from a Consensus of Updated Individual Analyst Earnings Forecasts', *International Journal of Forecasting*, 9(3): 345–53.

Stiglitz, J. E., and Weiss, A. (1981), 'Credit Rationing in Markets with Imperfect Information', *American Economic Review*, 71(3): 393–410.

Tirole, J. (1988), *The Theory of Industrial Organisation*, Cambridge, MA: MIT Press.

Tonks, I. (1996), 'The Equivalence of Screen-Based Continuous-Auction and Dealer Markets', Special Paper 66, LSE Financial Markets Group.

Wall, L. D. (1989), 'Puttable Subordinated Debt', *Federal Reserve Bank of Atlanta Review* (September), 58–69.

Wills, H. R. (1981), The Simple Economics of Bank Regulation', *Economica*, 45: 233–48.

Wilson, H. (1978), 'Evidence on the Financing of Industry and Trade', Committee to Review the Functioning of Financial Institutions, vol 5 (March).

Womack, K. L. (1996), 'Do Brokerage Analysts' Recommendations Have Investment Value?', *Journal of Finance*, 51(1): 137–67.

Index

Made in United States
North Haven, CT
20 March 2024

50211488R00157